Marxism and Ethics

SUNY series in Radical Social and Political Theory
—————
Roger S. Gottlieb, editor

Marxism and Ethics

Freedom, Desire, and Revolution

PAUL BLACKLEDGE

Published by State University of New York Press, Albany

© 2012 State University of New York

For information, contact State University of New York Press, Albany, NY
www.sunypress.edu

Production by Eileen Meehan
Marketing by Michael Campochiaro

Library of Congress Cataloging-in-Publication Data

Blackledge, Paul, 1967–
  Marxism and ethics : freedom, desire, and revolution / Paul Blackledge.
    p. cm.
  Includes bibliographical references and index.
  ISBN 978-1-4384-3991-4 (hardcover : alk. paper)
  ISBN 978-1-4384-3990-7 (pbk. : alk. paper)
  1. Socialism—Moral and ethical aspects.   I. Title.

  HX45.B53 2012
  171'.7—dc22   2011010773

10 9 8 7 6 5 4 3 2 1

To Kristyn, with love

Contents

Acknowledgments

Some of the arguments presented below were first rehearsed in articles published in the journals *Analyse and Kritik, Critique, History of Political Thought, International Socialism, Political Studies, Science and Society, Socialism and Democracy*, and *Studies in Marxism*. Thanks to the editors and referees of these journals for forcing me to sharpen up my ideas. Thanks also to the numerous other people who have helped along the way. These include the various organizers of, and contributors to, conferences and seminars organized by *Historical Materialism* in both London and New York, the Political Studies Association, Manchester Metropolitan University's annual Workshops in Political Theory, the University of Glasgow Centre for Socialist Theory, Nanjing University's Institute for Marxist Studies, the Department of Philosophy at Flinders University Adelaide, the London Socialist Historians, and the SWP's annual Marxism conference. Thanks also to my colleagues in the School of Social Sciences at Leeds Metropolitan University. For more detailed criticisms I am indebted to Colin Barker, Ian Birchall, Joseph Choonara, Neil Davidson, Sam Farber, Rob Jackson, Kelvin Knight, Rick Kuhn, Jonathan Maunder, Peter McMylor, and Victor Wallis. Chris Harman's untimely death in 2009 robbed the international left of one its most important thinkers, and me of an inspirational mentor. The arguments presented in this book are much stronger for his searching comments on an earlier draft. At a more mundane level, my colleagues on the Branch Committee of UCU lecturers' union at Leeds Metropolitan University are a practical example of the virtues of solidarity defended in the pages that follow. My thanks to them. Thanks to Michael Campochiaro, Janice Vunk and especially Bob Mouncer for their help. My sons Johnny and

Matthew are now old enough to ask hard questions about my work. They do, and they are inspiring. My daughter Kate isn't old enough to do anything but inspire; she's a beautiful reminder of the better world we're fighting for. She was born and almost died while I was writing this book. The staff at Leeds General Infirmary, particularly those on the children's intensive care unit, reminded me what a wonderful institution the NHS continues to be, despite all the attacks that market-driven politicians continue to make on it. My heartfelt thanks to them. Most of all, though, this book could not have been written without the unstinting support of Kristyn Gorton. Kristyn, you are my rock, and this book is dedicated to you.

Introduction

Marxism's Ethical Deficit

> We have found no way to replace capitalism as an effective mode of production, and yet that capitalist society as it actually functions violates all defensible conceptions of a rational moral order.
>
> —MacIntyre 1979, 4

Marxism and Contemporary Political Philosophy

In a recent and very powerful critique of the social and political irrelevance of much of contemporary political theory, Raymond Geuss somewhat idiosyncratically suggests that if "political philosophy wishes to be at all connected with a serious understanding of politics, and thus to become an effective source of orientation or a guide to action, it needs to return from the present reactionary forms of neo-Kantianism to something like the 'realist view, or, to put it slightly differently, to neo-Leninism'" (Geuss 2008, 99). Concretely, Geuss refers to Lenin's famous question "who whom?," or as he expands it "who does what to whom for whose benefit" (Geuss 2008, 23–30). If for Lenin, as for Geuss, the point of this question is to reconceptualize supposed value judgments as appeals to objectivity, the problems associated with this approach have been well rehearsed within the academy. For instance, Alasdair MacIntyre argues that Leninism tends to degenerate into a caricature of the capitalist managerial pseudo-expertise it is meant to counter (MacIntyre 1973, 341–2). Both Leninists and managers repeat, or so he insists, a more general failing of modern politics: its inability to transcend the nihilistic limitations which Nietzsche (mistakenly) claimed

1

to be a universal feature of the human condition: "that what purported to be appeals to objectivity were in fact expressions of subjective will" (MacIntyre 1985, 113).

This pseudo-objectivist cover for a nihilistic practice is often assumed to be an uncontroversial corollary of Marx's claim that the class struggle is characterised by "an antinomy of right against right" between which "equal rights, force decides" (Marx 1976, 344; cf MacIntyre 1985, 262). For instance, Simon Critchley criticizes Marxism precisely for its lack of a secure moral foundation. He claims that the present epoch has given rise not only to wars, poverty, and an impending environmental crisis, but also to a general "feeling of the irrelevance of traditional electoral politics," and that comparable historical situations generated one or both of two unfortunate responses: passive and active nihilism. Following Nietzsche (Nietzsche1967; Spinks 2003, 104–109), he argues that whereas the passive nihilist simply focuses on the "particular pleasures and projects for perfecting" herself, the active nihilist accepts that the world is meaningless "but instead of sitting back and contemplating" she counters the moral crisis with an attempt "to destroy this world and bring another into being" (Critchley 2007, 3–6). Critchley claims that Lenin's vanguardism reproduced a form of active nihilism which reflected "the silence or hostility to ethics that one finds in Marx and many Marxist and post-Marxist figures" (Critchley 2007, 5, 93, 146; cf Sayer 2000, 174). In an effort to overcome the limitations of these responses, Critchley argues that we now need "a conception of ethics that begins by accepting the motivational deficit in the institutions of liberal democracy, but without embracing either passive or active nihilism" (Critchley 2007, 8).

This assessment of the contemporary relevance and historical coherence of Marx's and Lenin's ethics and politics undoubtedly reflect the current academic consensus, even amongst the small minority of contemporary theorists who take the ideas of Marx and Lenin seriously (Wright 2010, 89–109). Perhaps the foremost contemporary representative of this tendency was, until his untimely death, Jerry Cohen. He argued that Marx developed what he called an "*obstetric* conception of political practice," according to which the role of a revolutionary socialist is, like that of a midwife, not to consider the "ideals" she wants to realise but rather more prosaically to "deliver the form that develops *within* reality" (Cohen 2000b, 43, 50, 54). Cohen identified what he believed were two devastating criticisms of this approach. First, it takes no account of the fact that the inevitability of an outcome does not guarantee its desirability. Second, he claimed that a number of Marx's most important scientific predictions had been falsified by history. For these reasons Cohen, as we shall see in Chapter 4, believed that the only realistic contemporary political option for socialists from the Marxist tradition is to embrace what Marx would have dismissed as utopian socialism.

Interestingly, those contemporary theorists who, like Cohen, are influenced by Marx, but, unlike him, remain optimistic about the possibilities for radical change tend to share his unease with the scientific claims of classical Marxism. Thus Antonio Negri has suggested snatching "Marxism back from its scientific status and restore it to its utopian, or rather ethical, possibility," while John Holloway has juxtaposed a more powerful tradition of workers' self-emancipation within Marxism to the pseudo-scientific attempts of Engels and Lenin to reduce it to a form of mechanical materialism (Negri 2008, 130; Holloway 2002, Ch. 7).

In what follows I argue that this interpretation of the relation between science and ethics in Marx and Lenin is mistaken, and that, by contrast, Lenin shared with Marx a commitment to an ethics of freedom which points toward a compelling ethical critique of capitalism. Against the general drift of theory's "return to ethics" since the 1970s (Bourg 2007), I argue that Marx's attempt to escape the impotence of moral theory is best understood not as a nihilistic rejection of ethics, but more narrowly as a refusal of the modern liberal assumption, best articulated by Kant, that moral behaviour involves the suppression of our naturally egoistic desires on the basis of a disembodied conception of reason. In opposition to this model, Marx suggested that through its collective struggles against exploitation and alienation the newly emergent working class both illuminates the historical (capitalist) character of the (un)freedom experienced by Kant's supposedly universal atomized individuals whilst simultaneously engendering virtues of solidarity which point beyond the narrow parameters of his account of morality. Against Kantianism, Marx's ethics amounts to a modern version of Aristotle's account of those practices underpinning the virtues through which individuals are able to flourish within communities. And just as Aristotle posited a natural movement from ethics to politics—"The science that studies the supreme Good for man is politics" (Aristotle 1976, 64)—Marx moved from formulating a model of human good to fighting for the political implications of this model. If this movement from ethics to politics was perhaps a little too quick both for many of

Marx's academic interlocutors and for some of his political followers, the fact that *Capital* is best understood as an extended study of the potential for and limitations of human freedom suggest it would be a mistake to deny either the first ethical step of this movement or the unity of the movement as a whole.

I argue that classical Marxism, once adequately reconstructed and disentangled from its Stalinist caricature, provides the resources to underpin an ethical political practice that is able to move beyond the negativity of anti-capitalism toward a positive socialist alternative to capitalism. Far from being a form of class reductionism, Marx articulated and justified a conception of social subjectivity in which the struggle for freedom (real democracy) is not only the imperative of free agency but is also rooted in the "new fangled" working class's emergent desire to overcome alienation through the concrete forms of collective struggle and solidarity which characterize the highpoints of class struggle. In arguing this case, I position myself in opposition both to traditional right-wing critics of Marx and to the arguments made by his much more impressive critics on the left.

The Turn to Ethics (and Back)

The arguments of Cohen et al. reflect a general movement within political theory toward a reinvigorated ethical discourse over the last few decades. Insofar as contributors to this theoretical turn have engaged with Marx, they tend to dismiss his ideas as a variant of mechanical materialism. Marx's claim that "[t]he history of all hitherto existing society is the history of class struggles" (Marx & Engels 1973, 67), is typically counterposed to, and found wanting by contrast with, moral theory's focus on "the recognition of the subjective freedom of individuals" (Habermas 1987, 17).

Nevertheless, though Marxism has been criticized for its supposed failure to theorize individual agency, modern moral theory has problems of its own. Of particular significance is the tendency of normative theorists to embrace a cacophony of incommensurable perspectives, each with little or no relationship to real politics (Geuss 2008). Indeed, Alasdair MacIntyre has powerfully made the case that modern moral discourse is but a "simulacra of morality." Whereas in the classical world ethics had an objective character, the associated imperatives of the various modern moral standpoints can be reduced to a series of more or less persuasive attempts to justify personal preferences (MacIntyre 1985, p. 2). Contemporary morality is consequently characterized by "interminable" disagreements which seem immune to rational closure: debates on war, rights, and justice, etc. each generate a multiplicity of rationally justified opposing positions which exclude reason as an independent arbiter (MacIntyre 1985, 6–7).

It was precisely to avoid this and other limitations with moral theory that Louis Althusser articulated an anti-humanist interpretation of Marxism in the 1960s (see Collier 1981, 6). And if it is undoubtedly the case that the coordinates of the left's embrace of the "return to ethics" from the 1970s and 1980s onward included the defeats suffered by the workers' movement in that period, it was also made in reaction to the breakdown of Althusser's earlier "return to Marx" (Wood 1995, 30–35; Elliott 2006, xiii).

Althusserianism itself emerged as the dominant voice of French Marxism in the early 1960s at the conjuncture of two events of global significance and a more local intellectual failure: Khrushchev's "Secret Speech," the Sino-Soviet split, and the waning of Sartre's star on the Left Bank in the wake of the Parisian reception of structuralism. These events combined to create an intellectual space on the Marxist left within which Althusser's voice rapidly became hegemonic (Poster 1975, 306; Callinicos 1983, 89; cf Blackledge 2006a, 162–166). If Khrushchev's speech opened the door to a variety of "socialist humanist" criticisms of Stalinism, Lévi-Strauss's powerful critique of Sartre's revolutionary humanism alongside a more general move by some of the milieu of 1956 socialist humanists toward liberalism in the 1960s informed Althusser's search for a standpoint from which to counter what he perceived to be the malign influence of humanism on Marxism. This project took him into the orbit of Maoism, even as he remained a member of the French Communist Party (Anderson 1980, 107).

Against the socialist humanists, Althusser rejected both the view that Marx's conception of the social totality could be equated with Hegel's analysis of the same (Althusser 1969, 107–116), and the idea that Marxism was in any sense a humanist ideology. He dismissed the suggestion that there might be a moral component to Marx's (scientific) thought (Althusser 1969, 219–247), and argued that the role of Marxist philosophy was to defend materialism against idealism: it was the "class struggle in the field of theory" (Althusser 1976, p. 64). Furthermore, he claimed that the "class struggle" was the motor of history, which was made by "the masses" and not by "man." In fact, he insisted that the concept of "man" was a bourgeois myth, and society, far from being made up of individuals, was constituted through "social relations," such that, crucially, "history is a . . . *process without a subject.*" From this perspective, Althusser argued that philosophy's role was a political one: to defend materialism by exposing the myths of idealism, including that of the human subject; for these myths would tend to turn "workers away from the class struggle" (Althusser 1976, 77, 79, 85, 83, 98). Althusser's project thus amounted to a nominally left-wing response to the liberalism supposedly inherent to socialist humanism (Althusser 1976, 77, 79, 85, 83, 98).

This interpretation of socialist humanism was doubly problematic. For although it was true that socialist humanism marked a point on a road toward liberalism for many of the generation of 1956 (Anderson 1980, 108), as we shall see in Chapter 5 this was by no means universally so. And by suggesting otherwise, Althusser, as Kate Soper points out, caricatured the complex historical movement that was socialist humanism in an attempt to justify his own allegiance to the Maoist variant of Stalinism (Soper 1986, 112–113).[1] More importantly, his variant of Marxism proved incapable of offering a coherent alternative to Sartre's thought that was able to account for either the mass upsurge in struggle associated with the year 1968 or the subsequent defeats of the struggles that flared up in the wake of that year.

If the defeats suffered by the workers' movement over the next couple of decades informed a widespread questioning of the idea that the class struggle was the motor of history, the fact that Althusserianism was particularly ill equipped to make sense of these defeats reinforced the view that Marxism was inadequate to modern conditions (Callinicos 1982, Ch. 1; 1989, 165; Eagleton 1996, 1). It is perhaps not surprising that as defeats opened the door to neoliberalism, the feeling of impotence and anger on the left lent itself toward a trend to increasingly abstract ethical discourse. Commenting on this tendency, Alain Badiou suggests that for many ex-revolutionaries the turn to ethics was experienced as a return from Marx (politics) to Kant (morality) (Badiou 2001, pp. 1–2, 4). More specifically, Dominique Lecourt explains this shift as

---

1. On the relationship of Maoism to Stalinism see Harris 1978, pp. 283–295.

a consequence of a narrowing "of the political vision" that had been expanded in 1968 (Lecourt 2001, 98).

David Harvey has articulated a particularly sophisticated Marxist variant of this trajectory. He argues that although contemporary socioeconomic trends generally tend to confirm Marx's damning indictment of capitalism, they simultaneously undermine the agency Marx believed would dig capitalism's grave. Whereas the old forms of capital accumulation depended upon the expansion of wage labour which in turn gave "rise to oppositional cultures," the new "accumulation by dispossession" leads to the fragmentation of oppositional forces (Harvey 2005, 178). This analysis informs his engagement with human rights discourse. Commenting on the problems associated with this concept, Harvey argues that though "the neoliberal insistence upon the individual as the foundational element in political-economic life opens the door to individual rights activism . . . by focusing on these rights rather than on the creation or recreation of substantive and open democratic governance structures, the opposition cultivates methods that cannot escape the neoliberal framework" (Harvey 2005, 176). Nevertheless, he argues that it is difficult to conceive of an alternative to the social fragmentation characteristic of neoliberalism without some reference to universal rights. Harvey accordingly suggests that, despite the power of Marx's criticisms of abstract moral discourse, the ideas of justice and rights could be deployed as a mechanism through which the formation of alliances amongst neoliberalism's opponents might be forged (Harvey 1996, 361; 2005, 179–180).

Jerry Cohen's embrace of egalitarian liberalism is rooted in a similar, though less sophisticated discussion of Marx's analysis of class. Cohen claims that, for Marx, the proletariat was that class of people who "constituted the majority of society," "produced the wealth of society," "were the exploited people in society," and "were the most needy people in society." It followed from these propositions that workers would have nothing to lose in a revolution and consequently "could and would transform society." Unfortunately, or so he insists, while there are today groups of people who fit into one or the other of these categories, because there is none that fits them all there is none that can play the role previously ascribed by Marx to the proletariat (Cohen 2000b, 107). It is for this reason that Cohen embraced a form of utopian socialism that converges with egalitarian liberalism.

From a very different perspective Alain Badiou has, despite his criticisms of the return to ethics—he insists "the Leninist passion for the real, which is also a passion for thought, knows no morality" (Badiou 2007, 13–14)—articulated his own ethical perspective; specifically a defence of fidelity to the "truth" of an "event." Hallward points out that Badiou follows Lacan in believing that the "real" can only be accessed through singular encounters or events, and that "a truth persists . . . solely through the militant proclamation of those people who maintain a fidelity to the uncertain event whose occurrence and consequence they affirm" (Hallward 2003, xxv). Concretely, for Badiou, a Maoist militant in his youth, this involves his continuing commitment to the idea of the Chinese Cultural Revolution in the context of its defeat (Badiou 2001, 40–57). Interestingly, his affiliation to a variant of Maoism informs his belief that the failure of this project marked the end of the possibility of a revolutionary alternative to capitalism. Consequently, although he continues to call himself a Communist he refuses the signifier Marxist as "the disorganised masses of global capitalism are no longer divided into classes" (Badiou quoted in Žižek 2008, 406). From this standpoint, Badiou defends the ultimately futile "imperative to 'Keep going!' ": Capitalism might be the only game in town, but Badiou will have no truck with it (Badiou 2001, 91).

This general perspective is shared by Simon Critchley, one of the foremost contemporary (anarchist) representatives of the ethical turn. Critchley argues that while "the truth of Marx's work" is to be found in his analysis of the "emergence and nature of capitalism," his discussion of the political implications of this critique was far less successful. Against Marx's (supposed) claim that social divisions were becoming simplified into an antagonism between the bourgeoisie and the proletariat, Critchley suggests that the proletariat has become increasingly fragmented, and that capitalism is now opposed by a "multiplication of social actors" (Critchley 2007, 90–91). He insists that this situation has had the effect of undermining not only the means by which Marx conceived the socialist struggle against capitalism but also his notion of the ends of communism itself. For, whereas workers' solidarity was the "condition of possibility for the Leninist withering away of the state," he points out that "if class positions are . . . becoming more complex . . . we are stuck with the state." Critchley attempts to square this pessimistic analysis with a call for action through the medium of what he calls "a politics of resistance," which although condemned to perpetual opposition need not, at least, degenerate into tyranny so long as radicals keep "a distance from the state"—he points to the Zapatistas as a concrete example of this strategy (Critchley 2007, 89, 92, 112).

If Slavoj Žižek agrees with Cohen and Critchley about the facts of the dissolution of the old working class, he disagrees with their respective utopian and perpetually oppositional political responses to this context. He goes so far as to call for a repeat of Leninism: although he is keen to point out that "to REPEAT Lenin does NOT mean a RETURN to Lenin" (Žižek 2008, 326, 420; 2002, 310). On the significance of this distinction, Žižek argues that he is not invoking, like the Trotskyists, a project of building renewed Leninist parties which might realise the unfinished business of 1917. Rather, he has the more limited goal of embracing what he calls a "politics of truth." He insists, against those postmodern relativists whose celebration of difference sits so easily with the contemporary liberal consensus, that to repeat Lenin today means to fight for the idea of truth and to challenge the liberal notion that any struggle for an alternative to contemporary capitalism will lead to a new Gulag (Žižek 2002, 168). Concretely, Žižek's attempted repetition of his politics both starts from and is intended to end with a negative act of resistance. In a discussion of Herman Melville's Bartleby, he suggests that just as Bartleby replied to his master's demands with the statement "I would prefer not to," today both the negative critique of the status quo and the positive construction of an alternative to it should be founded upon a similar refusal (Žižek 2006, 342, 382). This reference to negativity allows Žižek a medium through which to pass from Critchley's ethics of resistance to a new political space. As to the concrete shape of this alternative, Žižek criticizes those left neo-anarchists such as Critchley who refuse to engage with the state for what he labels their tacit "Fukuyamaianism." Žižek suggests that though few would explicitly embrace Fukuyama's end of history thesis, Critchley's political pessimism effectively involves a tacit acceptance of the claim that varieties of capitalism mark the parameters of modern politics. Their moral critique of the state serves to limit their radicalism to a form of perpetual resistance: "the contemporary liberal democratic state and the 'infinitely demanding' anarchistic politics are thus engaged in a relationship of mutual parasitism" (Žižek 2008, 349). In opposition to the type of abstract and impossible demands advocated by Critchley, Žižek insists that the left should make concrete demands which cannot so easily be dismissed, and which can be used to mobilize the new proletariat. He argues that Hugo Chavez's capture of the Venezuelan state through a project anchored in the politicization of the slum dwellers points to politics that is infinitely more appealing than the clean-hands characteristic of the postmodern left's anti-statism (Žižek 2008, 427).

Amongst the targets of Žižek's polemical advocacy of this project are Antonio Negri and Michael Hardt. If Cohen's and Critchley's variants of ethical politics reflect their pessimism about the possibility of radical sociopolitical change, Hardt and Negri's ethical anti-capitalism is almost willfully naive in its optimism. Like Cohen, Critchley and Žižek, they agree that the old proletariat is no more. However, they do not suggest that this class has ceased to exist, but rather that it has "been displaced from its privileged position in the capitalist economy." In place of the proletariat, which they characterize narrowly as the "industrial working class," Hardt and Negri locate the hegemonic form of production in the postmodern world to be the "immaterial labour" of the "multitude" (Hardt & Negri 2000, 53). They suggest that this type of labour produces "relationships and ultimately social life itself" and consequently view the multitude, rather than capital, as the dynamic force creating the modern world (Hardt & Negri 2004, 109). Following this proposition, and against the left's pessimistic interpretation of the dissolution of the proletariat, they insist that "the hegemony of immaterial labour creates common relationships and common social forms in a way more pronounced than ever before." This in turn means that, finally, Lenin's goal of the "abolition of the state" might now be realized in a way that was impossible in 1917. For whereas Leninism, in a reflection of the class structure of Lenin's age, involved the reduction of this desire to the "objective of the insurrectional activity of an elite vanguard" whose hierarchical structure consequently reproduced a new form of sovereign state, Hardt and Negri suggest that today this desire is expressed through the "entire multitude" which "needs to abolish sovereignty at a global level" (Hardt & Negri, 2004, 353–354). So optimistic are they about the potential of the multitude's role in creating "the common" that they tend toward a variant of the obstetric approach to politics which Cohen mistakenly ascribes to Marx (Hardt & Negri, 2004, 113, 189). Thus, Negri has gone so far as to claim that his model "abolish[es] any difference whatsoever between ethics and politics" (Casarino & Negri 2008, 151).

The goal of formulating an "ethical project" rooted in "an ethics of democratic political action within and against Empire" (Hardt, & Negri 2009, vii) is welcome. But, as David Camfield points out, the Hardt-Negri analysis of contemporary production tends to underestimate the barriers to building a unified anti-capitalist movement, leaving them with simplistic political perspectives that are little more than "wishful thinking" (Camfield 2007, 47; cf Callinicos 2006, 140–151). Developing a similar point, Žižek claims that Hardt and Negri, in a postmodern repetition of the limitations of the obstetric approach to politics, are too Marxist but not Leninist enough (Žižek 2008, 352, 360). Because they do not adequately address either the problem of state power or the mechanisms through which networking can lead to resistance, they grossly underestimate the difficulties faced by anti-capitalist activists, thus condemning themselves, despite their superficial differences with Critchley, to a similar perspective of perpetual opposition.

Although Žižek is surely right about this, because he accepts Cohen's analysis, the dissolution of the proletariat his politics is perhaps best understood as the flipside of post-Marxist utopianism rather than as a realistic alternative to it. Both sides agree that the state is here to stay, but whereas Critchley, for instance, seeks to wash his hands of this problem, Žižek distinguishes himself by his embrace of its political consequences: the left, he argues, should not fear "directly confronting state power"; it should forego "boring 'ethical' considerations" to "admit revolutionary violence as a liberating end in itself" (Žižek 2008, 339, 406; 2006, 380). He justifies this position through reference to Lacan's claim that "there is no big Other": that is, there is no ethical standard external to the act by which the act might be judged (Žižek 2007, xxiv). Thus, like "the Lacanian analyst, a political agent has to commit acts that can only be authorized by himself, for which there is no external guarantee" (Žižek 2004, 515). Thus Žižek defends a politics of "pure voluntarism," which he equates with Bolshevik practice in 1921 (Žižek 2009a, 154).

Alex Callinicos calls this perspective a form of "left decisionism," and justifiably complains that through it Žižek attempts to defend a return to a variant of what Trotsky labelled, in *Our Political Tasks* (1904), political "substitutionism"; the tendency of elites to substitute their activity for that of the mass of the working class. Given Callinicos's claim, made from a heterodox Trotskyist perspective, that this general approach has blighted much of the history of the left in the twentieth century (Žižek 2007; Callinicos 2006, 113, 119), it is perhaps surprising to note that Žižek has attempted to recruit Trotsky to this perspective. He does this, revealingly enough, through an engagement with what Ernest Mandel described as Trotsky's "worst book," *Terrorism and Communism*. Mandel suggests that whereas Trotsky was generally the most severe critic of all forms of elitism, this text marked an aberration in his career because in it he "justified and defended the practice of substitutionalism" (Mandel 1995, 83. For a powerful critique of this reading of *Terrorism and Communism* see Lih 2007).

If Žižek's reinterpretation of Trotsky as a substitutionist involves a fundamental distortion of the latter's contribution to Marxism, it does tend to fit with his repetition of Lenin without soviets. Against those who have judged both Stalinism and Western capitalism by the standard of the workers' councils, Žižek suggests that, to them, the "standard Hegelian answer is quite sufficient: the failure of reality to live up to its notion always bears witness to the inherent weakness of the notion itself" (Žižek 2004, 516). This argument allows him to bypass the importance of soviets to Lenin's project (Cliff 1976, 315–327) whilst simultaneously dismissing the reality of workers' councils as they have emerged at high points of workers' struggles throughout the twentieth century. This is the backdrop to his idiosyncratic claim that Chavez's government is "coming close to what could be the contemporary form of the 'dictatorship of the proletariat'" (Žižek 2008, 379). Whatever Chavez's merits, Žižek's use of the phrase "coming close" in this sentence hides a multitude of sins. Gregory Wilpert has pointed out that, although community and labour movement groups push for reforms from below while Chavez pushes for similar reforms from above, between these two forces the old state bureaucracy, which has remained relatively intact, acts as a barrier to continued radicalization (quoted in Gonzalez 2009, 57). A key weakness in Venezuela, from this perspective, is precisely that there is not a workers' state (dictatorship of the proletariat), and by suggesting otherwise, Žižek not only confuses changes in government with changes in the state, but also underestimates the powerful barriers that stand between Chávez and the realization of his most radical goals: the state on which he relies is integrated "into networks of capitalist social relations" (Holloway 2002, 14).

A consequence of the way the state is enmeshed in a web of capitalist relations is, as John Holloway argues, a tendency amongst even the most sincere revolutionaries who aim at conquering state power to reproduce the kinds of hierarchical thinking and practices that are characteristic of capitalism generally, and capitalist states more specifically, in a way that undermines their radicalism because it invariably leads to an "instrumental impoverishment of struggle" (Holloway 2002, Ch. 2, 17). This certainly seemed to be the case in 2007 when Žižek dismissed the mass anti-war demonstrations of 2003 as an irrelevant sideshow which merely allowed the protestors to "save their beautiful souls" whilst those in power carried on regardless (Žižek 2007). If this claim is the corollary of Žižek's suggestion that Bartleby's "no" should not simply be addressed to "Empire" but also to any forms of resistance that "help the system reproduce itself by ensuring our participation in it" (Žižek 2006, 383), its problem is not that there aren't faux acts of resistance to capitalism and imperialism, but that the anti-war movement certainly is not one of them. Nevertheless, if Holloway's arguments suggest real problems with Žižek's statism, his own embrace of the Zapatistas as an alternative model of revolutionary change is, as Žižek notes, no less problematic (Holloway 2002, 211; Žižek 2008, 372, 427): their refusal to challenge for state power leaves capitalist hierarchies in place just as much as underestimating the capitalist nature of the existing state does.

Back to Marx

Žižek's concern with politics has the great merit of focusing our attention on the practicalities attendant to the anti-capitalist slogan "another world is possible." However, by skirting over the weaknesses with Chavez's project he leaves unexamined the capitalist social relations embedded within the modern state. The limitations of this approach are, as we have suggested, the flipside of Critchley's stance of perpetual opposition: both agree that the state is here to stay, but disagree on how to respond to this situation. The pessimistic assumptions about not merely the resilience of capitalism but more importantly the fragmentation of the working class also informs the embrace, by David Harvey and Jerry Cohen respectively, of human rights discourse and abstract utopianism. While John Holloway and Antonio Negri and Michael Hardt are much more optimistic about the possibilities for the radical left, this is perhaps because they do not adequately engage with the problems highlighted by Harvey. So whilst Hardt and Negri's political optimism, as embodied in the concrete utopia of the multitude, is appealing, it also has the unfortunate character of being empirically suspect and politically weak (Callinicos 2006, 140–151). Similarly, despite his formal optimism, the reality of the problems faced by the left is reflected in Holloway's paralysis before the question of "what to do?": his answer, "we don't know" (Holloway 2002, p. 215; 2010, p.255).

There is an important sense in which Holloway is right to claim that for anti-capitalists "there is no right answer, just millions of experiments"

(Holloway 2010, 256). However, though past struggles do not provide a simple template of "correct" practice, they do provide an invaluable source of insight into the dynamics of anti-capitalism. For this reason, Holloway's rejection of a caricatured version of classical Marxism acts as a barrier to reassessing the lessons embedded within that tradition. In this book I argue that, once untangled from its caricatures, a renewed Marxism can overcome the limitations of these varied anti-capitalist perspectives. One aspect of this renewal is to rescue Marxist politics from its caricature as a lineal descendent of Jacobinism (see Blackledge 2010a, 148–153). Interestingly, Critchely, Hardt and Negri, Holloway, and Žižek all share a more or less explicit conflation of revolutionary (Marxist) with insurrectionary (Jacobin) politics (Hardt & Negri 2004, 250; Holloway 2002, 15; Critchley 2007, 60; Žižek 2007, viii–ix). This is an important issue, because it involves eliding over the ethical dimension of Marx's politics. From his earliest writings, Marx drew on Hegel's analysis of Jacobinism to criticise the one-sidedly political character of Robespierre's practice (Marx 1975e, 413). Despite Hegel's belief that the Terror was the inevitable excess which accompanied the progressive realization of the freedoms of civil society, he believed that the Jacobin dictatorship did not point toward a more free society because it was the culmination of the abstract political will's attempt to impose its vision on society from the top down, in a way that was not based upon a prior transformation of the nation's "dispositions and religion" (Hegel 1956, 446, 449, 450). It was because Marx took this criticism seriously that he rooted his politics in an analysis of immanent tendencies within capitalism. If these tendencies, as we shall see in Chapter 2, provide a solid answer to the charge that Marx was a nihilist, they are too often misrepresented as evidence of his supposed fatalism (i.e., Wright 2010, 89ff). I have challenged this interpretation of Marx's theory of history elsewhere (Blackledge 2006a), and in Chapters 3, 4, and 5 I argue that once classical Marxism is disassociated from both fatalism and Blanquism it is a relatively straightforward task to reconstruct an ethical Marxist politics that builds upon the contributions of Lenin, Lukács, Gramsci, and others. In this way, I point to a positive model of revolutionary socialist politics that escapes the related charges of nihilism and statism.

    If Althusser was right to suggest that Marx aimed at overcoming the limitations of moral discourse, he was mistaken to believe that this entailed a total rejection of the ethical dimension of action. Far from being a nihilist, I argue that Marx made a fundamental contribution to ethical theory.

In Chapter 1 I attempt to frame the problem of morality for Marxism. After a brief discussion of the emergence of modern moral theory through a comparison with classical Greek ethics, I survey the strengths and limitations of some of the most important modern moral perspectives. This chapter concludes with an overview of Alasdair MacIntyre's claim that no modern moral theory is able to provide a rationally justifiable guide to action, but rather that each approach is best understood as a more or less coherent justification of personal preferences. As we shall see, MacIntyre also claims that Marx's suggested alternative to this emotivist culture must ultimately be judged a failure. The rest of the book is best read as an extended discussion of and attempted answer to this criticism.

In Chapter 2 I argue that Marx was neither a nihilist nor that he held incoherent views on ethics, but that he is best understood as developing a critique of existing social relations from the point of view of the struggle for human freedom. If the theoretical foundation of this perspective involved a reworking of Aristotle's ethics through Hegelian lenses, this synthesis was made from the standpoint of workers' struggles against capital. Indeed, it was on the basis of the virtues of solidarity reproduced in these collective struggles that Marx both condemned capitalism and rejected modern moral discourse. If he took it to be uncontroversial that freedom was the human essence, the practical contestation of this concept through the class struggle informed his rejection of Kant's trans-historical and one-sided understanding of it. In its place, Marx embraced a model, as George Brenkert argues, of freedom as communal self-determination (Brenkert 1983, 88). And whereas Kant naturalized the modern experience of the atomized egoist who is fated to confront the world as a pre-given entity which limits her freedom to (at best) make minor local modifications, workers' struggles reveal a modern agency that is (potentially) able to remake social relations. It was from this perspective that Marx grasped, in Lukács' phrase, the "present as a historical problem" (Lukács 1971, 157). He suggested that, by contesting the freedom of civil society, collective working-class struggles simultaneously provided the standpoint which revealed the essence of capitalism as a system of exploitation and alienation and the basis from which to fight against its egoistic individualism in the name of the virtues of solidarity. He therefore implied a solution to the separation, characteristic of the modern moral theory, between "is" (science) and "ought" (ethics). So while Marx agreed with Kant that freedom was the universal human essence, because he historicized this concept he deepened it to be simultaneously the means to and end of the struggle against capitalism.

In the Chapter 3, I survey the Marxist debates on the ethics of socialism as they evolved within the Second and Third Internationals. I begin with a discussion of the debate between Kautsky, Bernstein, Bauer, and Vorländer occasioned by the emergence of revisionism in Germany at the turn of the last century. This debate signalled the appearance of a Kantian theme that has been repeated within the Marxist movement over the last one hundred years. I then move on to discuss the contributions made to a Marxist ethics of liberation in the inter-war period by Bloch, Gramsci, Lukács, Pashukanis, and Trotsky. These theorists articulated the most sophisticated responses to the problems with Second International Marxism. Specifically, I deal at length with the critique of Kantianism and defence of Leninism as outlined in Lukács' magnum opus *History and Class Consciousness*, before moving on to discuss both Bloch's and Gramsci's contribution to a Marxist ethics and the debate on revolutionary morality between Trotsky and Dewey in the 1930s. My aim is to point to the contribution made by these revolutionaries not only to a theoretical solution to the problem of the ethical status of socialism but also to the practical consequences of this model in an account of ethical leadership.

In Chapter 4, I discuss some of the main post-war (post) Marxist attempts to salvage elements of Marx's critique of capitalism after the apparent falsification of classical Marxism's wager on the proletariat. Theorists associated with both the Frankfurt School and Analytical Marxism, despite their implacably opposed methodological assumptions, agreed that Marx's politics were inadequate to the modern world. After discussing Adorno's specific question of how, if at all, it is possible to live a good life in a bad world, I analyze the normative shift in Analytical Marxism that occurred in the wake of the criticisms, made from within this School, of its founding text: Jerry Cohen's *Karl Marx's Theory of History* (1978). Between these two sections I outline Sartre's brilliantly flawed attempt to outline a revolutionary humanist ethics of liberation. To a greater or lesser degree, I suggest that in each case the retreat from classical Marxism informed an embrace of increasingly abstract ideals, which are susceptible to MacIntyre's criticism of the emotivist character of modern moral discourse.

In the final chapter, Chapter 5, I move on to discuss the debates on socialist humanism as they evolved in the wake of Stalin's death and Khrushchev's "Secret Speech." Focusing on this debate as it developed within the British New Left after 1956, I argue that it reached its zenith with the contribution of the young Alasdair MacIntyre. After surveying the debate, I argue that in the 1950s and 1960s MacIntyre pointed toward the ethical culmination of the all-too-brief renewal of Marxism associated with the works of Lenin, Trotsky, and Luxemburg in the period before the Stalinist counterrevolution, and that this contribution to Marxism points beyond the relativism characteristic of the contemporary turn to ethics.

This perspective provides me, finally, with the resources from which to trace the practical consequences of the argument thus far, and to apply this interpretation of Marx to contemporary trends. My aim in this concluding chapter is to suggest, via a brief survey of the literature on the continued salience of class politics to the modern world, a means through which we might learn from and build upon the lessons of classical Marxism for contemporary anti-capitalist politics.

1

Ethics as a Problem for Marxism

A moral philosophy . . . characteristically presupposes a sociology.

—MacIntyre 1985, 23

The refutation must not come from outside, that is, it must not proceed from assumptions lying outside the system in question and inconsistent with it. The system need only refuse to recognise those assumptions; the defect is a defect only for him who starts from the requirements and demands based on those assumptions.

—Hegel 1969, 581

Marx and Modern Moral Theory

Modern moral philosophy emerged, in part, as a reaction against those materialist models of human agency which, drawing on themes from the scientific revolution, attempted to explain human behavior reductively by reference to our materiality. If Thomas Hobbes' interpretation of human nature was perhaps the most powerful early attempt to articulate such an approach, the continued popularity of something like his reductive model amongst evolutionary psychologists and proponents of selfish gene theory is evidence that its appeal shows little sign of abating (Swarmi 2007; cf Rose & Rose eds. 2000). Whatever the merits of this type of explanation of human behavior, it is at its weakest when confronted with the problem of human freedom; the fact that we always choose how to respond to our natural urges and desires. It was in response to the dilemmas faced when making such reasoned choices that a counter-movement to the reductive paradigm emerged. Classically articulated by Immanuel Kant, the idealist alternative to reductive materialism attempted

to disarticulate the act of choosing from our human desires: the new
science of morality taught that an unbridgeable gulf existed between
what we ought to do and what we are inclined by our nature to do.

There is something appealing about both materialist and idealist
models. It seems intuitively right to suppose that underlying the complex web of our actions is a desire to meet our natural needs; while it
also true that on many occasions we choose to act so as to suppress
or order our desires. Nevertheless, despite the undoubted attraction of
these models of agency, neither seems adequate to the task of grasping
what is distinctive about our humanity. For if materialists reduce us to
little more than machines built for the satisfaction of our natural desires,
idealists suggest that we should repress our natural desires when we make
decisions about the ways we ought to act. These approaches therefore
look less like alternatives than they do two sides of the same mistake:
both analyze our activities in a way that makes them "unintelligible as
a form of *human* action" (MacIntyre 2008a, 58).

Marx, as Lukács argued, aimed to overcome the opposition between
materialism and idealism. His intention was to extend Hegel's attempt
to synthesize causal, materialist models of behavior with purposeful,
idealist accounts of agency, and, by divesting the result of its religious
coloration, provide a framework through which our actions could be
understood as *human* actions (Lukács 1975, 345). Marx's approach to
the problem of human action therefore involved an attempted sublation
(*aufhebung*) of materialism and idealism that is best understood, as we
shall see in the next chapter, through the lens of his Hegelian reading
of Aristotle's essentialism (Meikle 1985; cf MacIntyre 2008a). It was
from this perspective that he disassociated his theory of history from
both crude materialism and idealism (moralism).

"The chief defect of all hitherto-existing materialism," he wrote,
"is that the thing, reality, sensuousness, is conceived only in the form
of the object, or of contemplation, but not as sensuous human activity,
practice, not subjectively. Hence, in contradiction to materialism, the
active side was developed abstractly by idealism—which, of course, does
not know real, sensuous activity as such" (Marx 1975f, 422).

While this argument underpins Marx's famous formal solution to
the problem of structure and agency—"Men make history, but not of
their own free will; not under circumstances they themselves have chosen but under given and inherited circumstances with which they are
directly confronted" (Marx 1973c, 146)—perhaps more importantly it
illuminates the fundamental limitations of modern moral theory.

Contemporary Moral Discourse

The novelty of modern, post-Kantian, moral theory is perhaps best illuminated through a comparison with classical Greek conceptions of ethics. Greek ethics, especially as developed by Aristotle, was unlike modern moral philosophy in that it did not suppose that to be good entailed acting in opposition to our desires. Aristotle held to a naturalistic ethics, which related the idea of good to the fulfilment of human needs and desires (MacIntyre 1985, 122, 135). According to Aristotle the good is that "at which all things aim" and the good for man is *eudaimonia* (Aristotle 1976, 63). Literally translated this concept means something like being possessed of a "well-demon" or being "watched over by a good genius" (Knight 2007, 14; Ross 1949, 190). However, it is more usually, and usefully, rendered as happiness, well-being, self-realization, or flourishing. The latter of these translations perhaps gives the best sense of Aristotle's meaning of *eudaimonia* as a way of life rather than a passing sensation, not a transitory psychological state but an "objective condition of a person" (Norman 1983, 39). In this model, the virtues are those qualities which enable social individuals to flourish as part of a community (MacIntyre 1985, 148). And because Aristotle recognized that humans are only able to flourish within communities—he defines us as "political animals"—he made a direct link between ethics and politics. The question of how we are to flourish leads directly to questions of what form of social and political community would best allow us to flourish. Consequently, as against those who would suggest an unbridgeable gulf between ethics and politics, as we noted in the introduction Aristotle declared the subject matter of his book on ethics to be politics (Aristotle 1976, 64; MacIntyre 1966, 57). More concretely, Aristotle was prescriptive in his model of happiness. He believed that each thing in the world has an end, or *telos*, that is some role which it is meant to play. So, just as, according to his pre-Darwinian biology, eyes have the end of seeing, humans have a specific end which differentiates us from the rest of nature and at which we must excel if we are to be truly happy. Uniquely amongst animals, or so Aristotle believed, humans have the power to contemplate eternal truths. Consequently, he surmised, at its best human happiness involves a life spent developing and using this faculty in line with the virtues (Ross 1949, 191). He therefore distinguished between contemplative activity and more mundane acts of production; associating *eudaimonia* with the former and not the latter. The intrinsic elitism of this argument is all the more apparent when combined with his claim that the good life lived to its full was only open to those who had the leisure time to commit to a life of contemplation, and thus restricted to those who had the fortune to be born well, that is to be born a male member of an aristocratic family with enough wealth to underpin such an existence (Knight 2007, 26). Indeed, Aristotle's discussion of the virtues as the moderate mean between competing vices of extreme, at the peak of which is a virtue of magnanimity which by its very nature was only open to the rich, has led one commentator at least to label him a "supercilious prig" (MacIntyre 1966, 66). Nevertheless, if the substance of Aristotle's ethics is consequently colored by his own social location as a member of the elite of an elitist society—a type of "class-bound conservatism" in MacIntyre's opinion (MacIntyre 1966, 68)—its form implies much more radical conclusions, and indeed opens the door to a far-reaching critique of social relations. For instance, Kelvin Knight argues that the distinctions Aristotle draws between *theoria*, the contemplation of that which is eternal, *praxis*, the contemplation of those processes that are subject to human action, and *poiesis* or productive activity, are unstable, such that Aristotle's elitist conclusions are open to immanent critique from the standpoint of his own system (Knight 2007, 14ff; cf Nederman 2008). Nevertheless, beyond his elitism, Aristotle's account of what it is to flourish presupposes a pre-Darwinian model of human nature that is at odds with both modern liberal conceptions of individual egoism and Marx's historical humanism.

As opposed to Aristotle's social conception of individuality, liberal political theory has at its center a model of egoistic individualism. While this model is often assumed to be obviously true, the biological fact of our individuality should not be confused with the ideology of individualism, which was first systematically conceptualised in Hobbes' *Leviathan* (1651).

According to Hobbes the central fact of human nature is a desire for self-preservation. From this physiological starting point he concludes that in a situation of material scarcity individuals tend to come into conflict with each other over resources resulting in a "war of all against all" (Hobbes 1998, esp. Ch. 13). He argues that, in this context, concepts such as good and bad relate to the need for self-preservation. Accordingly, the might of the individual becomes the basis for what is right. Since the seventeenth century, moral theory has attempted to escape the relativistic consequence of Hobbes' thought while continuing to accept something like his model of competitive individualism.

Marx points to a fundamental problem with this approach. He insists that to perceive oneself as an individual in opposition to society is a product of specifically modern social relations. The further one looks back into history, "the more does the individual . . . appear as dependent, as belonging to a greater whole." Conversely, it is only in the eighteenth century, in the context of the newly emergent "civil society," that social relations between people "confront the individual as mere means toward his private purposes, as external necessity." One consequence of this fact is that "private interests," assumed as fundamental in the ethics of both Kant and Hobbes, are in fact "already a socially determined interest, which can be achieved only within the conditions laid down by society and with the means provided by society" (Marx, Karl 1973a, 156). Against the ahistorical assumption of the universality of modern egoistic individualism, Marx extended Aristotle's claim that we are "political animals" to suggest that it is because of our "gregarious" nature that we are able to "individuate [ourselves] only in the midst of society," and that this process occurs at a historically specific juncture (Marx 1973a, 84). This explains why, for instance, whereas in pre-capitalist societies individuals conceived themselves through mutual relations involving obligations, in modern capitalist society individuals appear "unconstrained by any social bonds" (MacIntyre 1966, 121–128).

Engels claims that in the medieval period, despite the fact that the bulk of peasant production and appropriation was carried out individually, local bonds of solidarity amongst feudal Europe's peasantry were underpinned by those forms of communal land which the peasantry needed in order to survive and which helped them resist lordly power (Engels 1972, 123, 216; Anderson 1974, 148). By contrast, the emergence and eventual domination of capitalist market relations has resulted in production becoming socialized while appropriation remains individualized (Engels 1947, 327–8). This generates a contradictory relationship. Socialized production means that humans depend for their very existence upon a massive web of connections through each other, whereas individual appropriation implies that these individuals confront each other merely as competitors. Modern moral theory arose against the background of this contradiction. Thus, whereas pre-modern thinkers had assumed that because people are social animals, individuals cannot be understood except as part of society, modern moral theory is confronted by the reality of society but can only conceive it negatively as a series of Hobbesian competitors.

Social contract theory, utilitarianism, Kantianism, deconstruction, and even modern virtue ethics can all be understood as attempts to provide an answer to the problem of how to formulate a common good in a world of egoistic individuals. Though Marx's criticisms of morality involve a rejection of these approaches, he follows Kant in putting human freedom at the center of his social theory, whilst arguing that Kant fails to understand real human freedom.

In Hobbes' version of the social contract, self-interested individuals would, in a hypothetical situation, agree to the rule of an absolute sovereign as the best way to guarantee their self-preservation. Although later contract theorists such as John Locke and more recently John Rawls have rejected Hobbes' (conservative) political conclusions, they continue to accept his (liberal) way of framing the question. How, they ask, can self-interested individuals agree to some moral and political order?

A similar problematic stands at the center of the dominant mode of English moral philosophy over the last couple of centuries: utilitarianism. Originating with Jeremy Bentham's defense of the principle of utility or greatest happiness, this approach aimed at providing a scientific basis for reforming society so as to ensure that the greatest number of individuals achieve the greatest pleasure for the least pain. Bentham argued that as "nature has placed mankind under the governance of two sovereign masters, pleasure and pain," it is these two sensations that provide not only "the standard of right and wrong," but also "govern us in all we do, in all we say, in all we think" (Bentham 1990, 9). He insisted that the principle of utility, or what is but another way of saying the same thing—the principle of greatest happiness, is that scientific approach by which we are able to restructure the social order so as to ensure that the greatest pleasure is provided for the greatest number of individuals for the least pain (Bentham 1990, 9–10). Bentham's community is a collection of individuals, and the importance of the concept of individuality to his moral theory cannot be overstated. He argued that it "is in vain to talk of the interest of the community, without understanding what is the interest of the individual" (Bentham 1990, 10). How, according to this model, can a plurality of pleasure seeking individuals avoid Hobbes' "war of all against all"?

An answer to this problem had been articulated by Adam Smith half a century earlier. Smith famously claimed that in a free market economy the general interest could emerge, not from the good intentions of individual actors, but rather as a consequence of the interaction of a plurality of individuals pursuing their own selfish individual interests. Although it might be true, he argued, that concrete individual business-men act selfishly; the consequences of these actions are improvements to the common good.

> He generally, indeed, neither intends to promote the public interest, nor knows how much he is promoting it. By prefer-ring the support of domestic to that of foreign industry, he intends only his own security; and by directing that indus-try in such a manner as its produce may be of the greatest value, he intends only his own gain, and he is in this, as in many other cases, led by an invisible hand to promote an end which was no part of his intention. Nor is it always the worse for the society that it was not part of it. By pursuing his own interest he frequently promotes that of the society more effectually than when he really intends to promote it. (Smith 1994, 484–485)

Smith's "invisible hand" provided a powerful consequentialist foundation upon which later thinkers were able to construct a utilitarian justification of capitalism. However, just as Smith naturalized the capitalist economy and capitalist individualism (Rubin 1979, pp. 167–175), at the core of their moral theory the classical utilitarians posited the existence of reified individuals whose desires were not only assumed to be unproblematically registered in the marketplace, but were also accepted as the proper basis for a moral community. Thus in a development of Bentham's ideas, John Stuart Mill argued that according to utilitarianism the only thing that is desirable as an end is happiness, and the only evidence that something is desirable is that "people do actually desire it" (Mill 1991, p. 168). By thus equating what is good with what people desire, Mill, or so G. E. Moore argued, committed "as naïve and artless a use of the naturalistic fallacy as anybody could desire" (Moore 1990, 21). While this is true, as will become apparent below, the key problem with Mill's argument is not his derivation of ought from is, but his assumption that our needs can be adequately registered through the alienated medium of the marketplace. Mill's approach is innocent both of the ways in which our desires are malleable, and of the fact that just because people are happy with their lot does not entail "that their lot is what it ought to be" (MacIntyre 1966, 237). Moreover, because markets have no mechanism for registering social desires, it is only by looking to those social forces that challenge these alienated relationships that we can begin to conceptualize a link between what is right and what is desired. In contrast to this, Bentham and Mill suggested that by our actions we show that we desire these benefits, that they make us happy, and that therefore they are good. Consequently, as Rawls pointed out, by defining the good "independently from the right" such that the right is defined as that which "maximises the good" it is not difficult to see why utilitarianism acts as a "tacit background" belief within contemporary society (Rawls 1971, 25; Kymlicka 2002, 10). It is no less obvious that it is an inadequate basis from which to articulate a satisfactory theory of social action in the modern world.

By focusing on the ends of actions rather than the means through which these ends are brought about, the broader family of consequentialist morality of which utilitarianism forms a part, is necessarily, in the words of Elizabeth Anscombe, "a shallow philosophy," because for them "the question 'What is it right to do in such-and-such circumstances?' is a stupid one to raise" (Anscombe 1981, 36). The idea that our unmediated desires can act as a basis for the good life is fundamentally problematic. For desires both change over time and exist as pluralities which do not necessarily pull in the same direction. We therefore must choose between them, and on these types of choices consequentialism has very little of interest to say. Indeed, by its focus on the ends of action, utilitarianism downplays just that aspect of our practice which is centrally important to moral theory: the means through which we aim to realize our ends. This lacuna goes a long way to explaining how, despite its radical roots, this approach has been used to justify all manner of inhuman acts in the name of their future consequences (MacIntyre 1964), and by conflating happiness with increased wealth it is blind to the way that modern societies generate so much unhappiness (Ferguson 2007; cf Frank 1999, Ch. 10; and Wilkinson 2005).

By far and away the most important alternative to utilitarianism and consequentialism is Kant's approach to morality. Indeed, to the extent that modern morality is typically understood as a series of strictures which are supposed to govern our conduct, the most sophisticated attempt to provide a rational justification for such a model was articulated by Kant. As Alasdair MacIntyre notes, "for many who have never heard of philosophy, let alone of Kant, morality is roughly what Kant said it was" (MacIntyre 1966, 190).

Following the Greeks, Kant divided philosophy into three parts: logic, physics, and ethics. Logic, he argued, was that formal aspect of philosophy whose domain was the nature of reason itself: it was concerned with *a priori* reasoning rather than with the empirical investigation of the real world. By contrast, because both physics and ethics deal with the material world they each involve empirical reasoning (Kant 1948, 53). Nonetheless, as physics and ethics deal with different parts of the material world, their methods are very different. Physics, according to Kant, is that aspect of philosophy whose subject is the natural world, whereas ethics involves the philosophical attempt to understand and guide our actions as free rational agents. While the overlap between physics and ethics is obvious—we are natural beings with natural needs and desires—it is less obvious why their methods should differ. He justified his attempt to conceptualize the differing approaches of these two parts of philosophy by reference to the limitations of our theoretical knowledge of the real world.

In the *Critique of Pure Reason*, Kant attempted to move beyond Humean scepticism by suggesting a transcendental method of argument which explained how scientists are able to move from empirical observations about the appearance of the world to suppositions about its essence or in his terms about the nature of the thing-in-itself. Nevertheless, he believed that because we are able to posit mutually contradictory yet equally plausible propositions about the thing-in-itself, there exist insurmountable limitations to our knowledge of it (Kant 1948, 111). The equally viable yet contradictory propositions or antinomies include, most importantly for our purposes, Kant's third antinomy between the assumptions that our actions are the product of free will and the assumption that they are conversely the necessary consequence of causal laws of nature (Kant 1933, 409ff). To the extent that our behavior is governed by natural laws, Kant proposed that it be understood via a branch of physics. However, he argued that because humans can be distinguished from the rest of nature by our possession of the faculty of reason, we should conceive our actions not as the effects of some natural laws, but as freely, autonomously chosen consequences of reasoned decisions (Kant 1948, 107ff). Thus, Kant suggests, the existence of a chasm between moral and natural laws—that is, between duty and desire.

Underpinning Kant's aim of disassociating morality or duty from human nature or inclination is his belief that our nature was essentially selfish. If Hobbes had asked how it was possible to "turn a state of war into a state of order and peace," Kant extended this question to ask how competitive individuals might mutually relate in a respectful manner (Reiss 1991, 10). As Allen Wood argues, according to Kant, "in society our inclinations, as expressions of competitive self-conceit, are inevitably a counter-weight to the moral law, which requires strength to overcome it" (Wood 2005, 149). For Kant, the moral law consists, as it did for the Protestant tradition in which he was raised, in essence as a series of limitations on or impediments to the actualization of our selfish and sinful desires. It was for this reason that he could not accept Aristotle's naturalistic approach to ethics: our selfish nature suggests that our needs cannot underpin a moral order. Indeed, the modern claim that there is no necessary connection between statements of fact (is) and value judgements (ought) is underpinned by this claim.

Because Kant sought to give theoretical rigor to existing moral opinion, his thought has been labelled "an essentially conservative view" (MacIntyre 1966, 191). This is, however, no mere contingent fact of his personal moral preferences; rather it follows from the fact that the categorical imperative—the universal moral law which reason teaches us we should freely follow—is a fundamentally negative law. As Alasdair MacIntyre has argued, Kant tells us what we should not do—we should not lie, or break promises, for instance, because if these acts were universalized then society would collapse into chaos—but not what we should do. Because of this, his doctrine is necessarily "parasitic upon some already existing morality" (MacIntyre 1966, 197). Specifically, Kant's ethics rest upon the common moral assumptions of his age. Indeed, the starting point for his moral theory is, according to Paton, "the provisional assumption that our ordinary moral judgements may legitimately claim to be true" (Paton 1948, 15). Thus, rather ironically, despite his insistence on the universality of the moral law, his own moral beliefs clearly have a historical (and, to the modern reader, disquieting) character. Wood points out that "Kant notoriously held some very extreme (even repellent) positions on certain ethical issues." For instance, "[h]e held that murderers should always be put to death, that suicide is contrary to a strict duty to yourself, that sexual intercourse is inherently degrading to our humanity, that masturbation is an even more serious moral crime than suicide, that no disobedience to duly constituted political authority is ever justifiable except when the authority orders you to do something that is itself wrong, and he once argued that lying for the purpose of adding to human welfare, even to save the life of an innocent person from a would-be murderer, is always wrong" (Wood 2005, 130).

Kant's conservatism is therefore manifest at two levels: first, he substantively held to a series of what most people today would consider conservative moral opinions; but second, and much more importantly if MacIntyre is right, this was no accidental reflection of influences of the milieu from which he wrote. The nature of his thought meant that he was compelled to look to the world around him to give positive substance to his morality, and therefore there exists a tendency for him and his followers to bend their views toward the dominant, conservative, morality of the order in which they lived.

Nevertheless, Kant offered much more than a moral justification for the status quo. Because he put the humane treatment of others at the center of moral philosophy, his ethics have appealed to many who would not otherwise share his substantive moral commitments. According to one of his formulations, to act in line with the categorical imperative meant to "[a]ct in such a way that you always treat humanity, whether in your own person or in the person of any other, never simply as a means, but always at the same time as an end" (Kant 1948, 91). One need only glance at this statement for a moment to grasp the power of its appeal to generations of radicals, who, like the Austro-Marxist Max Adler, could agree that "Kant's ethic represents a philosophical expression of the human aims of socialism" (Adler 1978, 63). However, herein lies another problem with Kant's approach: if both radicals and conservatives have been able to embrace his formulation of the categorical imperative, it appears that his theory of how we ought to act fails, ironically, to provide a concrete guide to action. This was the censure levelled at Kant by Hegel, who criticized the abstract nature of Kant's morality, which he characterized at one point by its "sublime hollowness and uniquely consistent vacuity" (Lukács 1975, 287; Taylor 1975, 371; cf Hegel 1952, 89–90). More generally, Hegel argued that Kant's standpoint, that is the moral standpoint, far from being the perspective of pure reason, reflected in fact "the ethical life of the bourgeois or private individual." Thus Kant understood "man" in abstraction not only from his natural needs and desires but also, in Wood's words, the "individual's role in ethical life," was understood "in abstraction from the whole of which it is a part" (Wood 1990, 132).

For all his formalism, Kant had recourse to the traditional Aristotelian concept of happiness when discussing the ends of our actions. He asserts, in MacIntyre's words, that it "would be intolerable if in fact duty were not in the end crowned with happiness." But this proposition makes a tacit link, despite what he writes elsewhere on the subject, between the concept of duty and the concept of human nature (MacIntyre 1966, 196). According to Robert Solomon, by thus suggesting that moral acts should not be executed in the name of happiness, but that happiness should be their reward, Kant generates a paradox which he nowhere resolves (Solomon 1983, 568). So despite Kant's good man being, in the words of Nietzsche, "the emasculated man, the man who has no desires" (Solomon 1983, 487), he ultimately finds it impossible to write on morality without some reference to the fulfilment of our desires.

Commenting on Hegel's criticisms of Kant, Lucien Goldmann suggests that "it is not Kant's ethic which is an empty form but that of actual man in bourgeois individualist society." He argues that Kant is right to suggest that there is a limit to practical egoism, for even the most evil or selfish men recognize the existence of a "universal moral law," even when they disregard it. The problem for Kant is that by assuming bourgeois individualism, he is compelled to conclude that the universal moral community posited by the categorical imperative can only exist at a formal rather than at a real level: our needs and desires are natural-ized as the needs and desires of atomized competitive individuals, and therefore there is no social basis for acting as he believed we should act except by way of some duty which acted against our needs and desires (Goldmann 1971, 174). From this bourgeois perspective moral theories tend to view morality and community as top-down impositions on people. And whereas conservatives embrace this authoritarianism, anarchists and liberals tend either to reject or seek to ameliorate it.

Because modern (liberal) moral theory tends to transpose into the distant past the latest manifestation of human nature (Ramsey 1997, 7–8, 12, 32–37), it effectively acts to naturalize the modern capitalist context within which both it and individualism emerged (Ramsay 1997, 7; Cf Archibald 1993, 45–56; Williams 1976, 133–136). Milton Fisk argues that it is difficult to overstate the importance of this perspective. For, in satisfying personal rather than social interests, the capitalist market is a mechanism which forces actors to relate "in a way that ignores any social links they may have." Markets therefore tend to obscure the social aspect of human nature, and this limitation is carried over into liberalism's "impoverished" model of human nature. One consequence of this facet of liberalism is that when liberals confront concrete ethical issues—Fisk gives the example of the debate on abortion rights—they tend to explain these conflicts superficially in terms of personal interests and values without enquiring as to the social roots of these preferences and values. More generally, it is liberalism's impoverished theory of human nature which underpins the substantive relativism of contemporary moral discourse. By pointing to the social basis of liberalism, Fisk argues, Marx points beyond the seemingly intractable character of debates such as these within contemporary political philosophy (Fisk 1989, 275–288).

If modern capitalist social relations underpin the inherent conceptual weaknesses in liberal approaches to morality, they also tend to undermine the virtues which helped reproduce pre-capitalist communities. In a critical discussion of Marxism, Alasdair MacIntyre has argued that although some of the evils endemic to the modern world arise in part from the character of those who commit them, others are generated by the "gross inequalities in the initial appropriation of capital" which bequeath a structural injustice to the labour market through the exploitative relations thus generated. However, the vices of capitalism go beyond this, for capitalism not only reproduces this exploitative system, it also "miseducates" people to perceive themselves primarily as consumers, for whom "success in life" is increasingly judged through the medium of the "successful acquisition of consumer goods." Consequently, whereas *pleonexia*, the drive to have more and more, was understood by Aristotle to be the very vice that was the counterpart of the virtue of justice, in bourgeois society it has itself become a virtue. This inversion of virtue and vice in turn "provides systematic incentives to develop a type of character that has a propensity to injustice." Consequently, MacIntyre suggests, the malicious character traits noted above are themselves reinforced by capitalist relations of production (MacIntyre 1995, xiii–xvi; 1985, 137; 2006, 39).

Capitalist social relations, according to both Fisk and MacIntyre, therefore inform not only liberalism's inherent moral relativism via its impoverished theory of human nature, but also reproduce the type of egoistic individualism which undermines those practices through which virtuous communities might emerge. And by naturalizing modern individualism and the capitalist social relations which underpin it, liberalism is unable to conceive of the transcendence of the system which undermines both the reproduction of virtuous behavior and the elaboration of an agreed-upon set of standards by which we should live. Furthermore, it offers a tacit apology for capitalism's characteristic power relationship. Jeffrey Reiman comments that liberal assumptions about the atomized, asocial, and ahistorical character of individualism act to smuggle into the supposed disinterested reason of modern moral theory the interests of those who benefit from the reproduction of modern, capitalist, social relations (Reiman 1991, 147).

While Kant's aim was to provide a universally valid argument for obeying the moral law, because we reason from concrete perspectives (MacIntyre 2008j, 314), in a fragmented world of competing interests reason itself tends to become fragmented into so many competing arguments for different visions of what is right. So, modern moral philosophers can agree, for example, that the world is an incredibly socially unequal place, but disagree as to whether or not this is a desirable situation. For instance, contemporary political philosophy is dominated by a debate between libertarians such as Robert Nozick who excuse social inequalities by defending private property rights and egalitarians such as John Rawls who justify such inequalities only insofar as they "benefit the least advantaged" (Callinicos 2000, 36–87). In a classic commentary on the historical roots of this situation, Alasdair MacIntyre points to the rational core of Nietzsche's universal nihilism as a false ahistorical generalization from a real characteristic of bourgeois society (MacIntyre 1985, 113): it is impossible from the standpoint of civil society for moral perspectives to escape the relativistic parameters of "emotivism"—the belief that the phrase "this is good" can essentially be translated as "I approve of it" (MacIntyre 1985, 12). This explains both the intractability of these debates, and the fact that moral and political philosophy tends to be a graveyard for political practice. By suggesting that there is no way of agreeing about the kind of world we should live in, these debates undermine any positive model of a better world and therefore tend to act as a tacit apology for the status quo (Reiman 1991, 147).

The deconstructive turn in ethical theory can be understood as but the latest variant of this tendency to moral relativism. Both Levinas and Derrida share with Kant a conception of morality as duty, because like their liberal forebear they reject ethical naturalism, and alongside contemporarary liberalism deconstruction tends toward a trite celebration of multiculturalism (Eagleton 2009, 223, 241, 247). Simon Critchley argues that because deconstruction starts not from abstract universality but from concrete particularity, a conception of duty derived from Levinas and Derrida is able to escape Hegel's critique of Kant's formalism (Critchley 1999, 41, 48). However, as Terry Eagleton points out, far from escaping the limits of Kantianism, deconstruction deepens them. He suggests that one of the ironies of the academic left's movement toward postmodernism since the 1980s is that it combined the deconstruction of the concepts of the autonomous individual subject and of universal reason alongside a return to Kantian ethical concerns. One consequence of this contradictory movement is that whereas Kant's moral theory presupposed as its point of departure the reasoning individual who was able to come to some universally valid moral conclusions, the poststructuralists' deconstruction of these concepts led them toward locating the moral law in "sheer arbitrary rhetorical force" (Eagleton 1993, 129; 2003, 152–3). More specifically, deconstruction's focus on the concept of the other has led to an extreme form of relativism which can if taken seriously, according to David Harvey, lead to the conclusion that "it would be just as unjust to try to override the cultural achievements of slavery, apartheid, fascism, or caste society as it would be to deny the rights to self-determination of native-Americans or Vietnamese peasants" (Harvey 1996, 351).

One attempt to escape this predicament involves a return to classical (Greek) virtue ethics (Slote 1997). Instead of focusing on the intentions of actors or the consequences of actions, virtue ethicists insist that the key ethical question should be "what kind of person ought I be?" While Aristotle was able to answer this question through reference to his pre-Darwinian model of human nature, an adequate modern virtue ethics must be rooted in a model of human nature that is compatible with Darwin without succumbing to the reductive temptations of social Darwinism. It was Hegel who first pointed toward a solution to this dilemma by suggesting a historical model of human essence.

Ethics beyond Aristotle and Kant

Despite their profound differences both modern and classical conceptions of ethics tend to naturalize the very different social contexts in which they were formulated (MacIntyre 1985, 159). Hegel's great contribution to moral theory was grounded in his historical comparison of these two contexts: he asked how and why moderns are different from ancient Greeks. By doing this he began a process, later completed by Marx, of synthesizing and overcoming the limitations of both Kantian morality and Aristotelian ethics.

As we will see in the next chapter, while Marx shared with Kant the idea that freedom was the essence of humanity, he also insisted upon the concrete natural and historical form taken by that freedom. This alternative to the reified conceptions of humanity common to much of modern moral philosophy drew upon the works of both Aristotle and Hegel. And if we follow Knight's suggestion that Aristotle's substantive elitism is open to an immanent critique from the standpoint of his own system, it is rather beside the point to claim, as does Rodney Peffer, that Marx's views on morality cannot be "completely assimilated to Aristotle's": the issue is rather that their methods converge in important ways (Peffer 1990, 102; Gilbert 1984, 155). For if humans have an essence, and if the aim of human life is to realize the potential of this essence, it follows that social structures which impede this should be challenged (Eagleton 1997, 17–33). Indeed, Richard Miller points out that Marx's theory of alienation recalls Aristotle's "description of deprivations which . . . would deny people a good life" (Miller 1989, 178; 1984, 76ff; cf Wood 1981, 126).

According to Allen Wood, Hegel's contribution to ethical theory is perhaps best understood as an attempt to synthesize the most powerful elements of Kant's and Aristotle's thought (Wood 1990, 7). Just as Aristotle sought to base his ethics on a model of human essence, Hegel insisted that ethics must start from a model of "what human beings *are*," for it is only when they are so grounded that they are able to say "that some modes of life are suited to our nature, whereas others are not" (Wood 1990, 17, 32). Nevertheless, while Hegel follows Aristotle in assuming that the goal of life is self-realization, he broke with him in a typically modern way by recognizing that it is only by way of freedom that this is possible. Consequently, whereas Aristotle insisted that happiness is the end of life, Hegel believed that the end of life was freedom (Wood 1990, 20, 33). Moreover, by linking the pursuits of happiness and freedom—for instance when he wrote that "the moral consciousness cannot forgo happiness"—Hegel suggested a solution to the paradox characteristic of Kant's morality noted above, whereby Kant believed that to act from a sense of duty meant repressing our desires but also that by thus acting we would be rewarded with happiness (Solomon 1983, 568).

For Hegel, to act freely involved acting in accordance with necessity, that is, in line with our human needs and desires (Lukács 1975, 354; Engels 1947, 140; Hegel 1956, 26; Adorno 1973, 249). He therefore criticized "Kant for seeing dichotomies in the self between freedom and nature . . . where he ought to have seen freedom as actualizing nature" (Wood 1990, 70). He believed that moral laws, far from being universal in a transhistorical sense, are in fact only intelligible "in the context of a particular community," and are universalizable only in the historical sense that "communities grow and consolidate into an international community" (Solomon 1983, 480–481). Indeed, Robert Solomon points out that when someone claims to act out of conscience, according to Hegel they are in fact engaged in behavior that is in line with beliefs which "echo" those of the moral community of which they are a part (Solomon 1983, 577). Hegel called this unity of the subjective and objective aspects of ethics in social life *Sittlichkeit*, or ethical life, which he understood to encompass both social institutions and "subjective dispositions" (Wood 1990, 196). Through this concept Hegel pointed to the social content of the idea of freedom by relating it to the movement of "a living social whole" (Lukács 1975, 153). Specifically, whereas liberals embrace an ahistorical conception of human nature, Hegel historicized the concept of essence by conceptualizing humans through their social relations. He nevertheless immunized his thought against possible relativistic consequences of this theoretical movement by reserving the idea of ethical life for those social orders that rationally articulated the relationship between the community and the freedom of the individual (Wood 1990, 205, 208). In this way he worked a dramatic change on Aristotle's conceptualization of happiness. For if there is an important sense in which human nature evolves with the cultural evolution of communities, then so too does the concept of self-realization. Wood consequently labels Hegel's theory as a form of "dialectical or historicised naturalism" (Wood 1990, 33). From this perspective, Hegel partially accepts Kant's argument that ethical norms be used as standards which act as a constraint on our desires. However, as opposed to Kant, he also argues that duties need not merely be things I ought to do but can in certain circumstances be things, in Wood's words, "I spontaneously want to do." Indeed, he insists that the good only truly becomes good when it is reconciled with our desires (Wood 1990, 210, 214). This approach involved a conception of desire that was both historical and critical, and therefore a conception of essence which escaped the abstractions of liberal political theory.

Unfortunately, if the great strength of Hegel's ethics was his attempt to overcome the opposition between Aristotle and Kant through a historicized conception of essence, his own positive account of the institutions through which the freedom of moderns could be realized was far from persuasive (MacIntyre 1966, 209). This reflected, as Marx suggested, a deeper limitation with his thought: despite his nominally historicized conception of essence, because he conceived the self-transformative labour at the core of his theory of history as intellectual labour while accepting the political economists' ahistorical conception of productive labour, in practice he was unable, as Chris Arthur comments, to "see beyond the horizon of capitalism" (Arthur 1986, 68). Consequently, according to Lukács, although Hegel criticised "the narrow and confined character of Kant's moral doctrine, he does not manage to surpass this limitation himself" (Lukács 1980a, 71). This contrasts with Marx's standpoint, which as we shall argue in the next chapter allowed him to recognize the specifically capitalist nature of alienation and therefore the anti-capitalist implications of the struggle for freedom. It is because Hegel conceived history as the history of consciousness rather than as the practical transformation of the world and humanity through productive labour he was ultimately unable either to "make a radical critique of the real world of estrangement" or to point to its "practical objective transformation" (Arthur 1986, 61).

The Crisis of Modern Moral Theory

The problem of how one might live a virtuous life in a world in which community and the virtues are constantly undermined by the rule of capital has taxed some of the most important moral philosophers of the twentieth century. Commenting on the culture in which deontological and consequentialist approaches to morality dominate, Elizabeth Anscombe famously argued that whereas consequentialism is obviously inadequate as a theory claiming to guide our actions, contemporary moral discourse more generally—that is morality understood in broadly Kantian terms—continues in the shadow of a past moral framework, but without the belief in a law-giving deity through which such an approach might be justified.

> To have a *law* conception of ethics is to hold that what is needed for conformity with the virtues failure in which is the mark of being bad *qua* man (and not merely, say, *qua* craftsman or logician)—that what is needed for *this*, is required by divine law. Naturally it is not possible to have such a conception unless you believe in God as a law-giver;

like Jews, Stoics, and Christians. But if such a conception is dominant for many centuries, and then is given up, it is a natural result that the concepts of "obligation," of being bound or required as by a law, should remain though they had lost their root; and if the word "ought" has become invested in certain contexts with the sense of "obligation," it too will remain to be spoken with a special emphasis and special feeling in these contexts. (Anscombe 1981, 30)

This argument greatly influenced Alasdair MacIntyre's claim, noted above, that in the modern world ethics has become but a "simulacra of morality," characterised by interminable debates where the arguments presented by either side are "incommensurable" while purporting to present "impersonal rational arguments," which in fact are premised upon a variety of distinct historical antecedents (MacIntyre 1985, 8–10).

In an early review of Rawls' *A Theory of Justice*, MacIntyre claimed that despite the undoubted power of Rawls' arguments, his thesis was undermined by his unwitting confusion of general and historically specific characteristics of human rationality: the "initial situation" which Rawls deployed as a convenient analytical tool from which to imagine "rational agents" agreeing upon the basic structure of society reflected not some pristine human rationality but a bias toward modern bourgeois individuality (MacIntyre 1972; 1988, 133). Beyond smuggling a bias toward bourgeois individualism into his moral theory, Rawls smuggled more specific aspects of his own egalitarianism into his first principles. While there was much that was subsequently persuasive about Rawls' arguments, these tacit assumptions would act as the Achilles' heel of his arguments, undermining their appeal to all who did not share his starting point.

More generally, MacIntyre argues that in the contemporary world, though we continue to use many of the concepts associated with classical ethical theory, these concepts have been unhinged from the social context in which they once made sense. It is as if, he argues, some dramatic catastrophe was to overcome our world, the consequences of which included the destruction of our existing scientific culture, right down to the teaching of elementary science in schools. Assuming that a movement arose in the wake of this event which sought to reinstitute science, but in a world without scientists or even a basic knowledge of science and with only a few fragments of surviving scientific texts, the resultant *pot pourri* of decontextualized snippets of scientific knowledge would be but a pathetic parody of the original, now lost, culture. Similarly, he argues that whereas conceptions of good and bad, etc. once had definite meanings within classical literature, today they have become disembodied. For instance, MacIntyre argues that Homer believed that to be good was to play a particular social role well—thus it would have been meaningless to ask "was he a good man?" in some generic sense rather than was he a good athlete/king/soldier, etc. in a sense that is partly comparable to modern questions such as "is she a good electrician?." It follows that to be virtuous involves work toward excelling in your social role. For Aristotle, the moral question has changed but is still recognizably related to Homer's. To be good, from his perspective, is to be a good citizen of the polis, and this involves carrying out some specific socially accepted role as part of the polis. In both of these cases the separation of facts and values does not exist in the way that it does within, and in large part defines, modern moral theory. MacIntyre suggests that where there had once been socially accepted norms, there exists today a cacophony of incommensurable moral perspectives which can be reduced to more or less coherent expressions of personal preferences (MacIntyre 1985, 122, 135).

Developing this argument, MacIntyre claims that Marx was "right when he argued against the English trade unionists of the 1860s that appeals to justice were pointless, since there are rival conceptions of justice formed by and informing the life of rival groups." Furthermore, although he was mistaken in his belief that contestations over the nature of justice were secondary social phenomena, he was "fundamentally right in seeing conflict and not consensus at the heart of modern social structure": "modern politics is civil war carried out by other means." Interestingly, MacIntyre argues that the pervasiveness of these conflicts in the modern world was classically expressed in the work of Nietzsche (MacIntyre 1985, 19, 113, 250, 252–3). However, he claims that Nietzsche's perspective on the world is best understood not, as Nietzsche himself would have it, as a radical alternative to eighteenth and nineteenth century liberal individualist ethical thinkers, but rather as a "representative moment in [the] internal unfolding" of this system of thought. As an alternative to the worldview which culminated in Nietzsche, MacIntyre suggests that some form of Aristotelianism is able both to account for the impasse of liberal individualism and to offer the basis for an alternative tradition through which we might restate our "moral and social attitudes and commitments" in such a way as to restore their "intelligibility and rationality" (MacIntyre 1985, 259). Commenting on a number of expected criticisms of this argument, MacIntyre predicted that although Marxists might accept his critique of liberal individualist—bourgeois—morality, they would reject his "realistic" political alternative to the status quo.

Against Marxism, MacIntyre posited a number of arguments. First, in the century since Marx's death, insofar as Marxists had taken "explicit moral stances" they tended to fall back on either one form or another of "Kantianism or utilitarianism." Second, Marx failed to conceptualize the means through which his vision of "a community of free individuals" was to be constructed. Third, Marxists in power had tended to become Weberians. Fourth, Marx's political optimism was undermined by capitalism's tendency to morally impoverish the human resources necessary to renew society. Additionally, MacIntyre insisted that anyone who took Trotsky's mature analysis of the Soviet Union seriously would be drawn to embrace a form of political pessimism that was incompatible with Marxism. Finally, he argued that in conditions of moral impoverishment, far from offering an adequate alternative to Nietzschianism, Marxists were wont to construct their own "versions of the *bermensch*": "Lukács's ideal proletarian," or "Leninism's ideal revolutionary" for instance (MacIntyre 1985, 261–2).

MacIntyre claims that the failure of Marx's politics was rooted in a systemic problem with his theory of history. His economic predictions had been found wanting by the test of history, and the working class had failed to become the self-conscious revolutionary agency that Marx had envisaged. In fact, Marx's analysis of capitalism was correct "only so long as the capitalist does not become conscious of those workings in a way that enables him to modify them." However, capitalists had in the second half of the twentieth century attained such a consciousness and consequently had suitably modified the system. Furthermore, the working class "was either reformist or unpolitical except in the most exceptional of situations." Indeed, Marx's failings as a political economist informed his failings as a politician: economic expansion underpinned a growth in the standard of living of workers, which in turn fostered an unpolitical and reformist way of life (MacIntyre 1995, 83–4, 119–120).

Marx had failed to see how politics and ideology could fundamentally affect economics in the way noted above because he had become hamstrung by his use of the base-superstructure metaphor, according to which, or so MacIntyre claimed in 1968, these two elements of the social totality "stand in external, contingent, causal relationship to each other." Repeating this claim in 1995, he suggested that this reified way of conceptualizing the relationship between politics, economics, ideology, and so forth reflected the extent to which Marx's thought was "distorted in a characteristically *bürgerlich* manner" (MacIntyre 1995, xviii, 136–137; 1970, 60–61). Marxism was a product of its time, and this was its undoing. For while Marx attempted to theorize praxis, his deployment of the base-superstructure metaphor saw him revert back toward crude mechanical materialism. Nevertheless, the base-superstructure metaphor was not the fundamental problem with Marxism; rather this prize was reserved for Marx's undeveloped model of praxis itself.

In his most developed mature criticism of Marx, "The *Theses on Feuerbach*: A Road not Taken," MacIntyre argues that Marx was too impatient when he left philosophy in 1845, and that had he developed the implicit Aristotelianism of his concept of working-class practice he might have recognised the limitations of this practice, and, consequently, the utopian nature of his own political optimism. It was to Marx's credit, MacIntyre argues, that he recognized that the standpoint of civil society could not be overcome by theory alone, but it was unfortunate that he had not given greater philosophical consideration to the nature of the practice through which it might be sublated (MacIntyre 1998, 230). While it was not fatal to the Marxist project that Marx had not made explicit the Aristotelian assumptions which underpinned his *Theses on Feuerbach*—MacIntyre notes that others, as we have noted above, have made explicit what was implicit—it was disastrous for his project that he left unexamined the nature of proletarian activity itself. He argues that the modern proletariat is unable to embody the type of social practice imagined by Marx, and illustrated by Edward Thompson in his *The Making of the English Working Class*. Indeed, he claims that the process of proletarianization, by contrast with Marx's expectations to the contrary, has simultaneously made resistance a necessary part of the lives of the working class, while robbing this resistance of its emancipatory content. Proletarianization, he claims, "tends to deprive workers of those forms of practice through which they can discover conceptions of a good and of virtues adequate to the moral needs of resistance" (MacIntyre 1998, 232). Developing this point, Kelvin Knight argues that because workers are not only exploited and alienated, but also find themselves, insofar as they act as workers, manipulated by managers, then their typical form of activity cannot generate those goods internal to practice which

MacIntyre believes are essential if a virtuous alternative to capitalism is to emerge in practice (Knight 2000, 86; 2007, 149). Consequently, MacIntyre has concluded that Marx's wager on the working class cannot today be justified, and, because Marxism cannot legitimately claim to be the theoretical expression of working-class practice, to the extent that Marxists articulate ethical critiques of capitalism they tend to revert to one or other form of modern bourgeois morality: typically either consequentialism or deontology.

According to MacIntyre, Marx's theories of exploitation and alienation imply that because capitalist production involves the separation of means and ends, working-class producers "cannot be understood as engaged in practices with internal goods" (Knight 2007, 149; 1998, 232). Even when workers combine in struggle to resist the dehumanizing effects of capitalism on their lives, they tend to do so within parameters set by capitalism. So, in struggling for a "fair day's wage," for instance, workers accept the separation of means and ends characteristic of capitalism. Consequently, MacIntyre concluded that both proletarian productive activity and the struggles of workers against that activity are conceived as being forever trapped within the confines of civil society.

It was for this reason that Marxism failed to become the theoretical expression of real workers in struggle, but rather became the pseudo-science of the self-appointed "leaders" of the workers' movement whose claims to understand the iron laws of history were but masks for another incommensurable moral framework in a world where ethical positions generally have become more or less coherent expressions of personal preferences (MacIntyre 1985, 19). It was the elitism of Marxism thus presented which tied it too closely to modern society, and which therefore opened it to subsumption amongst the traditions criticized in *After Virtue*. Thus, it was the consequentialist framework allegedly shared by Kautsky, Lenin, Trotsky, and Stalin, which revealed how far their critiques of capitalism were not simply marked by their origin within bourgeois society but had in fact failed to go beyond the typically bourgeois separation of means and ends. Although Marxists such as Guevara or Liebknecht broke with this framework, they did so only to replace Bentham with Kant: the bourgeois frame of reference was apparent at every turn (Knight 2007, 119–122). So while, in 1977, MacIntyre argued that "one Liebknecht [is worth] a hundred Webers" and "one Jaurès is worth a hundred Durkheims," he bemoaned the fact

that the Marxism of these virtuous men had undermined their attempts
to break free of bourgeois modes of thought (Knight 2007, 127, 172).

Conclusion

Given the content of this argument, it is perhaps surprising to discover
that in the late 1950s and early 1960s, as we shall see in Chapter 5, in
a brilliant contribution to the British New Left's debates on the nature
of socialist humanism, MacIntyre prefigured many of the criticisms of
contemporary moral philosophy that were later extended on the pages
of *After Virtue* but with one very important difference. In this period
he not only declined the suggestion that Marx's mature writings had
degenerated toward a form of mechanical materialism, but also argued
that a viable virtue ethics could be reconstructed from Marx's comments on the subject which could provide a powerful basis from which
to articulate an alternative both to Stalinism and liberalism. He argued
that Marx had provided a framework through which the limitations
of Kantianism and utilitarianism could be historically explained, whilst
simultaneously providing a framework to understand how human desires
might evolve to provide a materialist basis for the realization of something
like Kant's categorical imperative. He formulated this argument through
an attempt to disarticulate Marx's theory of history, including his use
of the base-superstructure metaphor, from what he then considered to
be its positivist caricature at the hands of both liberals in the West and
Stalinists in the East.

   He therefore pointed toward a solution to the paradox by which
Marx famously rejected the suggestion that socialism be grounded in
some abstract moral principles while simultaneously making ethical criticisms of capitalism. The question that I ask in this book is "Need we
accept MacIntyre's mature critique of Marxism, and if not, does Marxism indeed provide the resources which might help both to extricate
us from the crisis of modern moral philosophy, and also inform those
anti-capitalist struggles which could contribute to overcoming the social
basis for our contemporary moral fragmentation?."

   I attempt to show that Marx did succeed in overcoming the limitations of both modern moral theory and modern materialism while pre-
serving insights from each: he articulated a non-reductive, but scientific,
basis for human action that escapes the weaknesses of "commonsense"

morality. In so doing, Marx showed, contra the moralists, that although there are no disinterested reasons for action, in certain circumstances specific interest groups can act in the universal interest. Moreover, he showed that under modern capitalist relations of production working-class revolutionary practice could be in the universal interest whilst simultaneously realising such needs for solidarity which make socialism a real historical possibility. Indeed, I argue that Marxists have, in their most sophisticated writings on the subject, outlined a basis from which they are able to justify revolutionary socialist practice through reference to Marx's implicit Aristotelianism, by which the goods internal to working-class struggles are both the means and ends of virtuous activity. Specifically, I argue that Marx showed that collective working-class struggles against capitalism not only provide a viable, virtuous alternative to the consequentialist and deontological ethics that are hegemonic within contemporary political philosophy but also point to the concrete social content of the struggle for freedom in the modern world.

2

Marx and the Moral Point of View

The criticism of religion ends with the doctrine that *for man the supreme being is man*, and thus with the *categorical imperative to overthrow all conditions* in which man is a debased, enslaved, neglected and contemptible being.

—Marx 1975c, 251

Introduction

This chapter opens with a discussion of Marx and Engels' famously ambiguous comments on the issue of ethics and morality. Against the dominant reading of these texts, according to which "no interpretation of Marx's various remarks on justice and rights can make them all consistent with one another" (Elster 1985, 230), I follow those, such as Alan Gilbert and Roy Edgley, who have suggested that a coherent ethics can be reconstructed from their writings once they are adequately contextualized and understood (Gilbert 1984, 155; Edgley 1990, 24). Specifically, Marx and Engels' approach (Blackledge 2006a, 20) to the issue of morality is best understood as an aspect of a broader methodology which encompasses both normative and explanatory social theory: Marx's critique of political economy, his theory of history, his ethics, and his politics are all aspects of a greater whole which derives from viewing society from the standpoint of the working class. This aspect of Marx's work sets it apart from modern moral theory in a way that has confused so many who have interpreted his work from the moral standpoint. Marx not only claims that workers' collective struggles illuminate the historical specificity of capitalism's exploitative and alienated essence, he also suggests that through their collective struggles

workers are able to realize an emergent need for solidarity through
which they are able to reproduce virtues which begin to overcome
the dualism between the good of each and the good of all in a way
that points to a possible future beyond the capitalist mode of production. Ironically, it is precisely because Marx recognizes that everyone
(himself included) "believes" in morality, truth, justice, and so on that
these concepts cannot, as Hal Draper points out, act as "substitutes"
for concrete political analyses of concrete situations (Draper 1990, 29,
31). However, it does not follow from Marx's argument that morality
is an inadequate basis for action in socially divided societies that he
was a nihilist. It is better to understand him as an ethical thinker who
is a stern critic of moralism, where the term moral is understood to
emphasize an abstract imperative to action on the individual by contrast
with (virtue) ethics which stresses the development of "individual character" in a sociohistorical context (Williams 2006, 6). More generally,
Marx's criticisms of abstract moralizing do not reflect a tendency in
his work to dismiss purposeful human agency. Rather, they illuminate
the importance of such agency to his model of social transformation. It
is because, in Marx's view, the struggle for socialism involves concrete
and complex social movements whose outcome cannot be determined
in advance that abstract concepts, such as moral abstractions, must be
replaced by more concrete categories.

While this approach is a powerful counter to moralism, it has had
the unfortunate consequence of obscuring the ethical dimension of Marx's
thought. In fact, not only is this aspect of his work often only implied,
frequently it is actually denied. If these denials inform the manner in
which his contribution to the study of ethics is often dismissed within
the academy, the tendency to overlook his ethics also reflects the way
that his approach to such issues defies the categories of contemporary
moral discourse. For, whatever the undoubted differences between and
within modern social contract theory, utilitarianism, Kantianism, and even
contemporary virtue ethics, Marx characterised many of the seminal texts
of these traditions as examples of the type of reified thinking typical
of attempts to understand the world from "the standpoint of political economy" or, what is a synonym for this, "the standpoint of civil
society." By this, Marx meant that these theorists tended to naturalize
that which was a product of history; the modern notion that society is
made up of atomized and egoistic individuals. Whether modern moral
philosophers extend this assumption to derive egalitarian or libertarian,

deontological or consequentialist conclusions from their work is of secondary importance to this fact, for Marx shows that modern egoistic individualism, far from being a self-evident starting point for theories which aim to inform human behaviour, is itself a product of history.

Moreover, although modernity can be characterized, in part, by the rise of egoistic individualism, it has also witnessed a series of titanic collective struggles for freedom which do not fit easily with the models of selfish egoism assumed to be true by the classical political economists. Indeed Marx's ethics of freedom, while built upon insights taken from Hegel's attempt to deepen Kant's ethics through a synthesis of elements of his thought with aspects of Aristotelianism, was only possible from the perspective of these struggles. It was from this vantage point that Marx recognized the historical nature of modern individualism and the real unfreedom and alienation that lies beneath capitalism's formal freedoms. Marx wagered that the need for solidarity and collective organization amongst workers creates the potential not only to expose but also to overcome the narrow confines of bourgeois society: his was most definitely an ethical politics.

Marx and Morality

A fundamental problem common to any attempt to reconstruct a Marxist ethics from Marx's writings is that he nowhere wrote anything comparable to the classical works of ethical theory penned, for instance, by Aristotle, Mill, or Kant. Kamenka has claimed that if an anthology entitled "Marx on Ethics" were to be published, "it would contain no passages that continue to be strictly relevant for more than three or four sentences" (Kamenka 1969, 6). Nevertheless, while Marx did not write a work of ethics, he did engage with ethical themes throughout his *oeuvre* such that Brenkert is justified in claiming that "much of Marx's writings, for example the *Economic and Philosophical Manuscripts*, *The Communist Manifesto*, even *Capital* and the *Grundrisse*, sound very much like moral tracts—or at least significant parts of them do—even though little 'moral language' appears in them" (Brenkert, 1983, 15).

It is perhaps as a consequence of the scattered and unsystematic nature of Marx's remarks on ethical themes that academic discussions of his approach to issues of socialist morality tend to focus upon individual sentences which when taken out of context are easily misconstrued.

Thus, typically, Marx's "scientific" criticisms of moral theory and moralizing are juxtaposed to his own moral condemnations of capitalism and the like to suggest the irredeemably inconsistent quality of his thought (Kamenka 1969, 5). While this is an easy rhetorical ploy, it is an uncharitable one that serves to obscure more than it illuminates. By contrast, Brenkert points out that it is of the first importance when discussing Marx's views on morality to understand that his seemingly contradictory remarks on the subject are conceptualized as part of his broader social theory (Brenkert 1983, 132–3). For beneath the superficial contradictions manifest in Marx's comments on ethical matters, there is a deeper consistency to his approach to politics. To grasp this involves extricating oneself from the positivistic assumptions that underpin the caricatures of both Marx's political economy and his theory of history.

It is important to remember that although Marx wrote in a language inherited from Hegel and Aristotle, he has often been criticized as though he was a positivist and technological determinist. For example, in the 1859 preface to *A Contribution to the Critique of Political Economy*, he wrote that "[a]t a certain stage of development, the material productive forces of society come into conflict with the existing relations of production. . . . From forms of development of the productive forces these relations turn into their fetters. Then begins an era of social revolution" (Marx 1970, 20). Richard Miller points out that when statements such as this are interpreted through a positivist lens, Marx is construed as making hard technologically deterministic predictions which are not only falsifiable but have in fact been falsified. As Miller argues, neither Marx nor "most of his insightful followers" understood historical materialism in this way (Miller 1984, 7, 271ff). Developing a similar point, Scott Meikle suggests that historical materialism is best understood as locating *tendencies* within history (Meikle 1985, 57; cf Blackledge 2006a, 14–16). From this perspective, while the mode of production shapes the contours of social struggles, it is up to real men and women to fight for their desired ends, and such struggles necessarily have a normative dimension (Blackledge 2006a).

As to the nature of the normative dimension of his work, Marx is at least clear that it should not be conflated with bourgeois morality, which naturalizes capitalist social relations and the historically relative morality concomitant to these. In what was perhaps his most famous discussion of morality, Marx wrote to a number of his closest collaborators in Germany in 1875 to dismiss the claim as put forward in the new Social Democratic Party's *Gotha Programme*, for the "fair distribution of the proceeds of labour." Against this demand, he wrote: "Does not the bourgeoisie claim that the present-day distribution is 'just?' And given the present mode of production is it not, in fact, the only 'just' system of distribution?" (Marx 1974d, 344). This suggestion of the rights of the capitalist system itself was but a recapitulation of his claim, as laid forth in *Capital*, that within bourgeois society the class struggle manifests itself as a conflict of "right against right," and that between this antinomy of "equal rights" only "force decides" (Marx 1976, 344). Two decades earlier he and Engels, writing in *The German Ideology* (1845), had similarly argued that the emergence of a contradiction between capitalists and workers "shattered the basis for all morality, whether the morality of asceticism or of enjoyment" (Marx and Engels 1976, 419). Within a year they reaffirmed this position in a letter to Köttgen (15 June 1846), in which they argued that Communists must "have no truck with tedious moral scruples" (Marx and Engels 1984, 56). Similarly, in 1846 Marx criticised Proudhon for, amongst other things, his "mutton-headed, sentimental, utopian socialism" (Draper 1990, 23). More generally, he insisted in the *Civil War in France* (1871), that

> [t]he working classes have no fixed and perfect Utopias to introduce by means of a vote of the nation. They know that in order to work out their own emancipation—and with it that higher form of life which the present form of society irresistibly makes for by its own economic development—they, the working classes, have to pass through long struggles, a whole series of historical processes, by means of which men and circumstances will be completely transformed. They have no ideals to realise, they have only to set at liberty the elements of the new society which have already been developed in the womb of the collapsing bourgeois society. (Marx 1974d, 213)

This argument resonated with another put forward a quarter century earlier in *The German Ideology*:

> Communism is for us not a state of affairs which is to be established, an ideal to which reality [will] have to adjust itself. We call communism the real movement which abolishes the present state of things. The conditions of this movement result from the premises now in existence. (Marx and Engels 1976, 49)

These passages seem to prove beyond a doubt that Marx rejected moral discourse, which in any case his materialist conception of history showed to "no longer retain the semblance of independence" (Marx and Engels 1976, 37). Nevertheless, Marx did make use of moral concepts when he saw fit. Thus, the postface to the second edition of *Capital* includes a moral denunciation of that generation of economists who, writing in the wake of the scientific works of Smith and Ricardo, reduced themselves to "hired prize-fighters" for capital (Marx 1976, 97). Likewise, in the *Inaugural Address of the International Working Men's Association* (1864), he wrote of "the simple laws of morals and justice, which ought to govern the relations of private individuals" (Marx 1974a, 81). And while, as we shall see below, he famously claimed that this line was inserted into the address where it would do "no harm," no such ulterior motives can explain the moral praise heaped upon the British factory inspectors in *Capital* (Marx 1976, 406; cf Draper 1990, 32–3). Neither can it explain the existence, elsewhere in that book, of moral condemnations of traders and moneylenders alongside an outright moral denunciation of the "vampire"-like nature of capitalism itself (Wilde 1998, 34; cf Marx 1976, 416). In fact Marx condemned the way capitalism dehumanized even those whom he believed could become the agency to overthrow it:

> More than any other mode of production, [capitalism] squanders human lives . . . and not only blood and flesh, but also nerve and brain. Indeed it is only through the most enormous waste of the individual development that the development of mankind is at all preserved in the epoch of history immediately preceding the conscious organisation of society. (Marx cited in Cohen 2000b, 25)

In the *Critique of the Gotha Programme* Marx pointed to a historical model of ethics which provides the tools necessary to give coherence to these seemingly contradictory statements (Kain 1988, 176ff).

> We are dealing here with a communist society, not as it has developed on its own foundations, but, on the contrary, just as it emerges from capitalist society. In every respect, economically, morally, and intellectually, it is thus still stamped with the birthmarks of the old society from whose womb it emerges. Accordingly, the individual producer gets back from

society . . . exactly what he has given it. . . . Hence, equal right is here still—in principle—a bourgeois right, . . . In spite of such progress this equal right still constantly suffers a bourgeois limitation. The right of the producers is proportional to the labour they do; the equality consists in the fact that measurement is made *by the same* standard, labour. One person, however, may be physically and intellectually superior to another and thus be able to do more labour in the same space of time or work for a longer period. To serve as a measure labour must therefore be determined by duration or intensity, otherwise it ceases to be a standard. This equal right is an unequal right for unequal labour. It does not acknowledge any class distinctions, because everyone is just a worker like everyone else; but it gives tacit recognition to a worker's individual endowment and hence productive capacity, as natural privileges. *This right is thus in its content one of inequality, just like any other right.* A right can by its nature only consist in the application of an equal standard; but unequal individuals (and they would not be different individuals if they were not unequal) can only be measured by the same standard if they are looked at from the same aspect, if they are grasped from one particular side, e.g., if in the present case they are regarded only as workers and nothing else is seen in them, everything else is ignored. Further: one worker is married, another is not; one has more children than another, etc., etc. Thus, with the same work performance and hence the same share of the social consumption fund, one will in fact be receiving more than another, etc. If these defects are to be avoided rights would have to be unequal rather than equal, Such defects, however, are inevitable in the first phase of communist society, given the specific form in which it has emerged after prolonged birthpangs from capitalist society. Right can never rise above the economic structure of a society and its contingent cultural development. In a more advanced phase of communist society, when the enslaving subjugation of individuals to the division of labour, and thereby the antithesis between intellectual and physical labour, have disappeared; when labour is no longer just a means of keeping alive but has itself become a vital

need; when the all-around development of individuals has
also increased their productive powers and all the springs of
co-operative wealth flow more abundantly—only then can
society wholly cross the narrow horizon of bourgeois right
and inscribe on its banner: From each according to his ability, to each according to his needs! (Marx 1974d, 346–7)

In this passage Marx not only argues that the wage relationship is just
when viewed from the standpoint of civil society, but also that socialist
revolution cannot overcome the limits of the market without the prior
development of the forces of production. In a discussion of this argument,
McNally comments that postrevolutionary society will be characterised
by a developing mediation of those limits through "the increasing subordination of market transactions to non-market regulation" (McNally
1993, 215). How long this period will last is itself dependent upon
the material inheritance of the revolutionary regime (Rosdolsky 1977,
433–434; cf Trotsky 1972, 52–56). Nevertheless, despite pointing to
the historical and material basis of moral discourse, the needs principle
to which Marx refers predated Marxism as an organic demand of the
workers' movement. The fact that this demand was taken up within the
working class is evidence that once the discourse on equality and freedom was raised by representatives of the bourgeois revolution it created
a space within which the meaning of these terms could be contested.
Against the narrow, formal equalities and freedoms of the marketplace, in
the hands of workers and their representatives the demands for equality
and freedom were deepened, under the banner of the needs principle,
in a way that pointed beyond the historical limits of bourgeois society.
As Engels wrote:

The demand for equality in the mouth of the proletariat
has therefore a double meaning. It is either—as was the
case especially at the very start, for example in the Peasant War—the spontaneous reaction against the crying social
inequalities, against the contrast between rich and poor, the
feudal lords and their serfs, the surfeiters and the starving; as
such it is simply an expression of the revolutionary instinct,
and finds its justification in that, and in that only. Or, on
the other hand, this demand has arisen as a reaction against
the bourgeois demand for equality, drawing more or less

correct and more far-reaching demands from this bourgeois demand, and serving as an agitational means in order to stir up the workers against the capitalists with the aid of the capitalists' own assertions; and in this case it stands or falls with bourgeois equality itself. In both cases the real content of the proletarian demand for equality is the demand for the abolition of classes. (Engels 1947, 132)

Developing the historical themes of this argument, Engels suggests that hitherto "all moral theories" had been inherently marked by the context of the class divided societies in which they emerged. These ideologies consequently operated as class moralities which either "justified the domi-nation and interests of the ruling class," or represented the indignation and "future interests of the oppressed" class through their struggles "against this domination" (Engels 1947, 117). Nonetheless, although Engels dismissed the idea of some universal moral principle which could act as a neutral standard of the good in class-divided societies, he did believe that such a universal morality was possible under communism. He claimed that

a really human morality which stands above class antago-nisms and above any recollection of them becomes possible only at a stage of society which has not only overcome class antagonisms but has even forgotten them in practical life. (Engels 1947, 118)

While this schema might imply that contemporary moral standards were but relative justifications for various class interests, Marx suggested a link between sectional interests and deeper human interests. He argued that when workers rebel against the process of their dehumanization, they begin to act as *potential* agents, not only of their own liberation, but also of the universal liberation of humanity. So, as we noted in the previous chapter, whereas liberals effectively obscured the sectional inter-ests underpinning their approach to morality, Marx explicitly pointed to the particular interests that his approach represented whilst arguing that the universal interest is embodied in this particular interest. However, whereas Hegel merely assumed the bureaucracy to be the universal class (Marx 1975a, 136), Marx insisted that such a proposition must be grounded empirically: "this class liberates the whole of society, but only on condition that the whole of society finds itself in the same situation as this class" (Marx 1975c, 254). More specifically he also suggested a historical model of the relationship between a particular and a universal class, claiming that through history various classes at various junctures would, in fighting for their particular interests, act in the universal interest by overcoming the destructive conflictual relations into which society had become mired and thus cumulatively removing the barriers to human freedom: at specific historical junctures these classes consequently offered the hope of reconstructing society in a way that would avoid the alternative "common ruin of the contending classes" (Marx and Engels 1973, 68). If representatives of the bourgeoisie had furthered the cause of freedom in 1649 and 1789, by the 1840s their descendants' defence of property rights meant that they came to take a position against the further deepening of human freedom as represented by workers' struggles against these rights.

> The role of *emancipator* therefore passes in a dramatic movement from one class . . . to the next, until it finally reaches that class which no longer realises social freedom by assuming certain conditions external to man and yet created by human society, but rather by organising all the conditions of human existence on the basis of social freedom. (Marx 1975c, 255)

If the idea of a universal interest implies not only a shared interest in survival (Sayer 2009) but also some model of universal human nature, this latter implication appears to contradict Marx's sixth thesis on Feuerbach. Here Marx argued that "the essence of man (*menschliche*)[1] is no abstraction inherent in each individual. In reality it is the ensemble of the social relations." Nevertheless, although this statement has often been read as sure proof that Marx dismissed the concept of human nature, Norman Geras has convincingly shown that Marx in fact merely rejected Feuerbach's tendency to confuse human nature with one of its many manifestations (Geras 1983). Thus, he famously criticized Feuerbach

---

1. Whereas Marx used the non-gender specific words *mensch* or *menschen* (not the gender specific *der mann*), these are almost invariably translated into English as the gender specific "man" or "men." This accident of translation is a product of limitations of the English language rather than of Marx's supposed sexism (Arthur 1986, 150).

for substituting, in his *The Essence of Christianity*, historically concrete "men" with an abstract generic "Man." He claimed that because Feuerbach abstracted "Man" from the real historical process in this way, he ironically assumed exactly that which must be proved: namely that the contemporary form of behavior was universal. Feuerbach "presupposes an abstract—isolated—human individual," and confuses man's essence with "an internal, dumb generality which *naturally* unites the many individuals" (Marx 1975f, 422). Marx repeated a similar argument two decades later, when, in *Capital*, he criticized Bentham's "naivety" for assuming "that the modern petty bourgeois, especially the English petty bourgeois, is the normal man." Against this method, he argued that any analysis of human nature "would first have to deal with human nature in general, and then with human nature as historically modified in each epoch" (Marx 1976, 759).[2] Commenting on these lines, Erich Fromm

---

2. In a discussion of Marx's concept of social individualism, Carol Gould suggests that while Marx's ontology was built upon those of Aristotle and Hegel, he went beyond their ideas by breaking with all forms of essentialism (Gould 1978, 108). Underpinning this argument is the assumption that essences be understood as static things. This assumption has been challenged by Scott Meikle who insists that amongst his contributions to social science, Marx showed that human essence is "dynamic." Consequently, just as Gould argues that freedom is a process which is both a necessary condition for purposeful labour and its outcome, Meikle suggests that we should similarly understand our broader essence to include potentialities that can only be realized through history (Meikle 1985, 59). Indeed, Meikle claims that while Marx's essentialism is rooted in a reading of Aristotle, this interpretation was articulated through a Hegelian lens, such that, while "Aristotle considers essences as unities," for Marx essences are "unities in contradiction" (Meikle 1985, 37). Thus, Marx synthesised Aristotle's materialism with Hegel's dialectic to produce a materialist ontology which recognizes the existence of real contradictions within essences: a perspective from which he was able to articulate, if only in a rudimentary form, a naturalistic ethics rooted in a dynamic model of human nature (Meikle 1985, 37, 43; Sayers 1998). It was from this perspective that he conceptualized history as an ongoing struggle for freedom. This profound historical sense in Marx's ethical thought can thus be distinguished, much like Hegel's "self-actualisation theory," from both consequentialist and deontological moral theories. The distinguishing feature of Hegel's ethical theory, as Wood points out, is best understood by the fact that self-actualization is neither "an ultimate imperative," nor "the end or goal of the self," but rather relates morals to the human essence whose never ending process of realization through history is at once the imperative and the goal of morality (Wood 1990, 30–2).

points out that "Marx was never tempted to assume that 'human nature' was identical with that particular expression of human nature prevalent in his own society," because he was able to distinguish the essence of man from "the various forms of historical existence" (Fromm 1966, 24–5).

Following and extending Kant and Hegel, Marx insisted that "freedom is so much the essence of man that even its opponents realise it in that they fight its reality" (Marx 1975g, 155; Dunayevskaya 1988, 53). If this idea shaped his earliest work, it was profoundly deepened in *Capital* and in his mature political writings. At its simplest, Marx agreed with liberals that freedom must be historically grounded, first and foremost, in the satisfaction of our basic needs. Thus in the third volume of *Capital* he argued that "the realm of freedom really begins only where labour determined by necessity and external expediency ends . . . The reduction of the working day is the basic prerequisite" (Marx 1981, 959). However, Marx's model of human freedom is historical in a second sense; not only do increases in the productivity of labour create the potential for people to devote more time to the development of "human powers as an end in itself," but also, as labour productivity increases so too do human needs expand (Marx 1981, 959; Fraser 1998). And as human needs and powers expand through history so does the potential for the realization of human freedom (Sayers 1998, 136).

For instance, Carol Gould points out that the concept of freedom is a major theme of Marx's *Grundrisse* where it is understood as a process through which "social individuals" come to realize themselves through their labours (Gould 1978, 101; cf Gilbert 1981, 98). This idea is expressed in *Capital* thus: "Through this movement he acts upon nature and changes it, and in this way he simultaneously changes his own nature" (Marx 1976, 283). Freedom consequently is understood not merely as a necessary, negative, aspect of our relationship to nature, but also positively as a process of "self-realization" through work (Gould 1978, 101–128; Sayers 1998, 36–59; Marx 1973a, 611). Gould argues that Marx took Hegel's conception of freedom as self-realization and reinterpreted it in materialist language to explain how we not only realize our potential through labour, but also recreate our very nature as our needs and capacities expand through purposeful social activity (Gould 1978, 108). Lukács explains that, for Marx, the possibility of freedom is rooted in the historically conditioned way people produce to meet their needs: "freedom . . . appears for the first time in reality in the alternative within the labour process" (Lukács 1980a, 39). Freedom is thus rooted in the choices opened up within the productive process about how to meet our needs. Because Marx understood freedom in this historical and materialist manner he was able to grasp, contra Kant, its intimate connection with the realization of human needs through the medium of desire (Lukács 1980a, 58, 67, 114).

Moreover, because needs evolve through history, as Kain points out, Marx's ideal involved the emergence of humans who are rich in needs, such that our essence expands with the expansion of our needs, as at least some wants and desires are transformed through history into "directly felt needs" (Kain 1988, 28, 60). Sean Sayers writes that because Marx believed all things that are in fact needed by humans are part of our essence (Kain 1988, 25), then he is best understood as embracing "a historical form of humanism" (Sayers 1998, 128, 149). This is evident in the *Grundrisse* where Marx praised capitalism for creating the potential for a "rich individuality which is as all-sided in its production as it is in its consumption" (Marx 1973, 325). So, for Marx, as our needs and capacities change through history so too does our essence (Sayers 2009, 154). Commenting on this perspective, Allen Wood has argued that while the sixth of Marx's "Theses on Feuerbach" does not entail a denial of human essence, it does assert "that this essence is inextricably bound up with the social relationships in which those individuals stand, and must be understood in light of them" (Wood 1981, 17).

Thus historicized, the human essence as freedom is best understood as an immanent potential which evolves over time through a process of collective struggles shaped by the development of humanity's productive forces (Marx & Engels 1976, 74ff). Freedom, for Marx, is not reified as either one moment of this process, or simply as an attribute of individuals against the social. Instead, it has a concrete meaning which changes through history, as both the material parameters for its realization expand and as groups form through struggle to fight for the realization of these expanding demands (Fromm 1966). Against a unilinear reading of Marx's comment that history has moved through "the Asiatic, ancient, feudal and modern bourgeois modes of production," Eric Hobsbawm suggests that those stages be understood as a logical, not a historical, progression. This list of pre-capitalist modes of production was not intended to represent a unilinear path through history, it was meant to convey the idea of a logical progression toward the growing "individualisation of man" (Hobsbawm 1964, 36, 38; Cf Archibald 1993, 181–221). As Gould argues, the importance of this point for Marx cannot be overstated, for he insists that "although an individual cannot become free in isolation from others, nonetheless it is only individuals who are free" (Gould 1978, 108).

Nevertheless, Marx's mature conception of freedom does not end with individual self-realization—still less with a simplistic utopian understanding of the *all-round* realization of our capacities. The claim made in *The German Ideology* that under communism it would be "possible for me to do one thing today and another tomorrow, to hunt in the morning, fish in the afternoon, rear cattle in the evening, criticise after dinner, just as I have a mind, without ever becoming hunter, fisherman, herdsman or critic" (Marx & Engels 1976, 47), if not simply a witty barb aimed at the Young Hegelian idealists, is plainly utopian in the negative abstract sense of the term.

Our existence as social individuals presupposes some degree of the division of labour as the medium through which society itself is possible (Beamish 1992, 162). This social basis for politics means that it is impossible to develop *all* of our potential: there simply are not the hours in the day or the years in a lifetime to become a great concert pianist, and a great physicist, and a great novelist, etc. etc. What we can do, as we shall see in the discussion of the division of labour below, is remove most of the barriers to human self-realization that are a consequence of the technical or manufacturing division of labour, thus allowing people to flourish to a level that is presently denied the vast majority. Beyond this the necessary (social) aspects of the division of labour acts both as the material basis for our present (capitalist) alienation from the product of our labours, and the alternative potential that we might exercise real democratic control over society. It is for this reason that Marx concretely conceives the struggle for freedom as the struggle to win the battle for democracy. As George Brenkert argues, Marx's conception of freedom does not involve an impossible all-round conception of self-realization but rather self-realization that is best understood as social self-determination through democracy (Brenkert 1983, 87–88, 104; Wood 1981, 51). And the realization of human needs is the social content of this conception of freedom. This, for instance, is the meaning of Marx's angry rejection of the demand for a "free state" as presented in the *Gotha Programme*. Against this nonsensical claim, Marx insisted that freedom consists "in converting the state from an organ superimposed upon society into one completely subordinate to it" (Marx 1974d, 354). Thus, in volume three of *Capital* he wrote:

Freedom . . . can consist only in this, that socialised man, the associated producers, govern the human metabolism with nature in a rational way, bringing it under their common control instead of being dominated by it as a blind power; accomplishing it with the least expenditure of energy and in conditions most worthy and appropriate for their human nature. (Marx 1981, 959)

This collective control of society from the bottom up is the basis for Marx's claim, made in the *Communist Manifesto*, that communism would be characterized by "an association, in which the free development of each is the condition for the free development of all" (Marx and Engels 1973, 87). Thus, as István Mészáros argues, "the central theme of Marx's moral theory is how to realise human freedom" (Mészáros 1975, 162).

Marx's historical model of human freedom implies a critique of those superficial viewpoints which either conflate the atomized desires generated within bourgeois society with the good (utilitarianism), or, similarly assuming the existence of desires in this form, posit some universal moral code as a brake on their consequences (Kantianism). Mészáros contrasts Marx's attempt to understand the beliefs and actions of specific individuals in the concrete context within which they live, with modern ethical theory's ahistorical concern with "abstract 'Man'" (Mészáros 1975, 111). Of the two moral frameworks thus implicitly criticized, the power of Marx's dismissal of utilitarianism is most apparent. For, as we saw in his discussion of Bentham noted above, it essentially involves a call for concrete analyses of changing needs, capacities, and rationalities through history. Because Marx echoed Aristotle's insistence that human needs and activities are diverse, he was keen to insist that happiness cannot be reduced to a single factor (Gilbert 1984, 156). However, Marx's critique of Kantianism is famously more ambiguous: for while it is plain that he scores a hit when he rejects Kant's transhistorical moral claims, it also appears that his use of moral language commits him, implicitly at least, to his own version of just such a transhistorical moral claim.

Lukes has argued that this "paradox" in Marx's *oeuvre* can be "resolved" once we distinguish two types of moral claims which are unfortunately conflated in Marx—the morality of emancipation and the morality of justice or *Recht*: "it is the morality of *Recht* that [Marxism] condemns as ideological and anachronistic, and the morality of emancipation that it adopts as its own" (Lukes 1985, 29). Similarly, Mészáros argues, as we noted above, that Marx held to a morality of emancipation, and notes that while the "tone of moral indignation is very strong when Marx speaks about capital . . . its ground is not an appeal to an abstract concept of 'justice'" (Mészáros 1975, 185). Developing an analogous point, Allen Wood has claimed that Marx rejected the concept of justice because he understood it to be tied up with, and to sanction, particular historical modes of production (Wood 1981, 130–2).

Conversely, Rodney Peffer draws upon comments in the *Inaugural Address of the Working Men's Association* to argue, with some justification, that Marx held to a "deontological" ethics (Peffer 1990, 46). While Peffer acknowledges that Marx was very careful, as he wrote in a letter to Engels, that his use of rhetoric about justice in this speech did "no harm" to the central political message of the *Inaugural Address*, he dismisses this argument, suggesting that it is "most interesting that he chooses the occasions on which he has the most direct and immediate impact on the socialist movement to acquiesce and put them forward" (Peffer 1990, 206). Peffer has a point; Marx on many occasions seemed to betray his acceptance of an implicit conception of justice that moves beyond the morality of self-realization. On this issue Geras argues that Lukes' distinction between a morality of justice and one of self-realization is "unfounded," because individuals can only realize their true potential within a political context. Thus Geras argues that if postrevolutionary societies are not to be understood in a utopian manner, then they must include some conception of distributive justice (Geras 1989, 232). Geras insists that, rather than distinguish a morality of self-realization from one of justice in Marx, it is better to distinguish two conceptions of justice, one implicit and one explicit, which can help explain that while "Marx did think that capitalism was unjust . . . he did not think he thought so." So whereas Marx dismissed justice in its narrow "legal positivist fashion," he subscribed to a broader distributive justice based upon the needs principle: "from each according to ability, to each according to need" (Geras 1989, 245). Such a principle, Geras suggests, would act not merely as a benchmark against which capitalism is seen to be wanting, but would continue to operate in a socialist society as a transhistorical, distributive standard of "reasonable" need in a system without absolute abundance (Geras 1989, 264).

By conceptualizing justice in this broader sense, Geras argues, Marxists might be able to move beyond what he labels variously as the "pervasive contradiction" or the "real and deep-seated inconsistency" in Marx's writings which have, on the one hand, fostered a confused rhetoric amongst a number of his epigones, whilst, on the other, helped foster a "moral cynicism" amongst others of his followers, facilitating their justifications of the "crimes and tragedies which have disgraced socialism" (Geras 1989, 266). Geras suggests that this weakness with Marx's discussion of morality can be related to the residual Hegelianism in his mature writings. Commenting on the "dialectical wizardry" at the heart of Marx's discussion of the simultaneously just and unjust nature of the sale of labour power in Chapter 24 of the first volume of *Capital*, Geras argues that "as is so often the way with it, the dialectic here only muddies the water. A thing cannot be its opposite" (Geras 1989, 235–6).

Geras's attempt to disarticulate a defensible moral standpoint from Marx's dialectical terminology generates problems of its own. For although capitalism can undoubtedly be judged and found wanting by the standards of the needs principle, to show that such a judgment escapes the emotivist limitations of modern moral theory it is necessary to locate it as a concrete expression of a specific social practice that is able both to illuminate the historical character of and to point beyond the standpoint of civil society. This is what Marx alluded to in his *Critique of the Gotha Programme*. He was quite clear that far from being a transhistorical standard, the needs principle emerged with the struggle against capitalism and could only become operative on the basis of, first, a successful socialist revolution, and, second, further increases in the productivity of labour.

By contrast with Geras, both Kain and Wilde have pointed out that Marx's perspective is rooted in a specific social practice, and that the "dialectical inversion" he proposes in *Capital* is no act of wizardry, but reflects the way in which "the difference between capitalist and socialist morality stems from the difference between everyday experience of the surface phenomena determined by the prevailing mode of production and a scientific analysis which goes beneath this surface to grasp an essence," or that "[b]ehind the appearance of the exchange of equivalents is the essence of exploitation" (Kain 1988, 160; Wilde 1998, 43–4).

Despite Geras's suggestion to the contrary, Marx's discussion of this issue in *Capital* is eminently clear. His argument opens with the claim that from the "legal standpoint" commodity exchange presupposes nothing more than "the workers' power to dispose freely of his own capacities, and the money-owner or commodity-owner's power to dispose

freely of the values that belong to him." In this situation, labour power
and other commodities exchange at their "real value." However, while
there is an apparent relationship of equal exchange at the level of the
circulation of capital, within the production process something very different occurs. The wages paid to workers do not in fact originate with
the capitalist, but are rather "a portion of the product of the labour
of others which has been appropriated without an equivalent," while
the workers not only replace this capital but also add to it yet more
surplus. This appropriation of surplus value from workers by capitalists is
possible because, despite their formal freedoms, workers feel the "silent
compulsion" to work for capitalists (Marx 1976, 899), and once they
are set to work it is the unique nature of labour power as a commodity that it is able to generate surplus value. In fact, Marx argues, once
workers feel the *de facto* compulsion to work for the capitalist, factory
work itself "confiscates every atom of freedom" from them (Marx 1976,
548). This is a consequence of the very structure of capitalist production, where Marx recognized a mutual connection between the anarchic
relations between units of capital, and the despotic relationship between
capitalists and workers within the factory (Barker 1991, 207; see Marx
1976, 477; 1994, 29).

In a discussion of the first of these points Mészáros inverts traditional interpretations of Marx's famous claim that "men inevitably
enter into definite relations which are independent of their will," by
pointing out that far from being an example of his supposed crude
economic determinism these lines reflect his criticisms of the unfreedoms
of capitalism specifically and class societies more generally from the perspective of "considerations of real personal freedom" (Mészáros 1986,
204). Under these capitalist relations of production, labour power does
become a commodity and as a commodity it has both an exchange and
a use value. Exceptionally, the use value of labour power—its ability to
be put to work—has the characteristic of creating value. Consequently,
while wages may reflect the real exchange value of labour power, they do
not reflect a true significance of its use-value. If the buying and selling
of commodities at their real exchange values was all there was to the
wage relationship, then the exchange of equivalents could never lead
to the systematic increase in the wealth of the capitalist class relative
to the workers. However, it is the use-value of labour power to add
more to the production process than is its exchange value. So, whereas
the essence of the capitalist labur process is the constant appropriation

of surplus value, at the level of surface appearances there is a seeming exchange of equivalents through the buying and selling of labour power: "the separation of property from labour thus becomes the necessary consequence of a law that apparently originated in their identity." It is for this reason, as Marx argues, that a "dialectical inversion" occurs at the point of production between, on the one hand, the equal exchange of commodities and, on the other, the appropriation of value from the worker to the capitalist. By starting out from the buying and selling of equivalent exchange values there occurs an appropriation of value on the one side and relative poverty on the other: "social wealth becomes to an ever-increasing degree the property of those who are in a position to appropriate the unpaid labour of others over and over again" (Marx 1976, 725–734; Engels 1989b). Geras is wrong to claim that Marx's reference to dialectics allows an unfortunate aspect of Hegelian obscurantism to weaken his otherwise powerful arguments by leading him to suggest that a thing can be its opposite. Actually, this argument comes after about 400 pages in my Penguin edition of *Capital*, in which Marx excavates in great detail the process whereby the capitalists "consume" labour power (Marx 1976, Chapters 7–17, 291), and it is built upon what he claimed was one of "the best points in my book: . . . *the twofold character of labour*, according to whether it is expressed in use value or exchange value" (Marx 1987, 407). It is because Geras does not address the process of the consumption of labour power that he sees contradictions in Marx rather than in reality itself (Geras 1992, 48–52). Conversely, Marx recognizes that it is through this process of the production of absolute and relative surplus value that capitalists attempt to profit from their investment in labour power by forcing workers to work as hard and for as long as is possible. The ensuing struggle at the point of production—the "protracted more or less concealed civil war between capitalist class and the working class"—is the very basis for both Marx's politics and his ethics (Marx 1976, 412).

At this juncture Marx makes a fundamentally important argument. He suggests that the truth of this process is obscured so long as it is seen from the point of view of the individuals involved, and becomes fully apparent only when examined from the point of view of the totality of the capitalist system.

> To be sure, the matter looks quite different if we consider capitalist production in the uninterrupted flow of its renewal,

and if, in place of the individual capitalist and the individual worker, we view them in their totality, as the capitalist class and the working class confronting each other. But in so doing we should be applying standards entirely foreign to commodity production. (Marx 1976, 732)

This claim is of the utmost importance. For, by contrast with the sharp delineation between facts and values characteristic of modern moral theory, it provides the point of contact between Marx's scientific, explanatory account of the dynamics of the capitalist mode of production, and his normative critique of capitalism. Far from being mutually exclusive these two aspects of his social theory are best understood as two sides of the same coin: the labour theory of value conceived from the standpoint of workers' struggles underpins Marxism both as a social science and as a normative critique. Value theory therefore points beyond the incommensurable moral preferences which are the corollary of the liberal separation of facts and values (the "is-ought gap"), while simultaneously providing the key to understanding the problem of Marx's condemnation of morality.

If David Hume was the first moral philosopher to highlight the problems associated with the movement from statements of fact to value judgments (see Hume 1965, 196; MacIntyre 1966, 171–174; 1971), it was Kant who most fully realized the reified separation of science and ethics by insisting on an unbridgeable gulf between these two terms, arguing that there could be no non-moral reasons for a moral act. The problem with this claim, as Alasdair MacIntyre has pointed out, is that practice does not and cannot follow theory in the way Kant assumes. For it is universally true that we can theorize only from specific standpoints: "one cannot first understand the world and only then act on it. How one understands the world will depend in part on the decision implicit in one's already taken actions. The wager of action is unavoidable" (MacIntyre 2008j, 314). As we noted in the last chapter, because Kant naturalized the perspective of the egoistic individual he was unable to conceive of morality except as a limit to egoistic desires. By contrast, Marx suggested that socialist morality was not an abstract addition to a more or less mechanical model of historical progress, but rather was the flipside of the scientific critique of political economy. As Michael Löwy argues:

> At bottom what we have here is not even an interpretation
> "linked with" or "accompanied by" a practice but a total
> human activity, practical-critical activity in which theory is
> already revolutionary praxis, and practice is loaded with
> theoretical significance. (Löwy 2003, 109)

It was on this basis that Marx dismissed those moral attitudes that pretend to offer some mechanism through which a common model of the
good can be promoted in a world in which social divisions undermine
such a project, and he did this from the point of view of a class-based
ethics which, he believed, is in its purpose genuinely universal. This
universal normative ideal does not, as Geras claims it must, involve a
transhistorical conception of good (Geras 1989, 227). Rather, when Marx
conceives the proletariat as the universal class, this is best understood as
an extension of what Allen Wood calls Hegel's conception of "historicised
universalism" (Wood 1990, 204; cf Marx 1973a, 162). Indeed, the very
idea of a transhistorical concept runs counter to Marx's claim that "even
the most abstract categories . . . are . . . a product of historic relations,
and possess their full validity only for and within these relations" (Marx
1973a, 105). This is not to say that Marx thereby debars himself from
making ethical comparisons between different social formations and
between different modes of production. On the contrary, although
his rejection of bourgeois moral theory was informed by a keen sense
of the historical specificity of concepts, following Hegel's rejection of
ethical relativism noted in the previous chapter, he also suggests that,
because history is marked by continuity as well as change, earlier social
formations can be illuminated using categories specific to capitalism.
This is the basis of his famous claim that "[h]uman anatomy contains a
key to the anatomy of the ape" (Marx 1973a, 105). As is suggested by
his later praise for Darwin's articulation of a natural scientific basis for
historical materialism by dealing a "mortal blow" to "teleology" (Marx
quoted in Foster 2000, p. 197), this statement does not imply a teleological view of history.[3] Rather, it points to Marx's belief that although
the emergence of capitalism, and thus of the struggle for socialism,

---

3. Or rather although he does not believe there is a telos in history propelling
it inevitably to socialism, he recognizes that human essence does try to realise
itself (Eagleton 1997, 18).

were not preordained, once capitalism had emerged, workers' struggles provided the standpoint from which human history could for the first time be understood as a totality (Lukács 1971, 157). From this standpoint he was able to cognize not only the modernity and limitations of the bourgeois idea of freedom, but also the historical antecedents and potential basis for the deepening of this concept. Thus the standpoint of workers' struggles suggests a model of historical progress that allows Marx to successfully navigate between the twin dangers of historical anachronism and relativism. This approach therefore reveals the rational basis of teleology without implying either that capitalism or communism is the inevitable outcome of human history.

Marxism therefore both presupposes and reaffirms a historically constructed social practice—collective working-class struggles over the length of the working day—which reveals both the facts of exploitation and an alternative to the system of exploitation, while simultaneously suggesting a model of historical progress. As Terry Eagleton argues, "[i]n the critical consciousness of any oppressed group or class, the understanding and the transforming of reality, 'fact' and 'value,' are not separable processes but aspects of the same phenomenon" (Eagleton 1990, 225).

It is from this perspective that Marx criticized, amongst other ideas, Proudhon's concept of "eternal justice." Superficially, Marx's comment in *Capital* that we learn nothing new about the concept of usury, for instance, if we are told that it contradicts the concept of "eternal justice," may appear as yet more evidence of his dismissal of a normative for a scientific critique of capitalism (Marx 1976, 178–9). However, if we examine more closely Marx's criticism of Proudhon's moral theory, we see that things are not quite so simple. According to Marx, Proudhon attempted, in *What is Property?*, to criticize the classical political economists "from the standpoint of political economy" (Marx and Engels 1975, 31). According to McNally, Proudhon accommodated to political economy, first, by defining justice by "equal market exchange"; second, by using commodity exchange as "the model for the social contract"; third, by depicting exploitation not as a product of commodity production, but as its violation through monopoly; fourth, insofar as he aimed to foster equal exchange of commodities by opening a "People's Bank" which would use paper money to overturn "the royalty of gold"; fifth, by equating socialism with the "abolition of monopoly and the realisation of free trade"; and, sixth, by arguing within the workers' movement against strikes and political struggles against the state, and in their place for "mutualism and equal exchange" (McNally 1993, 141–143). From Marx's standpoint this schema is the most extreme muddle which reflects Proudhon's inability to look beneath the surface appearance of equal exchange in a system of generalized commodity production to the underlying appropriation of value from workers. Thus, Marx's criticism of Proudhon's concept of "eternal justice" involves not a rejection of ethical discourse *per se*, but rather a more simple rejection of Proudhon's confused moralism. "We may well," wrote Marx, "feel astonished at the cleverness of Proudhon who would abolish capitalist property—by enforcing the eternal laws of property which are themselves based on commodity production!" (Marx 1976, 734)

Interestingly, the chapter of *Capital* in which Marx makes these criticisms of Proudhon was almost doubled in length between the original 1867 edition and the 1872 French edition of that work. Part of the reason for this extension was Marx's aim of furthering his challenge to Proudhon's influence within the French workers' movement (Marx 1976, 733–734, McNally 1993, 166). The argument of this chapter is best understood not as an abstract discourse for the attention of the social scientific elite, but as an attempt to help win hegemony within the working class generally and the French working class specifically for the idea of class struggle against Proudhon's idea of class harmony (McNally 1993, 143, 145). At the core of this argument was that aspect of Marx's thought which Geras argues merely serves to muddy the waters: the idea of the dialectic. And the concept of "dialectical inversion" was no offhand remark in 1872, but can be traced back to Marx's claim, made in 1847, that in Proudhon's work "there is no longer any dialectics but only, at most, absolute pure morality" (Marx 1984a, 169; McNally 1993, 153).

Proudhon's "absolute pure morality" (Marx and Engels 1975, 31) followed from his inability to see beyond Smith's and Ricardo's blindness to the peculiar historical form taken by the production process under capitalism. They tended not only to naturalize the system of generalized commodity production, but also to obscure the nature of the appropriation of surplus value from wage labour (Meikle 1985, 63, 65, 69; Fraser 1998, 33; Marx 1972, 500). Whereas Smith and Ricardo, and following them Proudhon, took the capitalist form of production as the natural starting point of their analyses, Marx insisted upon discerning the specific historical forms taken by production to meet human needs. In a famous letter to Kugelmann (11 July 1868), he wrote the following:

Every child knows that any nation that stopped working, not
for a year, but let us say, just for a few weeks, would perish.
And every child knows, too, that the amounts of products
corresponding to the differing amounts of needs demand
differing and quantitatively determined amounts of society's
aggregate labour. It is **self-evident** that this necessity of the
distribution of social labour in specific proportions is certainly
not abolished by the specific form of social production; it can
only change its form of manifestation. Natural laws cannot
be abolished at all. The only thing that can change, under
historically differing conditions, is the form in which those
laws assert themselves. And the form in which this proportional distribution of labour asserts itself in a state of society
in which the interconnection of social labour expresses itself
as the private exchange of the individual products of labour,
is precisely the exchange value of these products.

Marx's discussion of the value form is the point in his *oeuvre* where not
only his moral and his economic analyses, but also his theory of history
are synthesized. Far from muddying the waters as Geras suggests, Marx's
use of dialectics to criticize Proudhon reveals the fundamental limitations
of the analytical methods used by the classical political economists. For,
although Proudhon aimed to outline a radical critique of capitalism, he
succeeded only in naturalizing it.

By contrast, Marx periodized history through the concepts of mode
of production and form of surplus extraction.

The specific economic form, in which unpaid surplus-labour is
pumped out of direct producers, determines the relationship
of rulers and ruled, as it grows directly out of production
itself and, in turn, reacts upon it as a determining element.
Upon this, however, is founded the entire formation of the
economic community which grows up out of the production
relations themselves, thereby simultaneously its specific political form. It is always the direct relationship of the owners
of the conditions of production to the direct producers—a
relation always naturally corresponding to a definite stage in
the development of the methods of labour and thereby its
social productivity—which reveals the innermost secret, the

hidden basis of the entire social structure and with it the
political form of the relation of sovereignty and dependence,
in short, the corresponding specific form of the state. This
does not prevent the same economic basis—the same from
the standpoint of its main conditions—due to innumerable
different empirical circumstances, natural environment, racial
relations, external historical influences, etc., from showing
infinite variations and gradations in appearance, which can be
ascertained only by analysis of the empirically given conditions. (Marx 1981, 927)

To understand the capitalist form of surplus extraction was, of course,
at the core of Marx's lifework. It was also at the core of his moral
critique of capitalism.

Capitalism, Alienation, and Freedom

As we noted in the introduction to this chapter, Hal Draper pointed
out that Marx dismissed not the ethical content of politics, but the idea
that moralistic abstractions could serve as an adequate substitute for
political analysis. Nevertheless, while Marx was quick to challenge those
moralistic pronouncements which he believed acted as an impediment to
the kind of clear social analysis necessary for the emergence of socialist
class consciousness, when even abstract moralizing emerged from the
real struggles of workers he was much more forgiving. For instance,
while he, as Draper puts it, "grumbled" about some moralizing that
found its way into George Julian Harney's Chartist newspaper *Friend
of the People* in 1852, he recognized that the class nature of Chartism
imbued these pronouncements with a content that overcame many of
the limitations of the rhetoric itself (Draper 1990, 27).

Similarly, when a decade later Marx came to write the *Inaugural
Address* of the First International, his use of moral language reflected
his unsectarian approach to building the most powerful possible international socialist movement. Collins and Abramsky have argued that
this involved an attempt to "reconcile the irreconcilable." As he saw it,
the International represented real social forces which were coming into
conflict with capital, and he believed it best to allow those forces to
coalesce into a coherent movement rather than to retard the evolution

of class consciousness by subjecting them to abstract criticisms from a purist perspective. To this end, he not only held back from making what would have been sectarian criticisms of the French Proudhonists, but instead welcomed them into the International in the hope of building the broadest possible mass movement (Collins and Abramsky 1965, 32, 39). This is not to suggest, as does Peffer, that Marx quietly retreated over his critique of Proudhon's definition of justice as fair and equal exchange of the products of labour; for Marx both restated his 1847 critique of Proudhon a year after the publication of the *Inaugural Address* and, as we noted above, he ferociously rejected similar ideas in his *Critique of the Gotha Programme* (Marx 1984a, 138; Marx 1985, 26; Gilbert 1981, 82–94). Rather, it is a sign that in making a concrete analysis of the balance of class forces in 1864, Marx, in what amounts to a precursor of the united front tactic, concluded that an abstract criticism of Proudhon would have perhaps scuppered the International before it had got off the ground, whereas allowing him and his supporters into that organization was the best hope of fostering the biggest possible mass movement in which their competing conceptions of politics could be tested in practice.

This approach to politics was not at all new to Marx. In the letter of 15 June 1846 to Köttgen referred to above, in which he and Engels argued that Communists must "have no truck with tedious moral scruples," the point of the argument was not to dismiss morality *tout court*, but to reject any tendency within the organization toward infantile refusals to compromise with groups and tendencies beyond it. Marx and Engels argued against purist sectarianism to suggest that "in a party one must support everything which helps towards progress." Concretely, the examples of the actions which he believed the party must support all involved the self-activity of the masses: the point was to not let abstract rhetoric get in the way of the concrete act of building a mass movement (Marx and Engels 1984, 56). Consequently, rather than marking instances of Marx's supposed nihilism, these examples illuminate his deep conception of social practice.

Underlying these political arguments was, of course, Marx's analysis of capitalism itself. One way of illuminating the difference between capitalism and previous modes of production is to look at the ways in which modern ethical discourse is a product, as we noted in the previous chapter, of a specific historical epoch, within which conceptions of good and bad, etc. have been both disembodied and reduced to more or less coherent expressions of personal preferences (MacIntyre 1985, 122, 135).

It is to the problem of characterizing the type of world where the concept of good has been simultaneously disembodied and individualized that Marx points us. Unsurprisingly, because his aim is to overcome this situation through revolution, his ethical theory cannot adequately be expressed in the terms which are characteristic of that world. Commenting on this situation, Bertell Ollman points out that while it is correct, in so far as it goes, to argue that Marx criticized moral theory by pointing out that conceptions of right and wrong change over time, that they do so in relationship to deeper changes in the mode of production, and that the dominant moral values tend to reflect the interests of the dominant classes within society, this does not in fact take us very far. More important, for Marx, is the way that in the modern world "moral" concepts such as love, for instance, lose the human specificity and become reified—either reduced, with the utilitarians, to but a manifestation of an overarching utility, or set against our human needs and desires as they are in Kant (Ollman 1976, 41).

For Marx, the key moral question is how this situation arose, and what chances there are, if any, that we might overcome it? His first systematic attempt to answer this question was articulated in the Paris or *Economic and Philosophical Manuscripts* (1844). This essay is of the first importance to our understanding of Marx's ethics both for the substance of what Marx writes and the method by which he reaches these conclusions. The manuscripts open with an immanent critique of political economy, in which capitalism is found wanting from the perspective of its greatest defenders. Marx pointed out that from Smith's "scientific" analysis of wages he effectively accepted the reduction of workers to the "same condition as the existence of every other commodity" (Marx 1975d, 283).

Beyond this conceptual treatment of workers as commodities, Smith's study of capitalism highlights the way in which the division of labour itself tends to dehumanize workers. He famously opened *The Wealth of Nations* with the argument that the tendency toward the division of labour was a basic facet of human nature: the division of labour "is the necessary, though very slow and gradual consequence of a certain propensity in human nature which has in view no such extensive utility; the propensity to truck, barter, and exchange one thing for another." This gave rise to great increases in the productivity of labour, and an increase in "that

universal opulence which extends to the lowest ranks of the people."
Smith recognized that in addition to this positive consequence of the
division of labour, there existed a negative corollary: those who worked
on the most menial tasks became intellectually debased by the deskilled
nature of their work. Smith argued that philosophers and manual workers differed less in natural abilities than do spaniels from sheep dogs,
and that it was the division of labour experienced from childhood that
gave rise to the differential educational capacities of the two groups in
later life (Smith 1994, 12, 14, 16–17). Furthermore, Smith went so far
as to suggest that "the man whose whole life is spent performing a few
simple operations . . . has no occasion to exert his understanding . . . He
generally becomes as stupid and ignorant as it is possible for a human
creature to become" (Smith cited in Marx 1976, 483).

Developing this argument, Marx showed how the modern division
of labour underpins a tendency to reduce workers "both intellectually
and physically to the level of a machine." He pointed out that while
Smith's and Ricado's variations on the labour theory of value entail that
capital "is nothing but accumulated labour," political economy justifies
a situation in which the worker, "far from being in a position to buy
everything must sell himself and his humanity." Consequently, whereas
Smith insisted that "a society of which the greater part suffers is not
happy," his own theory shows that within the present society the majority of the population, as wage labourers, are reduced to the status of
commodities: it appears, wrote Marx, "that society's distress is the goal
of the economic system" (Marx 1975d, 285–287). Smith was unable
to see beyond this situation, because he considered workers merely as
workers and not as human beings (Marx 1975d, 288).

If the tendency to treat workers as mere commodities is a characteristic of Smith's writings, it is even more so of Ricardo's. Thus,
according to Marx, Ricardo argued that "[n]ations are merely workshops
for production, and man is a machine for consuming and producing.
Human life is a piece of capital. Economic laws rule the world blindly.
For Ricardo, men are nothing, the product everything" (Marx 1975d,
306). Ricardo consequently outdid Smith in his treatment of workers
as mere things.

From the pens of the political economists, therefore, Marx learned
that through capitalist relations of production "the worker sinks to the
level of a commodity, and moreover the most wretched commodity of
all" (Marx 1975d, 322). Furthermore, Marx discovers that capital itself

is no neutral arbiter set up to mediate the exchange of commodities in the market place. Rather, it is a social relationship through which labour is controlled. According to Smith, "The person who acquires, or succeeds to a great fortune, does not necessarily acquire or succeed to any political power. . . . The power which that possession immediately and directly conveys to him, is the power of purchasing; a certain command over all the labour, or over all the produce of labour, which is then in the market." Marx commented, "Capital is, therefore, the power to command labour, and its products. The capitalist possesses this power not on account of his personal or human properties but insofar as he is an owner of capital. His power is the purchasing power of his capital, which nothing can withstand." Given Smith's claim that capital is nothing but "a certain quantity of labour stocked and stored up" (Marx 1975d, 295), it follows that as the store of labour expands then so does the power of the capitalist over the worker: "the misery of the worker is in inverse proportion to the power and volume of his production" (Marx 1975d, 322). This is quite the most perverse of situations. For just as the natural tendency with the increase in the productivity of labour would be for workers increasingly to realize their potential to free themselves from the necessity of working to meet their needs, social relationships conspire to invert this relationship. They make workers more and more powerless before the demands of capital just as they become ever more productive. Increasing social wealth therefore goes hand in hand with decreasing autonomy!

What is more, while the direct costs of this mode of production are felt most acutely by the working class, the capitalists are by no means immune from the power of capital. The market imposes its logic upon them just as much as it does upon workers: while "the capitalist, by means of capital, exercises his power to command labour; . . . capital, in its turn, is able to rule the capitalist himself" (Marx 1975d, 295). Capital acts as an ever-expanding power over everyone within the capitalist system. This, broadly speaking, is the meaning of Marx's concept of alienation. That which we produce through our labours comes to stand opposed to us "as *something alien*, as a *power independent* of the producer" (Marx 1975d, 324). Marx explains alienation as a fourfold process: by selling their ability to work, workers are alienated, first, from the product of their labours; second, from the labour process itself; third, from their own human essence; and, finally, from their fellow human beings (Marx 1975d, 326–330; Mészáros 1975; Ollman 1976). Through the

wage-labour system, proletarians not only lose control over what and
how they produce, they also invert their very nature by converting their
life essence—the social and purposeful act of producing to meet their
needs—into the means by which they maintain their existence. Capitalist
relations of production therefore warp their very nature:

> Production does not produce man only as a commodity,
> the human commodity, man in the form of a commodity; it
> also produces him as a mentally and physically dehumanized
> being . . . Immorality, malformation, stupidity of workers and
> capitalists . . . the human commodity. (Marx 1975d, 336)

Alienation can be understood, as Richard Norman argues in an Aristotelian register, as "the obverse of self-realisation" (Norman 1983, 174).
But, as we have seen, it is perhaps better understood as the obverse of
self-determination. This is as true of the capitalist class as it is of workers.
Despite being in an infinitely more comfortable and desirable position
than the latter, capitalists have no more real control over the product
of industry than do workers. Production for the market means that they
are just as alienated from the product of labour, the production process, and their human essence as are workers. The ends of production
are therefore alienated from both workers and capitalists alike, and the
act of producing becomes for both groups a mere means to maintain
their existence. The division between means and ends proves to have
social roots: just as facts and values are separated in the modern world,
alienation means that whereas life had once been lived as a totality it
was now split into various contradictory spheres of existence—the moral,
the economic, and so forth—each with its own distinct standards. Marx
illustrates this situation with an example taken from contemporary French
society. When the wives and daughters of French factory workers felt
compelled to prostitute themselves so that the family might eat, they
de facto experienced the contradictory pressures of moral and economic
demands: whereas the former taught them to respect their humanity, by
the standards of the latter they were mere commodities to be sold to
the highest bidder in the marketplace (Marx 1975d, 362).

   This example illuminates the differential experience of alienation
both between classes and along lines of gender within classes. It is perhaps for this reason that Marx and Engels praised as "masterly" Fourier's

critique of marriage and his claim that "the degree of emancipation of woman is the natural measure of general emancipation" (Marx and Engels 1975, 196). Nevertheless, Marx and Engels suggest that the class division is the more fundamental of these divisions, and that whereas the capitalist class, which acts as the medium through which capital exercises its control over the process of production, feels at home in this situation, workers feel the increasing demands of the market as an attack on their humanity.

> The propertied class and the class of the proletariat present the same human self-estrangement. But the former class feels at ease and strengthened in this self-estrangement, it recognizes estrangement as its own power and has in it the semblance of a human existence. The class of the proletariat feels annihilated in estrangement; it sees in it its own powerlessness and the reality of an inhuman existence. It is, to use an expression of Hegel, in its abasement the indignation at that abasement, an indignation to which it is necessarily driven by the contradiction between its human nature and its condition of life, which is the outright, resolute and comprehensive negation of that nature. (Marx and Engels 1975, 36)

It is this differential experience of alienation that is, on the one hand, the reason why there can be no universally accepted moral standpoint in a capitalist society, and on the other, the basis for the modern form of class struggle. On this issue, Marx was keen to point out that while socialist writers ascribe both a revolutionary and an emancipatory role to the proletariat, this should not be understood as implying that they believed the workers to be "gods." On the contrary, it was precisely because the humanity of the proletariat has almost been extinguished by the capitalist system that they were ascribed such a positive role. Unfortunately, those radical and socialist writers who dismissed the emancipatory potential of the working class because of the inhuman conditions of proletarian life made the mistake of reifying this situation. Marx, by contrast, argued that capitalism's inhumanity compelled workers to rebel against their situation and to grasp toward those forms of association through which they could make concrete that which for Kant was merely an abstract proposition: the goal of treating others not as means to their ends but as an end in themselves (Goldmann 1971, 199, 211). This was no abstract deduction on Marx's part, but rather was an empirical observation of existing tendencies.

> It is true that the English and French workers have formed associations in which they exchange opinions not only on their immediate needs as workers, but on their needs as human beings. In their associations, moreover, they show a very thorough and comprehensive consciousness of the "enormous" and "immeasurable" power which arises from their co-operation. (Marx and Engels 1975, 52)

In fact, what the French and English workers reminded Marx was that the abstract egoistic individual "Man" of liberal political theory was not merely derived from reality but was also imposed upon it. He elaborated this point in his "pre-Marxist" essay *On the Jewish Question* (1843). In this article he argued that the evacuation of the social content from the concept of "Man" in bourgeois society was no simple mistake, but rather reflected the nature of liberalism as it emerged as an ideological challenge to the political barriers to freedom characteristic of feudal society. It was a fundamental characteristic of bourgeois revolutions that, while they involved a struggle for political emancipation, they did not deliver "the complete and consistent form of human emancipation" (Marx 1975b, 218). So although the English and French revolutions were won through mass collective struggles from below, the formal political communities thus created at the level of the state existed in a symbiotic tension with the egoism entrenched through Lockean constitutions within civil society. And by having at its core the idea of the atomized property owning individual, the doctrine of human rights became a double-edged sword: not only a progressive weapon to be used by individuals to defend themselves against the abuses of state power, but also a reactionary barrier to the realization of the social aspect of our individuality. By institutionalizing the liberal, egoistic conception of individuality at their core, the newly formed bourgeois states both held up the flag of liberty against their feudal forebears and simultaneously acted as a brake on the realization of our social individuality, that is, on full human emancipation. Commenting on the rights to liberty, equality, and security that were enshrined in the constitutions of these liberal states, Marx pointed out that these were primarily property rights: the right to do with one's own property what one wills; the right to equal treatment before the law; and the right to security of property (Marx 1975b, 229–230). This reflects the class character of the social forces that made the bourgeois revolutions. The newly emergent "middling sort" in England and "sans-culottes" in France were small property owners who fought for property rights (Manning 1992, 230–241; Rudé 1988, 47–58). Their victories were consummated through the creation of states that fixed egoistic relations within civil society through the maintenance of property rights (Marx 1975b, 230). Far from being universal truths, concepts such as the *Rights of Man* and the *Rights of the Citizen* embody the demands for freedom and equality as they were articulated by representatives of these groups. However, while these ideas involved a progressive critique of the limitations to human freedom and equality under feudalism, they simultaneously reified the empty egoistical nature of humanity in bourgeois society such as to obscure the way that "individuals obtain their freedom in and through their association" (Marx and Engels 1976, 78). Subsequent revolutionary movements from below, by challenging the social relations that underpin these theories, cannot but act in "flagrant contradiction" to the theories themselves (Marx 1975b, 231).

Nevertheless, Marx's critique of the idea of human rights did not involve a simplistic dismissal of this concept. Rather, as Jay Bernstein has argued, he illuminated and criticized the tacit social assumptions that underpin the individualism of rights-based discourse. He showed that because rights "have their force and meaning through being recognised" they are best understood not as natural entities but in fact as presupposing some historically constituted community (Bernstein 1991, 102–3). The problem with liberal conceptions of rights is that they presuppose and naturalize a community of egoistic individuals as it is represented in the modern alienated state. If the essence of these rights is the maintenance of modern property relations, the fact that there is more to liberal rights than this essence implies that socialism, understood as a free association of individuals which will be characterized in part by non-class conflicts, will necessarily involve a deepening of individual "rights" along lines suggested by Lucien Goldmann in his critique of Kant. Indeed, this type of reasoning explains Ernst Bloch's claim that the formula of the Declaration of Human Rights "goes far beyond the revolutions that took place in America and France" (Bloch 1987, 65). It also illuminates Mészáros's suggestion that, for Marx, despite the ideological limitations of rights-based discourse, the concept of human rights retains a progressive social content because of the existence of a contradiction between the vision of freedom, equality, and fraternity expressed within it and the actuality of capitalist social relations. Social-ism, from this perspective, is best understood as a movement from below which begins to overcome in practice the contradiction between the ideals expressed in the idea of human rights and the reality of capitalist alienation (Mészáros 1986, 197, 199, 210).

Marx became a "Marxist" when he linked the struggles of the proletariat to the process whereby the idea of freedom was concretely being deepened in the modern world (Perkins 1993, 33). It was from the standpoint of this class that the split between facts and values on the one hand, and means and ends on the other were historicized, whilst the conception of individual rights was challenged from the point of view of associative activity. The formal equality and freedom of the system of commodity production was exposed not simply as a myth but as a partial truth from the point of view of the individual which can be overcome only through the point of view of the totality. The truth of these claims, of course, depended upon the validity of the standpoint from which the totality was gleaned: the revolutionary workers' movement.

Alienation and Class Struggle

The importance of the class basis of socialism to Marx is nowhere more apparent than in the section on "true socialism" in *The German Ideology*. True socialism was the name taken by a movement of German intellec-tuals in the 1840s who sought to overcome the "crudities" of English and French class-based socialism through an appeal to the rationality of the general idea of socialism (Wood 1986; Gilbert 1981). In the words of one of their number, Hermann Semmig:

> It seems that the French do not understand their own men of genius. At this point German science comes to their aid and in the shape of socialism presents the most reasonable social order, if one can speak of a superlative degree of reasonable-ness. (Quoted in Marx and Engels 1976, 458)

The true socialists developed what they believed were the socialist implications of Feuerbach's humanism. Feuerbach rejected the egoistic conception of individualism, arguing that "man is conscious of himself not only as an individual, but also as a member of the human species" and that "God is really the perfected idea of the species viewed as an individual" (McLellan 1969, 92). Extending this claim, the true socialists argued that socialism was in the general human interest irrespective of class and other antagonisms.

Although the young Marx was influenced by these ideas, from a very early stage he was aware that the naturalistic morality which Feuerbach extrapolated from it was inadequate to the needs of modern politics (McLellan 1969, 113). Interestingly, Max Stirner engaged with this weakness with Feuerbach's moralism in *The Ego and His Own* (1844) (McLellan 1969, 131; Hook 1962, 174). And it was through answering Stirner's criticisms of Feuerbach that Marx moved beyond the limitations of the latter's perspective.

Stirner argued that all political systems, conservative, liberal, socialist, or whatever, led in practice to authoritarian suppression of the individual ego. Even revolutions, by claiming to be in the common interest, involved the suppression of individual egoism. Consequently Stirner conceived "self-liberation" to be possible through an act of rebellion rather than revolution (Martin 2005, xiii; Thomas 1980, 130). Drawing on Hobbes, but in a way that prefigured Nietzsche (Hook 1962, 165), he insisted that "because each thing *cares for itself* and at the same time comes into constant collision with other things, the *combat* of self-assertion is unavoidable. . . . The victor becomes the *lord,* the vanquished one the *subject* . . . But both remain *enemies*" (Stirner 2005, 9). Nevertheless, in contrast not only to Hobbes but also to his liberal critics, Stirner did not extend this argument into a justification for some form of political state. Quite the reverse, he suggested that "political liberty" amounts to nothing less than the "individual's *subjugation* in the state" (Stirner 2005, 106, 196, 255). In a comment on the French Revolution, which he believed to have general salience, he suggested that this upheaval was not directed against "*the establishment,* but against the *establishment in question,* against a particular establishment. It did away with *this* ruler, not with *the* ruler." That the French Revolution ended in reaction should therefore come as no surprise: for it is in the nature of revolutions that one authority is merely exchanged for another (Stirner 2005, 110). "Political liberalism's" embrace of the postrevolutionary state revealed its authoritarian implications, implications which were also inherent in socialism and communism (ideologies he subsumed under the heading "social liberalism"), for these too would merely repeat the transference of power from one authority to another (Stirner 2005, 122, 130). Even the "humane liberalism" of the best of the Young Hegelians was suspect because it too saw the egoism of others as a weakness while denying it in itself.

In contrast to Hegel's sociohistorical understanding of the conception of freedom, Stirner argued that "*freedom* can only be the whole of freedom, a piece of freedom is not *freedom*" (Stirner 2005, 160). From this perspective, he concluded that all moral approaches, including Feuerbach's, because they preached self-sacrifice in the name of some metaphysical notion—god, man, the state, class, nation, etc.—were the enemies of freedom. If "the road to ruin is paved with good intentions," the correct egoistic response was not revolution in the name of some "good" but a more simple rebellion of the ego against authority (Stirner 2005, 54, 75). Communism was not so much a radical alternative to the *status quo* as its latest moralistic variant (Stirner 2005, 18, 164, 258).

The vast bulk of the almost universally unread sections of Marx and Engels' *The German Ideology* is a critique of Stirner's book. Against Stirner's claim that socialists had embraced a static model of human essence, which provided them with a moral basis for criticising existing society, Marx outlined a Hegelian historicised transformation of his earlier Feuerbachian materialism. In the modern world this process underpinned the emergence both of egoistic and more social forms of individualism. Morality, as it was understood by Stirner, was an essential authoritarian characteristic only of communities made up of the former. By assuming the universality of egoism, Stirner was unable to comprehend the concept of workers' solidarity. Conversely, because Marx recognized that solidarity had become a real need and desire for workers he concluded that it was unnecessary to impose the idea of community on them. This is why, in stark contrast to modern liberal criticisms of the implicit authoritarianism of his ideas,[4] he argued that "communists do not preach morality"

---

4. It is precisely because Isaiah Berlin, for instance, criticizes Marxism from such a perspective that he talks past his subject. In "Two concepts of Liberty" Berlin dismissed Marx as a "utopian" believer in a form of "positive freedom" whereby the idea of freedom, understood as individual self-mastery, is transposed from the individual to the social to become the tyrannical attempt on the part of those who control the state to impose their authority upon those poor wretches below them whose desires do not conform to "reason" (Berlin 1997, 204). Against this degenerate form of freedom, Berlin championed the idea of negative freedom, according to which "I am normally said to be free to

(Marx and Engels 1976, 247). As Wilde points out, this argument has been misconstrued by those such as Jerry Cohen who have taken this line out of context to claim that Marx was a nihilist who embraced an "obstetric" conception of historical progress. What Marx was criticizing here was specifically the abstract conception of morality deployed both by Stirner and the utopian socialists, and counterposing to it ideals that are rooted in the real practice of workers in struggle (Wilde 2001, 4).

Marx and Engels therefore criticized the abstract moralism of the true socialists, because that which was to be liberated according to their models was always some disembodied "Man" rather than really existing men and women (Marx and Engels 1976, 468). This tendency, by abstracting the human essence from its real manifestation in history, acted as a barrier to the real diffusion of socialist consciousness, which could only arise out of a recognition of the class-divided nature of society.

---

the degree to which no man or body of men interferes with my activity" (ibid., 194). While this argument has been widely cited as the authoritative rebuttal of Marxism, it has in fact been definitively criticized by, amongst others, C. B. Macpherson. According to Macpherson, the problem with Berlin's model is that it "takes little or no account of class-imposed impediments" to individual activity (Macpherson 1973, 101). Indeed, by naturalizing the socially produced distribution of resources by which one section of society is compelled to work for another as the only means to their survival, Macpherson points out that far from acting as a theoretical defence of the individual against social power, the concept of negative liberty as articulated by Berlin "has become the cloak for un-individualist, corporate, imperial, 'free enterprise'" (Macpherson 1973, 116). Developing a related line of argument, Maureen Ramsay points out that Berlin is only able to maintain his position by, on the one hand, naturalizing the poverty of those who are compelled to sell their labour power, and on the other hand, by reducing freedom to the absence of intentional interference and thus by dismissing the "unintended but nevertheless inevitable and foreseeable effects of social arrangements and capitalist property relations" (Ramsay 1997, 48–53). Similarly, Andrew Collier shows that Berlin conflates Marx's and Kant's concepts of freedom. In opposition to this move, Collier points out that while Berlin is right to claim that Kant believes that reason and desires conflict, he is wrong to impute this idea to Marx. For whereas Kant juxtaposes desire and reason, Marx insists that socialism can only come through the class struggle of the proletariat because it is only through the struggles of this class that solidarity can become a real human desire (Collier 1990, 54). Indeed, this conception of socialism not only acts as a practical critique of liberalism it also acts as an immanent critique of the socialist pretensions of Stalinism and Maoism (Thomas, 1980, 122).

If, then, the theoretical representatives of the proletariat wish their literary activity to have any practical effect, they must first and foremost insist that all phrases are dropped which tend to dim the realisation of the sharpness of this opposition, all phrases which tend to conceal this opposition and may even give the bourgeois a chance to approach the communists for safety's sake on the strength of their philanthropic enthusiasms. (Marx and Engels 1976, 469)

Marx and Engels insisted that the "true socialists" worked with "arid abstractions" which they compared with the "philosophers . . . choice of terms" (Marx and Engels 1976, 478, 480). Consequently, the true socialists, like Kant and other moralists before them, forget

that the "inward nature" of men, as well as their "consciousness" of it, "i.e.," their "reason," has at all times been an historical product and that even when . . . the society of men was based "upon external compulsion," their "inward nature" corresponded to this "external compulsion." (Marx and Engels 1976, 480)

Nevertheless, Marx was keen to stress that human nature was not infinitely pliable, and that throughout history one consistent characteristic of the human condition was that the different skills and abilities possessed by various individuals at any particular historical juncture did not entail that they had different needs.

But one of the most vital principles of communism, a principle which distinguishes it from all reactionary socialism, is its empirical view, based on a knowledge of man's nature, that differences of brain and of intellectual ability do not imply any differences whatsoever in the nature of the stomach and of physical needs; therefore the false tenet, based upon existing circumstances, "to each according to his abilities," must be changed, insofar as it relates to enjoyment in its narrower sense, into the tenet, "to each according to his need"; in other words, a different form of activity, of labour, does not justify inequality, confers no privileges in respect of possession and enjoyment. (Marx and Engels 1976, 537)

If Marx's deployment of a version of the needs principle appears to tie him to a transhistorical moral standard, once this statement is read in the context of the broader argument of *The German Ideology* it is clear that it is meant not as an ideal to be imposed upon society in a top-down manner, but rather as a concrete criticism of another manifestation of the true socialists' faith in the power of abstract reason: their belief in their own privileged position as intellectual leaders. Marx's argument here is best understood, therefore, as a concrete expression of what Draper famously called "socialism from below" (Draper 1992). It was because Marx held to such a model of socialism that he expended so much energy exploring the barriers to working-class socialism.

Nonetheless, although Marx believed that proletarians were impelled to revolt against their alienation, the division of labour itself tended, as Smith noted, to make them unfit for rule. In *Anti-Dühring*, Engels pointed out that "in the division of labour, man is also divided. All other physical and mental faculties are sacrificed to the development of one single activity. This stunting of man grows in the same measure as the division of labour, which attains its highest development in manufacture" (Engels 1947, 355; Draper 1978, 483; Braverman 1974, 73). So, while Engels insisted that the development of society's productive forces created the conditions whereby the division of labour might be "swept away," and in *Capital* Marx argued that the increases in the productivity of labour associated with the growth of capitalism ensured that "the technical reason for the lifelong attachment of the worker to a partial function is swept away," Marx also added that, simultaneously, "the barriers placed in the way of the domination of capital by this same regulating principle now also fall" (Engels 1947, 342; Marx 1976, 491). Marx consequently argued that whereas the increases in the productivity of labour associated with the deepening of the division of labour under capitalism had created the objective potential for socialism, he also saw that the existence of the division of labour acted as a barrier to the realization of this potential.

Furthermore, in *Capital* Marx registered his sympathy with Hegel, when, against the stupefying consequences of the division of labour, he quoted the latter's claim that an educated person is one who "can do what others do" (Hegel quoted in Marx 1976, 485). More radically, in *The German Ideology*, he and Engels suggested that the system of alienation could be overcome only by "the abolition of division of labour," and that this was the precondition to the "all-round development of individuals" (Marx and Engels 1976, 438–439). Unfortunately, one can only do what others do if there is no division of labour, and if there is no division of labour then it follows from Smith's argument that humanity will revert back to a primitive, in fact even an impossibly pre-social, state.

This certainly was not Marx's mature vision of the socialist future. In the two decades after penning *The German Ideology* Marx articulated a much more sophisticated conception of the division of labour that provided a basis from which to escape the limitations of his earlier writings on the subject without retreating in his criticisms of capital.[5] In his mature writings, Marx squared his critique of the division of labour with the view that socialism required a relatively high level of economic development through a conceptual distinction he drew between two distinct aspects of the division of labour: the manufacturing (what later commentators tend to call the technical) and the social.

In *Capital* and the notebooks he wrote in preparation for it, Marx insisted that although social or occupational divisions within the production process were a near universal feature of human history, the most dehumanizing element of the modern division of labour—the manufacturing or technical division of labour—is a product of modern capitalist production. Thus he differentiated between the social division of people into various specialist occupations, and the technical division of individual jobs, and thereby the people who worked them, into increasingly simple component parts. In the *Economic Manuscripts of 1861–1863*, he argued that Smith "constantly confuses these very different senses of the division of labour, which admittedly complement each other, but are also in certain respects mutually opposed" (Marx 1988a, 266). It was as a consequence of this confusion that Smith "did not grasp the division of labour as something peculiar to the capitalist mode of production." Therefore, as Marx argued in *Theories of Surplus Value*, whereas occupational specialization was a universal feature of human history, the subdivision of jobs into their relatively unskilled component parts, whilst built upon this earlier division, was a peculiar

---

5. Marx's views on the division of labour and the parameters of its possible suppression developed from a utopianism that is evident in his earlier work toward a more realistic analysis in his mature work. Unfortunately, considerations of space preclude a full discussion of this intellectual evolution (cf Ratansi 1982; Beamish 1992).

product of capitalist manufacture (Marx 1972, 268). Whereas Smith equated the manufacturing division of labour with both the social division of labour and the tendency toward increased productivity, Marx argued that the development of the manufacturing division of labour is better understood as that process through which the subsumption of labour to capital moved from its formal to its real phase. Marx insisted, the manufacturing division of labour was not instituted primarily as a means of increasing labour productivity, but was rather used as a means of enforcing capitalist discipline on the labour force by deskilling the labour process (Braverman 1974, 119; Thompson 1989, 75). Whereas the social division of labour facilitated increases in the productivity of labour by occupational specialization, the technical division involves the subdivision of jobs such that individual workers perform increasingly simple tasks for which they require only a minimum of training (Ratansi 1982, 150). For while capitalism had emerged, in part at least, out of pre-capitalist modes of production by enforcing the discipline of the market upon existing labour processes—the formal subsumption of labour to capital; with the development of factory production the nature of the labour process was itself transformed such that labour was deskilled and becomes really "subsumed under capital" (Marx 1988a, 271, 279; Marx 1976, 1019–1024). In this new situation, Marx argued, "the division of labour within the workshop implies the undisputed authority of the capitalist over men" (Marx 1976, 477).

Accordingly, for Marx, the social and the manufacturing divisions of labour could be differentiated thus: while the former is a necessary aspect of social life and social development through increases in labour productivity, the latter was primarily designed to facilitate the appropriation of surplus-value from workers by increasing capital's control over the labour process. "The machine," he wrote, "is a means for producing surplus-value" (Marx 1976, 492). Marx suggested that whilst the former process was an inevitable precondition of economic and social advance, the tendency immanent in it toward "crippling of the body and mind" by occupational specialization was taken to an extreme in the factory for reasons that had little to do with increasing the "universal opulence." Rather, the manufacturing system emerged to ensure capital's control over the labour process and was an "entirely specific creation of the capitalist mode of production" (Marx 1976, 480, 484).

In stark contrast to those who claim that Marx predicted a simplification ond homogenization of social class relations, the logic of his

discussion of the division of labour appears to imply that the condition
of the proletariat is both too fragmented and too intellectually narrow
for it to act as a realistic agency of its own emancipation. Nevertheless,
as Braverman has shown, while the aim of the technical division of
labour is to reduce workers to the position of cogs in a machine, the
intelligence and humanity of those performing even the most menial
tasks is never completely extinguished (Braverman 1974, 325). Similarly,
Marshall Berman points out that *Capital* contains the voices of many
workers who, when interviewed by factory inspectors exhibited a "stoi-
cal endurance" and "austere intelligence" in the face of the overbearing
pressures of manual labour in nineteenth-century England (Berman 1999,
83). It was Marx's contention, based upon his experience in socialist
workers' circles in the mid-1840s, that the irrepressible intelligence and
the humanity of these workers acted as the mainspring of the struggle
for freedom, and that through their struggle for freedom workers could
break the sociological binds that alienated them from each other and the
rest of society. Consequently, whereas Hegel had argued that this process
merely created a fragmented rabble (Taylor 1975, 407, 436), Marx suggested that workers could move, through their engagement in combined
struggles for a better life, from being an atomized and dehumanized
group, toward becoming a potential collective agency of universal social
and political emancipation. Marx therefore differentiated himself from
the utopian socialists in conceptualizing workers not merely as victims
of the system but also as agents of its possible overthrow: "they see
in poverty nothing but poverty, without seeing in it the revolutionary,
subversive side" (Marx 1984a, 178).

Nevertheless, Marx stressed that the workers' potential for revolt
should not be confused with their potential to rule, for it was only
through struggle that the latter was realized. The revolutionary nature
of workers' struggles was therefore crucial to Marx's political theory
because it was only through such struggles that workers could overcome
the intellectually and morally debilitating consequences of the division
of labour. Marx and Engels argued that revolutions were necessary to
overthrow capitalism not simply because the ruling class could not be
removed in any other way, but more importantly because it was only
through the tumultuous struggles associated with a revolution from
below that the proletariat could rid "itself of all the muck of ages and
become fitted to found society anew" (Marx and Engels 1976, 53).
So, it was only through the act of making a revolution that working

people, socialized by their class location to assume subservient social roles, could become masters of their own destiny. As he wrote in the *Theses on Feuerbach*, "[t]he coincidence of the changing of circumstances and of human activity or self-change can be conceived and rationally understood only as **revolutionary practice**" (Marx 1975f, 422).

If, as Marx believed, it was through revolutionary practice that workers were able to remake themselves fit for self-government, this form of activity also provided the framework which allowed him to uncover the contradictory essence of capitalist society. As we suggested in our discussion of Proudhon, Marx argued that his own perspective could be differentiated from Proudhon's specifically, and that of classical political economy more generally, through his deployment of the concept of totality: from the standpoint of the individual within civil society commodity exchange seems free and fair, whereas from the standpoint of the totality it was a form of exploitation.

It was Marx's belief that Smith and Ricardo, in cutting through the many and varied manifestations of wealth within capitalist society to uncover the labour theory of value, made a fundamental contribution to social science. Nevertheless, following Engels he claimed that just as Luther had stymied the humanism inherent in his overthrow of the external religiosity of Catholicism by internalizing faith as the "inner essence of man," the classical political economists, while recognizing that labour is the source of wealth, undermined the power of this insight by internalizing "private property into the very being of man" (Marx 1975d, 342). Marx insisted that this was no mere error of reason, but in fact was the ideological consequence of the reified way the world looks from the standpoint of the modern division of labour.

In *Capital* Marx explained the social basis for reification through an extension of his theory of alienation by means of the concept of commodity fetishism (Perkins 1993, 126ff; Rees 1998, 87ff). While he continued to suggest that it is workers who produce wealth which becomes "an alien power" that "dominates" them (Marx 1976, 716, 1054), he developed this argument to claim that within a system of generalized commodity production this alien power presents itself in a fetishized way: "the commodity reflects the social characteristics of men's own labour as objective characteristics of the products of labour themselves" (Marx 1976, 164–5). This fetishistic relationship emerges as a consequence of the twofold nature of the commodity: its use-value and its exchange-value. While the commodity's individual material form is its use-value, its social form is expressed through the market only as exchange-value. In the marketplace, the commodity's exchange-value appears as an objective property which bears no relation to its use-value. It is this false objectivity which obscures the social aspect of production, the concrete forms of cooperation through which we produce and without which we would die, thus giving the impression that the world is a ready-made thing which dominates the powerless individual consumer. Commodity fetishism transforms "the social, economic character that things are stamped with in the process of social production into a natural character arising from the material nature of these things" (Marx 1978, 303). Subsequently, whereas capitalist relations of production are a product of history at a specific moment of development, they appear as natural relations between people. Production of commodities for the market entails, or so Marx argues, that "the relationships between the producers, within which social characteristics of their labours are manifested, take on the form of a social relation between the products of labour." So, just as the idea of god is a product of the human mind which is endowed by the religious with its own agency, commodities are a product of human industry that appear not as a manifestation of our productive powers but rather as a power over us. Concretely, capitalism is a mode of production whose social aspect is manifested through the exchange of commodities between otherwise private individuals. When such commodities are exchanged, they appear to exchange in ratios that are determined by "the nature of the products" themselves (Marx 1976, 163–177). Reflecting on this state of affairs, the classical political economists articulated the labour theory of value in recognition that there must be something common to all commodities which facilitates their commensurability. However, partly as a consequence of the way that these relations manifest themselves, Smith and Ricardo (and Kant and Bentham) naturalized the capitalist mode of production (Mészáros 1986, 174). Because they were interested primarily in explaining the prices at which commodities exchanged, their analyses stopped at the point where they recognized money as the common expression of value (Marx 1976, 168). By contrast, Marx argued that it is precisely the monetary exchange of commodities that conceals the appropriation of surplus value at the point of production. He thus wrote that

[t]he crude materialism of the economists who regard as the natural properties of things what are social relations of

production among people, and qualities which things obtain because they are subsumed under these relations, is at the same time just as crude an idealism, even fetishism, since it imputes social relations to things as inherent characteristics, and thus mystifies them. (Marx 1973a, 687 quoted in Mészáros 1986, 138)

Because their analyses did not look beneath the level of the circulation of capital, the classical political economists, notwithstanding Ricardo's comments on the rationality of workers' struggles against the introduction of new technology (Ricardo 1973, 263–271), were blind to the systematic nature of the exploitation of wage labour. They therefore failed to explain the rationality behind, and the social significance of, one of the most important movements of the nineteenth century: the struggle to reduce the working day.

It was the struggle over the working day that informed the framework from which Marx moved beyond the standpoint of political economy, and thus beyond the perspective of modern moral philosophy, which like political economy naturalized and reified capitalist social relations. As we have noted, Marx argued that beneath the surface appearance of the fair exchange of labour power the struggle over the working day revealed a "civil war between the capitalist class and the working class" which showed that workers came "instinctively" to recognize what was concealed from the political economists: they and the capitalists stood in opposition to each other. This struggle exposed the gap between capitalism as it presents itself at the level of circulation and as its real social content. In the marketplace, workers encounter capitalists freely and equally as commodity owners, but "when the transaction was concluded, it was discovered that [the worker] was no 'free agent.' " Rather, they are forced to sell their labour power to capitalists, who, vampire-like, "will not let go" (Marx 1976, 411–416; cf 1981, 966). When seen from this perspective, the "pompous catalogue of the inalienable rights of man" whose formal political equality masks real social inequality, gave way, under pressure of real social movements from below, to the "modest Magna Carta of the legally limited working day" (Marx 1976, 416).

Marx's critique of liberalism thus arose out of his keen sense of those collective movements of real men and women against the power of capital, which threw into relief the hollowness of traditional liberal

conceptions of individuality in general and individual rights more specifically. This perspective not only allowed him a deeper understanding
of capitalism than was evident in the works of Smith and Ricardo,
but also a basis from which to explain the limitations of their theories
(Weeks 1981, 41). Marx already made this point explicit in the tenth of
his theses on Feuerbach: "[t]he standpoint of the old materialism is
civil society; the standpoint of the new is human society or social
humanity."

It is plain from what we have written above that the concept of
social humanity is no abstraction that overrode society's class divisions.
In Capital Marx repeated the argument first encountered in The Holy
Family that the differential experiences of alienation on the part of
workers and capitalists meant, when seen from the point of view of
capital accumulation, that both groups acted as personifications of their
social roles: capitalists feel empowered by their role whereas for the
workers their role "was just effort and torment" (Marx 1976, 989).
Thus, as Chris Arthur argues, "both in the 1844 Manuscripts and
Capital it is clear that the political location of Marx's critique is that
of the proletariat." In neither case does Marx choose this standpoint
because the workers are the most oppressed section of society, but rather
because of "its strategic position in the economic order" (Arthur 1986,
145). As Marx wrote, insofar as his own critique of political economy
"represents a class, it can only represent the class whose historical task
is the overthrow of the capitalist mode of production and the final
abolition of all classes—the proletariat" (Marx 1976, 98; quoted in
Arthur 1986, 172).

The gap between this standpoint and that of political economy
(and modern moral theory) could not be greater (Mészáros 1986,
143). Whatever their differences, both Kant and Mill shared a reified
idea of "Man" and a "frozen" conception of history (Mészáros 1986,
144, 147). It is for this reason that Marx cannot be labelled a moralist, for the moralistic conception of human agency is a hollow and
indeed ideological reflection of the formally free and equal individualism
characteristic of the capitalist mode of production (Reiman 1991). As
opposed to those who suggest that Marxism lacks a moral aspect as a
consequence of Marx's economic determinism and crude materialism,
it is precisely because Marx's conception of agency is so much more
profound than Kant's or Mill's that his ethics cannot be reduced to one
or other of their systems.

Against the reified abstractions of bourgeois social theory, Marx recognized when workers came together to resist their exploitation they began to realize a new form of humanity, which in turn created the basis from which the social world could be conceived as a changeable product of their labour. Marx came to this conclusion through his engagement in 1844 with the Silesian weavers, who rose against their bourgeois masters. If it was in light of this movement that Marx became a Marxist (Marx 1975e, 415; Blackburn 1977, 27–30), it is because modern moral theory fails to recognize the importance of this kind of practice that it cannot see beyond bourgeois egoism.

Virtues and the Struggles of the Working Class

Daniel Brudney has recently argued that because Marx failed to justify the ethical significance of working-class practice he wrapped himself in a contradiction from which he was unable to escape (Brudney 1998, 197). According to Brudney, Marx's theory of alienation simultaneously implies that "knowledge of human nature gives the standard for political change," but that our alienation from this nature prevents workers from developing such a knowledge (Brudney 1998, 4, 224–226). Consequently, whereas Marx's eleventh thesis on Feuerbach famously suggests a break with philosophy—"the philosophers have only interpreted the world in various ways, the point is to change it"—this is an impossible dream because alienated human life cannot provide a window to some supposed real humanity (Brudney 1998, 361). If valid, I think that this argument would entail that socialism, at least in its Marxist variant, could be dismissed as a utopian dream.

Brudney's suggestion of a dichotomy within Marx's thought between nature as it could be under socialism and nature as it is under capitalism seems to miss the point: for Marx our nature evolves in a context of humanity's developing productive powers, and the struggle for democratic control over those powers. Thus, he argues against any romantic notion of a natural human solidarity with the claim that "individuals cannot gain mastery over their own social interconnections before they have created them." He insists that whereas "in earlier stages of development the single individual seems to have developed more fully," this was only because these individuals had not yet fully worked out their mutual "relationships." Marx therefore points out that while it is "ridiculous to yearn for a return to that original fullness," because bourgeois thought is unable to grasp the historical character of these relationships it tends to confront the horrors of bourgeois society with an impotent, romantic alternative (Marx 1973a, 161–2). The problem that Marx addresses by contrast is not whether workers might be able to recreate some pristine species being from the standpoint of their alienated existence. Rather, he criticizes the existing social order from the point of view of real struggles against it, and judges that in the present epoch workers' struggles point toward a fuller realization of human freedom. It is because of this that Marx and Engels, as Draper points out, rather than use the abstract word socialism to describe their goal, more usually wrote of workers' power (Draper 1978, 24).

In this context it is important to remember that Marx was keen to stress, as we noted above, both that socialists should not reify the proletariat as "gods," and that even these ungodly folk would tend to feel their alienation as dehumanization, which in turn would underpin their collective struggles for self-realization. As Terry Eagleton argues:

> The means and ends of communism are interestingly at odds: a traditionally conceived *Humanität* will be brought to birth by those whose humanity is most crippled and depleted; an aesthetic society will be the fruit of the most resolutely instrumental political action; an ultimate plurality of powers flows only from the most resolute partisanship. (Eagleton 1990, 206)

Although Eagleton is right to stress the "ungodly" characteristics of the modern proletariat, it would be one-sided to leave the analysis of the working class at this point. For Marx also recognized that the collective struggles of workers underpinned the emergence of virtues of solidarity and sociability which pointed beyond the limitations of liberalism's world of egoistic individuals. Indeed, he suggested that workers' consciousness tended to change through their experience of collective struggles as they realized their objective need for solidarity in ways that fostered socialistic attitudes.

There are numerous examples throughout Marx and Engels' work that point to the historical emergence of the need and desire for association as actualized through the struggles of workers for freedom against exploitation. Thus, in 1853 Marx wrote that "the continual conflicts between masters and men, are, . . . the indispensable means of holding up the spirit of the labouring classes, of combining them into one great association against the encroachment of the ruling class, and of preventing them from becoming apathetic, thoughtless, more or less well-fed instruments of production" (Marx 1979, 169). Six years earlier he had pointed out how the struggle to form associations (trade unions), while being partially explicable from the point of view of classical political economy as a means of improving wages, became inexplicable once workers began to turn over to the associations, for the sake of association, "a good part of their wages." Marx argues that this process is evidence that "the domination of capital has created for this mass a common situation, common interests." Consequently, whereas political economy was able only to understand atomized individualism, Marx showed how a new social rationality emerged within the working class (Marx 1984a, 211). While written prior to his mature reflections on the division of labour, this argument continues to illuminate important aspects of working-class life. Marx accepted that the political economists were right, from their point of view, to point to the irrationality of workers forming unions, but also that, from their point of view, workers "are right to laugh at the clever bourgeois schoolmasters" (Marx 1984b, 435; Hyman 1984, Ch. 5). For Marx, therefore, the core of the socialist project is, of course, the movement from below which begins to realize in however a limited form the negation of capital: "In order to supersede the idea of private property, the idea of communism is enough. In order to supersede private property as it actually exists, real communist activity is necessary" (Marx 1975d, 365). Marx suggested not only that workers feel compelled to struggle against the power of capital, but that in so doing they begin to create modes of existence which also offer a virtuous alternative to the egoism characteristic not only of capitalist society generally, but also of working-class life within that society more specifically.

> When communist workmen gather together, their immediate aim is instruction, propaganda, etc. But at the same time, they acquire a new need—the need for society—and what appears as a means had become an end. This practical development can be most strikingly observed in the gatherings of French socialist workers. Smoking, eating, and drinking, etc., are no longer means of creating links between people. Company,

association, conversation, which in turn has society as its goal,
is enough for them. The brotherhood of man is not a hollow
phrase, it is a reality, and the nobility of man shines forth
upon us from their work-worn figures. (Marx 1975d, 365)

As Sean Sayers points out, Marx condemns capitalist society not
from some abstract concept of right, but from the standpoint of workers' struggles immanent to it (Sayers 1998, 124). Because this model
of revolutionary politics is rooted in immanent forces within capitalism,
it stands in opposition to traditional top-down conceptions of insurrectionary politics. Thus, as Michael Löwy points out in his discussion
of the French Revolution, although Marx obviously showed admiration
for Robespierre's "historical greatness and revolutionary energy," he
explicitly rejected Jacobinism "as a model or source of inspiration for
socialist revolutionary praxis" (Löwy 1989, 119). Indeed, from his earliest writings, Marx drew on Hegel's analysis of Jacobinism specifically
and the French Revolution more generally to criticise the one-sidedly
political character of Robespierre's practice (Marx 1975e, 413). According to Hegel, Robespierre's Terror was the necessary counterpart of
his attempt to impose a vision on society from the top-down that was
not rooted in a prior transformation of the nation's "dispositions and
religion" (Hegel 1956, 446, 449, 450).

Marx recognized the power of Hegel's argument, but disagreed
with him that Jacobinism exposed the limits of the revolutionary project
(Taylor 1975, 437). Rather he argued that this gap between the revolutionary leadership and the mass of the population was not a general
characteristic of revolutions, but reflected the bourgeois nature of the
French Revolution. He distinguished this type of revolution from modern
proletarian revolutions in a way that pointed to the qualitative difference
between his politics and Jacobinism (Marx 1973c). According to Marx,
bourgeois revolutions were born of developing contradictions between
emergent capitalist relations of production and existing pre-capitalist
states, and where they were successful resulted in the removal of fetters to further capitalist development. Although these revolutions were
generally marked by a progressive break with pre-capitalist hierarchies,
because they were characterized by the transference of power from one
ruling class to another they involved at best a contradictory relationship
between their leadership and the mass of the population. For instance,
bourgeois revolutions "from above" such as Bismarck's unification of

Germany involved no mass action at all, whereas England's, America's, and France's bourgeois revolutions "from below" were won through the involvement of the lower classes but ended similarly with the exclusion of the poor from power. Proletarian revolutions, by contrast, because they are made for and by the working class—"the emancipation of the working classes must be conquered by the working classes themselves" (Marx 1974b, 82)—were necessarily qualitatively more democratic in both their execution and outcome. Their triumph required the workers to be organized as a political force (a workers' state), but because the workers exploit no social group below them once the bourgeois counterrevolution was suppressed the workers' state would begin to "wither away" (Blackledge 2006, 127–139; cf Callinicos 1989b; Draper 1978, 28–32; Hobsbawm 1986, 26; Lukács 1971, 282).

Contrary to the superficial contrast between the two, the ideas of socialism from below and a vanguard party actually complement each other. Thus, as shall see in the next chapter, Marx's argument for the creation of "an independent organisation of the workers' party" (Marx 1973b, 324), does not betray a closet Blanquism. In fact, far from negating the idea of socialism from below, the idea of a revolutionary vanguard is an essential component to it. Accordingly Lars Lih argues that because Marx insisted that socialism can only come from below he realized that it will necessarily emerge out of sectional and fragmented struggles, and it is the sectional and fragmentary nature of the struggle that creates differences between more and less advanced workers, and consequently results in the emergence of socialist leaders. Lih points out that whereas "[s]ometimes the dictum [socialism is the self-emancipation of the working class] is viewed as the opposite of the vanguard outlook . . . in actuality, it makes vanguardism almost inevitable. If the proletariat is the only agent capable of introducing socialism, then it must go through some process that will prepare it to carry out that great deed" (Lih 2006, 556). Concretely, the vanguard could not be a sect of self-appointed leaders, but would develop as different activists took on leading roles within the workers' movement. Stephen Perkins argues that thus understood the "vanguard is ever changing as it responds to the vicissitudes of the class struggle" (Perkins 1993, 170). The revolutionary workers' party, in Marx's conception, aimed at overcoming both the division between mental and manual workers within its own ranks, and the tendencies toward the fragmentation of the workers' movement more broadly (Löwy 2003, 134, 146). As Michael

Löwy points out, for Marx "the proletariat tends towards the totality through its practice of the class struggle" and this process is necessarily mediated through "its communist vanguard" (Löwy 2003, 137). The role of this vanguard is not to preach "the truth" but to "participat[e] closely in the process of class struggle, helping the proletariat to find, through its own historical practice, the path to communist revolution" (Löwy 2003, 136). As John Molyneux has argued, Marx's conception of the revolutionary party "absolutely ruled out" both the "conspiratorial" idea of the party of as a small elite acting for the working class and the "authoritarian view" of the party handing orders down to the class from above. Against both of these models, Marx firmly established "the concept of leadership won on the basis of performance in the class struggle" (Molyneux 1986, 17). As Marx wrote, whereas Proudhon and other anarchist and socialist sectarians aimed to prescribe a set course, deduced from doctrine, to the workers. movement, he himself aimed to root his "agitation in the actual elements of the class movement" (Marx 1988b, 133). It was from this perspective that the famous lines from the *Communist Manifesto* were written:

> The Communists are distinguished from the other working-class parties by this only: 1. In the national struggles of the proletarians of the different countries, they point out and bring to the front the common interests of the entire proletariat, independently of all nationality. 2. In the various stages of development which the struggle of the working class against the bourgeoisie has to pass through, they always and everywhere represent the interests of the movement as a whole. (Marx and Engels 1973, 79)

If the revolutionary party, thus conceived, fights for an ideal that is immanent to the practical solidarity of workers' collective struggles, it is precisely because the division of labour generates divisions within the working class as well as the potential for solidarity across the proletariat that this role cannot be reduced to a mere act of midwifery. For instance, both in the 1840s and in the period of the First International, Marx fought for, and helped create, a spirit of internationalism which was intended to contribute to the shape of the new society (Collins and Abramsky 1965; Gilbert 1981).

From this perspective the moral dimension of politics is neither an abstract imperative imposed upon individuals in the name of some supposedly disembodied reason, nor is it a distraction from an otherwise automatic process of the growth of working-class socialist consciousness. Rather, socialist morality is the flipside of the scientific critique of political economy, and both of these aspects of socialist theory are intended to help workers realise *a* potential, the socialist potential, inherent to the spontaneous acts of solidarity which characterize life within capitalist society just as much as do acts of selfish egoism. The collective struggles on the part of the proletariat are simultaneously, therefore, the basis for Marx's critique of political economy and the precondition for his parallel critique of moral theory.

Marxist ethics therefore presuppose an unbreakable unity between the facts and the condemnation of exploitation and alienation on the one hand, and the means to and end of socialism on the other. While modern moral philosophy is a reified reflection of our alienated existence under capitalism, Marxism, both as an explanatory account of the dynamics of capitalism and as a condemnation of this system, is rooted in the collective struggles of workers for freedom. Practice does not and cannot follow theory in the way that modern moral theory would have us suppose, for it is universally true that we can theorize only from specific standpoints. Marx thus criticized liberal moralists for naturalizing the standpoint from which they wrote, and consequently for being unable to offer an adequate account of human action. By contrast, because he made his own standpoint explicit he revealed not only the limitations of modern moral theory, but also the unity, but not identity, of socialism, social science, and moral realism.

Conclusion

In the *Grundrisse*, Marx famously compared the modern world negatively to the period of antiquity. Arguing that, whatever their manifest limitations, because the Greeks and Romans almost universally asked of production not was it the most efficient creator of wealth, but what kind of citizen did it foster, their world, despite its relative poverty could appear to be and was indeed "loftier" than modern capitalism

> Thus the old view, in which the human being appears as the aim of production, regardless of his limited national, religious, political character, seems to be very lofty when contrasted to the modern world, where production appears as the aim

of mankind and wealth as the aim of production. In fact, however, when the limited bourgeois form is stripped away, what is wealth other than the universality of individual needs, capacities, pleasures, productive forces etc., created through universal exchange? The full development of human mastery over the forces of nature, those of so-called nature as well as of humanity's own nature? The absolute working-out of his creative potentialities, with no presupposition other than the previous historic development, which makes this totality of development, i.e., the development of all human powers as such the end in itself, not as measured on a predetermined yardstick? Where he does not reproduce himself in one specificity, but produces his totality? Strives not to remain something he has become, but is in the absolute movement of becoming? In bourgeois economics—and in the epoch of production to which it corresponds—this complete working-out of the human content appears as a complete emptying-out, this universal objectification as total alienation, and the tearing-down of all limited, one-sided aims as sacrifice of the human end-in-itself to an entirely external end. This is why the childish world of antiquity appears on one side as loftier. On the other side, it really is loftier in all matters where closed shapes, forms and given limits are sought for. It is satisfaction from a limited standpoint; while the modern gives no satisfaction; or, where it appears satisfied with itself, it is vulgar. (Marx 1973a, 487–488)

Commenting on these lines, Eagleton suggests that "Marx does indeed possess an 'absolute' moral criterion: the unquestionable virtue of the rich, all-round expansion of capacities for each individual. It is from this standpoint that any social formation is to be assessed" (Eagleton 1990, 223, 226). Because Marx recognizes that workers' struggles give con-crete shape to the struggle for freedom of social individuals, he implies a model of discrimination between various powers: "we should foster only those powers which allow an individual to realize herself through and in terms of the similar free self-realization of others. It is this, above all, which distinguishes socialism from liberalism" (Eagleton 1990, 224). In fact, Marx shows that liberalism, far from representing the disinterested power of reason has the effect of naturalizing the modern, capitalist social relations and thus, implicitly, of legitimising the power of those who gain from these relations (Ramsay 1997, 7).

Marx's socialism, by contrast, is not a moral doctrine in the modern liberal sense because it does not pretend to be disinterested. Rather, it explicitly reflects the real, *interested* movement of workers to gain democratic control of the alienated product of their labours. It is, however, ethical in an Aristotelian sense because its challenge to the system of alienation is in the universal interest: it points to the potential for us all to "excel at being human" (Eagleton 2003, 142; 2007b). Workers' struggles are consequently of the first importance not only because they simultaneously illuminate and point beyond our alienated existence, but also because in so doing they provide some concrete content to the idea of universality in a way that begins to overcome the limitations of liberalism's abstract conception of the same.

If it follows from the theory of alienation, especially in the modern context when alienated relations appear to leave us powerless before an impending environmental catastrophe, that the modern categorical imperative is to join the struggle for socialism, one of the roles of intellectuals in this movement is to make explicit that which is implicit to workers' struggles: Marx's socialism is, in Engels words, "nothing but the reflex, in thought," of the social conflicts endemic to capitalism (Engels 1947, 325). Or as Marx wrote three decades earlier; "we do not say to the world: Cease your struggles, they are foolish; we will give you the true slogan of struggle. We merely show the world what it is really fighting for, and consciousness is something that it *has to* acquire even if it does not want to" (Marx 1975h, 144).

By highlighting the intimate link between Marxist theory and working-class struggle these quotations suggest that Marxism is best understood not as an ideology that is presented to the workers' movement from "without," but rather as the theory of the generalized lessons of the struggles of ordinary workers against capitalism. According to Patrick Murray, Marx "seeks a science that will find the 'ought,' the rational, in the actual world and its immanent contradictions, rather than dictate an abstract, external moral code to the world" (Murray 1988, 222). So although Marx did not hold the naive belief that workers in struggle would automatically see beyond capitalist reification—he insisted on the fundamental importance of the concept of mediation as a corollary of the "irreparable gap" between thought and actuality, essence and appearance (Murray 1988, 31, 225)[6]—he did believe that social science was possible only if it is rooted in the standpoint of these struggles. And the most important mediation between the workers' movement and his scientific analyses is involvement in political practice itself (Murray 1988, 92). Marx deepened and developed his analysis of alienation and the concrete form of the movement against it (see Draper 1977; 1978; 1986; 1990; Gilbert 1981 and Thomas 1980) through participation in political organizations which fought for the working class to become an independent political actor (Molyneux 1986, 15).

From this perspective, Marx's ethics is best understood not as a more or less coherent addition to his scientific account of the inevitable collapse of capitalism, but as a fundamental aspect of the "sensuous human activity, practice." This concept of practice sits at the heart of his social theory, which is necessarily ethical as well as scientific. If the collective struggles of workers illuminate the essence of the capitalist mode of production, their historical specificity simultaneously denaturalizes this order. Beyond revealing capitalism to be a novel, alienated mode of production, workers' solidarity also points to the concrete possibility of freedom. This provides the ethical foundation for Marx's politics, which is predicated on the hope that by realizing both the new need and desire for solidarity the collective struggles of workers against exploitation and oppression offer the basis for a socialist alternative to capitalist alienation.

Paradoxically, despite Marx being "above all else a revolutionary" this most important practical aspect of his work was the least theoretically elaborated. It was left to the second generation of Marxists to make good this lacuna, and it is to their work that this study now turns.

---

6. Marx argues that because "vulgar economics" takes as its starting point the consciousness of agents within bourgeois society it remains "trapped within bourgeois relations of production." Against this method, Marx famously wrote that "all science would be superfluous if the form of appearance of things directly coincided with their essence" (Marx 1981, 956).

3

Ethics and Politics in
Second and Third
International Marxism

Walking upright, this distinguishes men from animals, and it cannot
yet be done. It exists only as a wish, the wish to live without exploitation and masters.

—Bloch 1986, Vol. III, 1367

The thought of the ideal passing into the real is profound: very
important for history.

—Lenin 1961b, 114

Introduction

In the wake of the collapse of the International Working Men's Association
(the First International) after the defeat of the Paris Commune, Marx and
Engels' most direct influence on the European workers' movement was
through the German Social Democratic Party (SPD). This organization
was created through a merger of existing Marxist and Lassallean groups
at the 1875 Gotha Unity Congress and in 1889 it played a key role in
the formation of a new international grouping of socialist parties, the
Socialist International (Second International). Formed in Paris on the
centenary of the storming of the Bastille, from its inception until its
collapse at the outbreak of the First World War the Second International
was dominated by its German section, and the interpretation of Marxism dominant within this party became increasingly hegemonic within
European socialist politics (Abendroth 1972, 51–68). When academics

101

write of "orthodox Marxism" or "orthodox historical materialism" it is usually some variant of Second International Marxism, or Stalin's caricatured version of the same, to which they refer.[1] Moreover, the claim that Marx failed to offer a viable ethical alternative to liberal moral perspectives is often substantiated by reference to the ethical debates within the Second International (MacIntyre 1995, 131), and the fact that many of the contributions to these debates were relatively crude lends weight to this argument. However, the degree of discontinuity between Marx's revolutionary politics and Second International Marxism is such as to cast severe doubt on this rhetorical ploy. Additionally, the fact the revolutionary left within the International explicitly broke with the "Marxism" of that organization in the name of a return to Marx, and formalized this break through the creation of the Third International or Comintern in 1919 poses questions of how far, if at all, it is reasonable to label Second International Marxism as orthodox historical materialism, and to what extent the Marxists associated with the pre-Stalinist Comintern managed to renew Marxism through a break with the categories of Second International thought.

The tension between Second International Marxism and Marx and Engels' politics was first signalled in an exchange over the compromise at the center of the SPD's initial Gotha Programme (1875), and was repeated when this compromise was reproduced in its reformulated Erfurt Programme (1891). In both of these documents the Marxist case for revolution was skirted over, and consequentially the political strategy of the organization was fudged. Insofar as these programmes outlined a strategic perspective it was reformist, and whereas Marx had posited a sharp break between capitalist and communist societies the programmes implied a more gradual and evolutionary transition. This separation of theory and practice meant that Second International Marxism functioned, as George Lichtheim argued, less as a "theory of action" and more as an "integrative ideology" (Lichtheim 1970, 251–2).

---

1. In fact, the most philosophically sophisticated version of this interpretation of historical materialism is Jerry Cohen's *Karl Marx's Theory of History: A Defence*, and it is to this that most contemporary references to orthodox historical materialism refer (Cf Wright 1992, 11, 14, 16; Roberts 1996, 1; Callinicos 2004, 54). I discuss this modern articulation of Second International Marxism in Chapter 5.

This shift away from Marx's revolutionary politics implied a similar shift away from his revolutionary ethics: while Marx posited the standpoint of the working class as a perspective from which both to understand the immanence of virtuous practice within working-class struggle and to overcome the modern bourgeois separation of facts and values, the shift within the Second International toward a *de facto* reformism undermined this perspective and informed a reengagement by a number of its most important theorists with modern moral theory.

Nevertheless, the process whereby intellectuals within the Second International explored the theoretical implications of their practice was by no means uniform, and was certainly not so uniformly crude as it is often presented. If the debate on the merits of integrating Kant's ethics with socialist practice was classically championed by Eduard Bernstein and Karl Vorländer, their arguments opened a debate which initially drew responses from Karl Kautsky, Georgi Plekhanov, and Otto Bauer, before extending with contributions from Rosa Luxemburg, Vladimir Lenin, Leon Trotsky, Georg Lukács, Evgeny Pashukanis, Henryk Grossman, Ernst Bloch, and Antonio Gramsci. This debate was overdetermined by broader political struggles within the International which saw, first, the more moderate wing of the movement criticize the Erfurt Programme from the right, before, second, the left-wing defenders of Erfurt bifurcate between a centrist tendency which eventually ossified to become politically marginalised as it attempted to hold to the Erfurt compromise, and a revolutionary left which slowly and falteringly broke with Erfurt to reembrace Marx's revolutionary theory. It was this process that eventually led this group generally, and Lenin preeminently, in the words of Bloch, to "renew authentic Marxism" (quoted in Anderson 2007, 123). Throughout this period there existed a dialectical relationship between political and ethical matters, and consequently the contributions to debates on the latter cannot adequately be understood without recourse to discussions of the former. Unfortunately, this process of theoretical growth was cut short by the rise of Stalinism, such that on ethical matters especially the implications of the Third International's break with Erfurt were never fully explored. As we shall see in Chapter 5, some of these themes were developed within the British New Left in the 1950s. Consequently, while this chapter examines these earlier debates, it also points forward to the New Left's debates on socialist ethics in the wake of the crisis of international Stalinism in 1956.

Second International Marxism

The programme agreed to by the German Social Democratic Party at the Gotha unity congress in 1875 was in many ways an odd amalgam which brought together some ultra-radical verbiage, the content of which was either meaningless or simply wrong—for instance its claim that "[t]he emancipation of labour must be the work of the working class, in contrast to which all other classes are only one reactionary mass"—alongside a series of practically moderate political demands. Both aspects of this "synthesis" were evident in the programme's central demand for a "free state" (Gotha Programme 1875). In response to a draft of the programme, Marx famously penned *The Critique of the Gotha Programme* in which he subjected the document as a whole to a brutal interrogation. Marx pointed to the authoritarian implications of the claim that the SPD would fight for a "free state," and insisted that in the transitional period from capitalism to communism the state could only exist as "the revolutionary dictatorship of the proletariat," and that in avoiding this issue the SPD had opened itself up to a possible evolution toward liberalism (Marx 1974d, 355).

He consequently opened *The Critique of the Gotha Programme*, which took the form of a letter to a number of his closest comrades in Germany, with the statement that "after the unity congress Engels and I are going to publish a short statement dissociating ourselves from the said programme" (Marx 1974d, 339; Engels 1989a, 71). Interestingly, in a letter written later that year, Engels explained why neither he nor Marx had found it expedient to break with the new party in the wake of its adoption of the Gotha Programme. He pointed out that the bourgeois press had, in fact, read into it his and Marx's views. More importantly, the workers had done the same, and, as Engels writes, "it is *this circumstance alone* which has made it possible for Marx and myself not to disassociate ourselves publicly from a programme such as this" (Engels 1991).

In this context, Marx and Engels wagered that, despite the shortcomings of the party's program, the general superiority of the perspectives of the party's Marxist tendency would lead to its eventual hegemony within the organisation. This, in the medium term, was precisely the turn taken by events. Thus Schorske points out that as Bismarck "unleashed his fury" against the socialist left in the period between 1878 and 1890, the party "became really receptive to Marxism" (Schorske 1983, 3).

Bismarck's authoritarian turn coincided with the publication of Engels' *Anti-Dühring* (1878), which took up the fight for hegemony within the party, and which won over many of the organization's cadre to Marxism (Steger 1996, 3). This process culminated with the revision of the party's programme at the Erfurt congress of 1891 (Erfurt Programme 1891).

However, while Engels welcomed the Erfurt Programme as an improvement on Gotha, he once again criticised the failure of the Germans to address the question of state power scientifically: "The political demands of the draft have one great fault. It lacks precisely what should have been said" (Engels 1990, 225). Noting that "opportunism" (reformism) was "gaining ground in large sections of the Social-Democratic press," Engels argued that it was incumbent upon the framers of the programme to spell out clearly to the German workers that the transition to socialism could only come "by force" (Engels 1990, 226). He insisted that if the SPD did not make this clear then, in the long run, the party would go "astray": "The forgetting of the great, the principal considerations for the momentary interests of the day, this struggling and striving for the success of the moment regardless of later consequences, this sacrifice of the future of the movement for its present, may be 'honestly' meant, but it is and remains opportunism, and 'honest' opportunism is perhaps the most dangerous of all!" So, just as he and Marx had argued in 1875, in 1891 he reminded his comrades that "our party and the working class can only come to power under the form of a democratic republic. This is even the specific form of the dictatorship of the proletariat" (Engels 1990, 227).

Schorske points out that the Erfurt Programme essentially included two related messages to members of the SPD. If it said be "patient" to the revolutionaries, to the reformists it said "reforms are the first task. Pursue them. But remember, you must fight for them. And the faith in the bright new society is a weapon in your struggle. Do not ignore it." Schorske goes on to say that this compromise could hold so long as, on the one hand, the working class was maintained in its "pariah" status by the German state, whilst, on the other hand, revolution was not on the immediate political agenda as economic growth gave rise to improvements in the living standards of the working class (Schorske 1983, p. 6).

Whereas the unity of the various factions of the SPD was maintained on this basis in the decades up to the war, the tensions that exploded after 1914 and which saw the party fragment over the following years had deep roots going back over the previous two decades. A half decade of economic boom from the mid-1890s underpinned a massive expansion of trade unionism, which in turn strengthened the social base of reformism within the party (Schorske 1983, 12ff). Thus, within a few years of the party's formal embrace of Marxism at Erfurt, events conspired to draw it away from Marx's politics. It is an accident of history that the party's *de facto* reformism came to be justified theoretically by one of the two co-authors of the Erfurt Programme: Eduard Bernstein. Elsewhere, the emerging reformist tendency within the European socialist movement had simply got on with its reformist practice, leaving the revolutionary rhetoric for party congresses. It was with an eye to the benefits of this approach that Ignaz Auer, the general secretary of the SPD, famously wrote to Bernstein that "one doesn't formally decide to do what you ask, one doesn't say it, one does it" (Auer quoted in Mészáros 2005, 309). Ignoring this advice, Bernstein provided German reformism with a theoretical cloak, and from the late 1890s onward his name dominated all subsequent political debate within the party.

At the core of Bernstein's critique of Marxism was the claim that contemporary economic trends had disproved Marx's theory of crisis, thus making irrelevant his concept of revolution. In particular, he argued that as Marx's "theory of breakdown" and his "theory of immiseration" had been refuted by the test of history, hopes for a revolution were utopian and a more realistic strategy would require the formalization of the SPD's existing practical reformism (Bernstein1993, 56ff, 79ff). This argument was countered by the second co-author of the Erfurt Programme, Karl Kautsky, who, alongside other leading theorists within the International, pointed out that Bernstein's Marx was in fact a caricatured version of the real thing. In fact, Kautsky argued, Marx had formulated neither a "theory of breakdown" nor a "theory of immiseration" (Kautsky 1983a; Colletti 1972, 52). As we shall see in the discussion of Grossman below, this argument was theoretically weak. It also missed the point, for the force of Bernstein's arguments came not from their intellectual merits, but from the fact that they represented a real and growing tendency within German Social Democracy, and Kautsky's arguments did nothing to address this issue. Schorske suggests that in an effort to maintain the unity of the party Kautsky was happy to win a formal acceptance of his position at the party's national level, while ceding the real leadership of the German workers' movement to the increasingly reformist trade union and party bureaucracy (Schorske 1983, 115; Salvadori 1979, 63, 113).

Because she recognised this, Rosa Luxemburg's response to the rise of revisionism was much more powerful than was Kautsky's. In her books *Social Reform and Revolution* (1900) and *The Mass Strike* (1906) she argued that revisionism was not simply a theoretical error in the context of economic expansion, but that it was deeply rooted in the structure of modern trade unionism. Accordingly, revisionism grew as the theoretical expression of the growing strength of the trade union bureaucracy: a layer whose condition of life not only diverged from that of the mass membership of the unions, but whose very existence represented the institutionalisation of working-class struggle within the confines of civil society (Luxemburg 1986, Ch. 8).[2] One might expect that, given Marx's critique of the standpoint of civil society, in writing from this perspective Bernstein would be drawn to cement his break with Marxism with a rejection Marx's revolutionary ethics. And this is what he did.

For and Against Kant

Bernstein argued that the political failings of Marxism could in part be understood as a consequence of its simplistic deduction of political conclusions from economic premises. He claimed that this method betrayed the malign influence on Marxism of the Hegelian idea of the "self-development of the concept," which all too easily lent itself to arbitrary deductions (Bernstein 1993, 30–31). Bernstein also claimed that just as Hegelian philosophy was "a reflex of the great French Revolution," insofar as

---

2. For instance Luxemburg's claim that trade unionism is a "sort of labour of Sisyphus" (Luxemburg 1989, 67). Schorske argues that "if we look back over the great issues on which the Socialist movement divided in the years 1906–1909, we discover that in all those in which the trade-unions threw their weight into the scales the reformist attitude was the one to prevail." He explains this, as did Luxemburg, by the conservative function and structure of the union bureaucracy (Schorske 1983, 108, 127). Similarly, Salvadori notes that Kautsky failed to comprehend, that which Luxemburg so clearly perceived: "that a cleavage was arising between a 'goal' that was socialist and a 'means' that was ever more thoroughly administered by a conservative and moderate bureaucracy, which was now concerned to fortify the organisation solely within the dominant system" (Salvadori 1979, 144).

Marxism failed to go beyond this framework, it too remained politically tied to those far-left tendencies, represented classically by Babeuf and Blanqui, which emerged from that revolution (Bernstein 1993, 36ff). This is not to say that Bernstein believed that Marx and Engels were uncritical of Babeuf and Blanqui. Rather, he thought that their attempt to synthesize the "destructive" politics of these early socialists with more modern and more "constructive" tendencies was a failure which succeeded only in bequeathing an unstable compromise to their followers (Bernstein 1993, 40–41). It was thus against the harmful consequences of the Hegelian dialectic that Bernstein famously called for socialists to embrace "Kant against cant" (Bernstein 1993, 189). The cant to which he referred was the meaningless revolutionary rhetoric of what was in practice a reformist organization, while the interpretation of Kant with which he sought to replace it included a combination of the championing of the workers' movement with "a high degree of that scientific impartiality which is always ready to acknowledge errors and recognise new truths" (Bernstein 1993, 210). This argument was first rehearsed in a series of essays published between 1896 and 1898, before being revised for republication as *The Preconditions of Socialism* in 1899 (the original essays can be found in Tudor and Tudor 1988). Unfortunately, Bernstein wrote little of substance about his positive interpretation of Kant in this book, though in one of the preceding essays he suggested that Marxists had been wrong to conflate bourgeois and civil society, for "the morality of developed civil society is by no means identical with the morality of the bourgeoisie" (Bernstein 1988, 243; see also Bernstein 1993, 146). Developing this point in "How is Scientific Socialism Possible?" (1901), he pointed to a perceived contradiction between the implicit morality of Marx and Engels' oft-repeated claim that capitalist production involved the exploitation of workers and their suggestion that this was not unjust. Against what he believed was the incoherence of this position he argued that socialists, if they were honest, would be forced to engage with Kant to the extent that they asked what sort of society ought we to fight for (Bernstein 1996, 91, 94–5). He claimed that it was as ridiculous to posit liberal, conservative, or socialist social sciences as it was to imagine similarly political variations of the natural sciences. Furthermore, he claimed that political conflicts arise atop a generally accepted and politically neutral social scientific foundation, and these conflicts are informed by differing ideas about what ought to be.

Consequently, because socialist politics "carries within itself an element of speculative idealism" the label scientific socialism was best discarded (Bernstein 1996, 96, 100).

Many commentators have noted that Bernstein's brief discussion of Hegel and Kant was far from sophisticated (Kolakowski 1978, 111; Gay 1962, 159ff). Nevertheless, Bernstein did point to weaknesses within the Second International interpretation of Marxism. Indeed his embrace of Kant was, in part, a reaction against the crude empiricist model of science assumed by many of the leading theoreticians of the Second International, including most prominently Bernstein himself. According to Lukács, neo-Kantianism emerged as a reaction not against the failings of Marx's work but against the mechanical and fatalistic distortion of his ideas within the Second International (Lukács 1978, 149). As McLellan argues, "the very barrenness of [Bernstein's] positivist approach led him to seek a separate moral basis for his socialism" (McLellan 1979, 35). Bernstein did so from a perspective that was informed both by the growth of reformism in Germany and Britain, and by the revival of neo-Kantianism in Germany from the 1870s onward (Sheehan 1985, 70; Gay 1962, 151 ff; Kolakowski 1978, 98ff; Steger 1996, 6ff; Walicki 1995, 212). So, while his own arguments were fairly crude, he represented a broader tendency which forced a theoretical response from within the International. This process eventually informed a root and branch critique of the Erfurt compromise from the revolutionary left of the organization. The socialist, but not Marxist, neo-Kantianism position was originally articulated by the Marburg School of Hermann Cohen and Paul Natorp (Van der Linden 1988). These two argued that Kant's categorical imperative to treat others as ends and not merely as means could provide socialism with an ethical basis (Kolakowski 1978, 246). This perspective was developed within the Marxist movement by Karl Vorländer who, in a lecture titled "Kant and Marx" (1904), argued that while Marx's rejection of moralism was an understandable counterpart to his break with "true socialism" it was nonetheless incoherent, and in any event Marx and Engels in their "scientific" works were incapable of avoiding ethical questions. Socialism, he concluded, "cannot free itself from ethics historically and logically, neither on the theoretical level nor in fact" (Vorländer quoted in Goldmann 1968, 15). Lucien Goldmann argues that it was as a response to the growing hegemony of Vorländer's neo-Kantianism on the reformist wing of social democracy that Kautsky was forced to reply in the name of orthodoxy (Goldmann 1968, 15).

According to Kautsky's commentary on the Erfurt Programme, "socialist production must, and will, come. Its victory will have become inevitable as soon as that of the proletariat has become inevitable" (Kautsky 1892). It was against the background of the fatalism of this perspective, a fatalism that was no less real for all it was explicitly denied by Kautsky, that Bernstein's call for a return to Kant became so influential. In the place of Erfurt's fatalism, Bernstein seemed to offer a positive basis for active politics.

If Bernstein's most powerful *political* critic was Rosa Luxemburg— she pointed out that his reformism did not posit a different road to the same end as that imagined by revolutionaries but a different road to a very different end (Luxemburg 1989, 75)—the most important early *philosophical* critique of his thesis was penned by the Russian Marxist Georgi Plekhanov. However, Plekhanov's criticisms of Bernstein's revisionism focused on his break with materialism and said little explicitly about his claim that socialism required an ethical dimension (Plekhanov 1976, 326ff). Plekhanov did stress to Kautsky the importance of these debates, and he insisted, against his German counterpart's reluctance to include philosophical debate within the party press, that "it is essential to *force* the readers to interest themselves in philosophy . . . it is the *science of sciences*" (Plekhanov quoted in Baron 1963, 178). While Kautsky's reluctance to engage with this debate was perhaps rooted in an awareness of his own limitations—"philosophy was never my strong suit" he wrote to Plekhanov in 1898—the growing strength of revisionist inspired "ethical socialism" over the next few years meant that he felt compelled to engage with this issue, and consequently he wrote the only book-length study of ethics from the point of view of Second International orthodoxy.

Kautsky's *Ethics and Materialist Conception of History* (1906) has often been dismissed as, in the words of Rodney Peffer, "a rather unsophisticated brand of utilitarianism" (Peffer 1990, 81). Leszek Kolakowski suggested that in this book Kautsky "failed to understand the epistemological problem of moral values or the fact that, when a historical process has been presented as inevitable, the question of its value remains open" (Kolakowski 1978, 39). In contrast to the generally dismissive tone of the commentary on Kautsky's ethics, Tony Burns has pointed out that Kautsky did have something interesting to say about this issue

(Burns 2001). Burns follows Jules Townsend in finding Kautsky's work much more attractive than the standard caricature of his *oeuvre* suggests (Burns 2001, 30; cf Townsend 1989). Rather than dismiss him as a crude utilitarian, Burns points out that in his book on ethics Kautsky attempted to synthesize (while perhaps only succeeding in mixing) elements from utilitarianism with Kantian deontology (Burns 2001, 42).

When first engaging with Kautsky's book the reader cannot help but be struck by the contrast between the standard academic dismissal of Kautsky as a political fatalist and the sense of political urgency that infuses this work. Thus he opened the study with the claim that it was written "not to serve . . . contemplative knowledge," but rather as a weapon of struggle: it was "for the fight, a fight in which we have to develop the highest ethical strength as well as the greatest clearness of knowledge" (Kautsky 1918, 7). Later in the text he argued that because "action implies continual choice" so it follows that "moral judgement . . . is unavoidable in the world of the unknown future—of freedom" (Kautsky 1918, 60). He then accepted Kant's claim that the realm of freedom is the realm of moral law. However, he insisted that "the world of freedom . . . is no timeless and spaceless and no super-sensual world, but a particular portion of the world of sense seen from a particular point of view." By radically separating the realms of freedom and necessity, Kant, or so Kautsky argued, closed off access to a true understanding of the moral law, such that if we were to hope to understand it then we must go beyond him (Kautsky 1918, 64–5). Against Kant's claim that the moral law should be imposed upon us by reason against our desires, Kautsky attempted to root the moral law in our nature as social animals (Kautsky 1918, 98). And in a discussion which Burns rightly suggests is reminiscent of Marx's comments on the biologically rooted but historically conditioned character of human nature in the as yet unpublished Paris Manuscripts (Burns 2001, 21–2), Kautsky pointed out that it is precisely because it is our essence to be social that society and morality will have a history. A key problem with Kantianism from this standpoint is that it naturalizes modern individuality, and as such confuses the relations between people at a certain moment in history with the universal relations between people throughout history (Kautsky 1918, 156, 184). Kant and the neo-Kantians also were blind to the way in which in class-divided societies, differing and conflictual moralities emerge as class moralities. In fact, Kautsky claimed, while capital has created the "material foundations for a general human morality," it undermines this by "treading this morality continually under its feet." Alternatively, because the proletariat does not exploit any other class below it, when it fights for its particular interests it is capable of realizing this "general human morality" (Kautsky 1918, 160). This, Kautsky insisted, was no abstract academic hope, but reflected the real evolution of the workers' movement: "The content of the new moral ideal . . . does not emerge from any scientific knowledge of the social organism . . . but from a deep social need, a burning desire, an energetic will for something other than the existing, for something which is the opposite of the existing." By its nature, therefore, the new moral ideal is a "negative" force, reflecting "opposition" to the status quo. Thus, Kautsky concluded, while its "importance is recognised as the motor power of the class struggle," the negative character of the new moral ideal implies that it cannot "direct our policy," for policy must be formulated on the basis of a scientific analysis of social relations (Kautsky 1918, 195, 200–201). Commenting on this argument, Dick Geary observes that Kautsky did not believe that "moral judgements were irrelevant for a Marxist . . . It was just that on its own it could not serve as the basis of socialist theory" (Geary 1987, 12).

Of course, for all Kautsky's criticisms of the ahistorical nature of Kant's morality, by accepting the separation of facts and values he was at one with Kant and the neo-Kantians in being "equally far removed from the Hegelian origins of Marx's own thought" (Lichtheim 1964, 295; Goldmann 1968, 15). And, whereas Kautsky claimed that differing moral ideals represented differing social standpoints—Marxism the standpoint of the working class, Kantianism the standpoint of the individual (Kautsky 1918, 114, 156)—he at no point attempted to uncover the social basis of revisionism. Instead, the structure of his argument suggested that he saw it merely as an intellectual error through which ethics rather than science was placed at the center of the socialist project. As for his own scientific understanding of the socialist project, the book closed with a contradictory denial that his own perspective was fatalistic and a reiteration of Erfurtian fatalism: "socialism is inevitable because the class struggle and the victory of the proletariat is inevitable" (Kautsky 1918, 206).

The contradiction between the fatalism of this sentence and Kautsky's earlier claim that the book was aimed at contributing to the struggle of the working class is of course very real. Nevertheless, Kautsky was sure of his own role in the struggle for socialism: it was to contribute to the scientific analysis of social relations that would help maintain and extend the unity of the SPD specifically and the working class more generally. Unfortunately, whatever the undoubted merits of his contribution to this debate, its power was undermined by his failure to move beyond the Erfurt compromise (Blackledge 2006f).

The fundamental problem with this approach was highlighted by another Second International theorist, Rudolph Hilferding. In the introduction to his classic *Finance Capital* (1910), he famously wrote that Marxism "is only a theory of the laws of motion of society," and "acceptance of the validity of Marxism . . . is one thing," it is "quite another to work for that necessity." Further, he suggested that "it is quite possible for someone who is convinced that socialism will triumph in the end to join the fight against it" (Hilferding 1981, 23; 1981, 127; see also Colletti 1972, 229–36; and Anderson 1980, 6). A similar position was first expressed within the International by the Austrian Marxist Otto Bauer in his contribution to the debate on ethical socialism. In a review of Kautsky's book he asked if Kant was really a threat to socialism. His answer opened with the claim that while science might point to the eventual victory of the working class, it said nothing as to the desirability of this situation. Thus, when confronted by the question of which side to take in the class war, Marxists who rejected ethical concerns weakened their hand. Bauer suggested that it was a failing on Kant's part that he did not notice the existence of competing class moralities, but that, given the existence of such moralities, his categorical imperative might act as an objective criteria through which individuals could escape the radical ethical scepticism inherent to such a situation. So while Bauer proclaimed himself to be at one with Kautsky's defence of the scientific status of Marxism, he also suggested that Kant's morality could aid the socialist cause by "protect[ing] us from the stream of scepticism unleashed by the enemies of the working class" (Bauer 1978, 84).

While this argument has an obvious appeal, it was rejected by Kautsky, who, in a reply to Bauer, pointed out that because Kant's morality was merely formal it could not bear the weight of Bauer's argument. In fact, he claimed, "despite their categorical imperative, the Kantians have so many different opinions about bourgeois and proletarian ethics, that every ethical sceptic finds it a matter of amusement." By contrast, "despite their ethical relativism, Marxists, because they have a definite economic outlook, all stand firmly behind the proletariat and its ethic" (Kautsky 1983b, 52). If the power of Kautsky's critique of

Bauer's attempt to recruit Kant for the socialist cause is undeniable, the weakness of his own alternative is equally palpable. By assuming both a dualism between science and ethics, and the necessarily relativistic character of ethics, Kautsky's scientific socialism veered toward an objectivist parody of Marx's thought. And while he insisted that his interpretation of Marxism was not fatalistic, the activists within the movement increasingly came to break with him both to the right and to the left. This process was most pronounced in Germany where, first, Bernstein and the Right broke with his defence of Erfurt, to be followed, second, by Rosa Luxemburg and the left (Nettl 1969, 284ff; Schorske 1983, 191ff). These developments came to a head in 1914, when the gap between the SPD's formal revolutionism and real reformism was cruelly exposed by the test of war. If, in the wake of the collapse of the Second International in 1914, Lenin famously went back to Hegel—"It is impossible," he famously wrote, "completely to understand Marx's *Capital*, and especially its first chapter, without having thoroughly studied and understood the whole of Hegel's *Logic*. Consequently, half a century later none of the Marxists understood Marx!" (Lenin 1961b, 180)—to help him think through his break with Kautsky, this moment is probably best understood as the culmination of two decades of bifurcation between his interpretation of Marxism and that dominant within the International.

Toward a Renewal of Marxism: Lenin, Lukács, and Grossman

Thus far we have noted how socialists within the Second International pushed at the political limits of the dualistic relationship between science and ethics. While their activity assumed an, albeit implicit, form of ethical commitment, their dualism undermined any attempt to formulate a morality that went beyond the relativism characteristic of bourgeois ethics. And where they attempted to outline a scientific justification for action, their objectivist model of science was subversive of political practice. If Bernstein was amongst the first to recognize the incoherence of this system, his attempt to unify reformist theory and practice succeeded only in combining economic and political impressionism with ethical relativism. Nevertheless, it was the growing challenge of revisionism that sparked a movement on the left of the International to raise theory to the level of revolutionary practice. If the central contribution to this process was made by Lenin, it was substantially added to by Lukács and Grossman.

At the turn of the last century Lenin was centrally involved in the attempt to build a Russian party along the lines of the SPD. Because political conditions in Russia were obviously much less amenable to socialist activity than they were in Germany, although the emerging revisionist wing of Russian social democracy argued against placing revolutionary politics at the center of the new party's programme, he could not simply copy the German model. Consequently, whereas from the 1890s onward Kautsky was active in a party with a formally revolutionary programme but which operated in an increasingly reformist manner, Lenin was attempting to build an organization whose membership was constantly under threat of arrest, and in which he was forced to fight for a revolutionary programme. If this context informed a growing tension between his Marxism and Second International orthodoxy, the break between the two centrally involved the reinsertion of the active human element back into Marxism such that it laid the basis for overcoming the separation between facts and values that had been characteristic of Second International Marxism.

In *What is to be Done?* (1902), Lenin painted a picture of the previous two decades of socialist activity in Russia. He characterized the decade from 1884 as one in which the Marxist left coalesced as a coherent theoretical tendency. The next half-decade saw this theoretical tendency engage successfully with Russia's growing workers' movement. This trajectory culminated in 1898 with the formation of a socialist party. However, state repression meant that this organization was quickly crushed. In the wake of this process, the fragmented remnants of the revolutionary movement came to concentrate their activities on supporting local campaigns for immediate reforms. And it was this practice which informed a move by many of the activists to distance themselves from the long-term aims of the revolutionary overthrow of tsarism. The group around the newspaper *Iskra*, with whom Lenin was associated at the turn of the century, responded to this context by calling for the creation of a national organization built around a national socialist newspaper through which the myriad local campaigns could be unified into a national revolutionary movement (Lenin 1961a, 517–520).

Lenin's consistent attempt to overcome sterile abstractions by bringing theory to the level of practice had been evident long before he wrote *What is to be Done?*. In an early critique of the "legal Marxist" Peter

Struve, he argued that, while it was a weakness with traditional moral theory that it failed "to connect its 'ideals' with any immediate interests," Struve ran the "risk of becoming an apologist" for the status quo because he erred in the opposite direction by reducing materialism to its objectivist caricature. In opposition both to moral subjectivism and economic objectivism, Lenin suggested that materialism, because it examined the contradictions of any social process, "includes partisanship . . . and enjoins the direct and open adoption of the standpoint of a definite social group in any assessment of events" (Lenin 1960, 400–401). The break with any form of dualism between science and morality implicit to this argument was subsequently reinforced through his attempt to realize the project of *What is to be Done?*. Because Lenin had to build a party from scratch against the opposition of the Russian revisionists, he entered into a much sharper relationship with revisionism than did Kautsky. Consequently, he extended the practical side of Second International Marxism much further than occurred in Kautsky's theoretical texts.

It is one of history's ironies that a core constituent of the myth of Leninism, constructed by the Stalinists from the mid-1920s onward to justify their own power and accepted by Western liberal intellectuals thereafter for their own ideological reasons, includes a key constituent part of the Bernsteinian revisionism which Lenin fought from the outset: that which Mészáros calls Bernstein's "patronizing treatment of the working classes" (Mészáros 1995, 4). According to what Lars Lih labels the "textbook interpretation" of Leninism, Lenin's contempt for the intellectual capacities of workers was reflected in his insistence on building a party of professional revolutionaries who would bring socialist ideas to the working class from without and subsequently lead this class in a top-down manner. By contrast with this myth, Lih shows that Lenin's underlying assumption in the text that is paradigmatic of the myth, *What is to Be Done?*, was an optimism about the possibility of the growth of socialist consciousness within the Russian working class, combined with scathing criticisms of the weaknesses of Russia's radical intelligentsia generally and the Russian socialist movement specifically, which, he claimed, were in grave danger of failing the workers' movement in the coming revolution (Lih 2006, 27, 615; Blackledge 2006e).

Concretely, Lenin argued against a reemerging economism within Russian social democracy—the local variant of Bernsteinian reformism. A crucial constituent part of Bernstein's revisionism included his rejection of what he believed to be Marxism's romanticization of the working class. Against Marx, Bernstein claimed that the working class was "not yet sufficiently developed to take over political power," and that the only people who disagreed with this prognosis were those pseudo-revolutionaries "who have never had any close relationship with the real labour movement" (Bernstein 1993, 206). Similarly, the Russian "economist" Krichevski accused the *Iskra* group of "being over-optimistic about the possibility of proletarian awareness and organisation," and insisted that workers were interested only in basic bread-and-butter issues, not socialist politics. Against Krichevski, Lenin argued in Lih's paraphrase, that "worker militancy is not the problem because it is increasing in leaps and bounds all on its own. The problem, the weak link, is effective party leadership of all this militancy" (Lih 2006, 316–317). Lenin suggested that socialists who spoke only of bread-and-butter issues to workers both patronized them whilst simultaneously failing to challenge the hegemony of bourgeois ideology within the working class (Lih 2006, 226).

Unfortunately, in so far as Lenin theorized this position he borrowed concepts from Kautsky who insisted that "socialist consciousness is something introduced into the proletarian class struggle from without" (Lenin 1961a, 384). Similarly, and infamously, Lenin posited Marxism as a science which was to be introduced to the working class by intellectuals: "The history of all countries shows that the working class, exclusively by its own effort, is able to develop only trade union consciousness, i.e., the conviction that it is necessary to combine in unions, fight the employers, and strive to compel the government to pass necessary labour legislation, etc. The theory of socialism, however, grew out of the philosophic, historical, and economic theories elaborated by educated representatives of the propertied classes, by intellectuals" (Lenin 1961a, 375).

Given the preponderance of crude nonsense written about this argument, two points are worth stressing. First, the relationship between spontaneity and consciousness is *not* the central thesis of *What is to be Done?*. Rather, Lenin's discussion of this point was hurriedly added to the text as a response to Krichevski's discussion of the relationship between spontaneous movements and conscious leadership in an article published as Lenin was writing *What is to be Done?*. Second, understood in the context noted above it is clear that, as Lih points out in his exhaustive study of the subject, on this issue Lenin meant the opposite of what he is typically taken as meaning. It was his opponents who dismissed the socialist potential of working-class struggle, whereas he defended it.

While this is not the place to go through the minutiae of the debate on the significance of *What is to be Done?*, elsewhere Lenin did address the question of the relationship between socialism and the movement from below in terms which both confirm Lih's interpretation of that text and which point to his developing break with Second International dualism. Thus, in contrast to the dualistic formulations found in *What is to be Done?*, in 1899 Lenin wrote that "[e]very strike brings thoughts of socialism very forcibly to the workers' mind" (Lenin quoted in Cliff 1986, p. 81). Similarly, in 1905 Lenin reiterated that "[t]he working class is instinctively, spontaneously Social-Democratic" (Lenin 1962, 32; Molyneux 1986, 59; Dunayevskaya 1988, 182). So, in contrast to Kautsky, who posited a sharp separation between the ethical life of workers and the science of socialism, in these formulations Lenin suggests a dialectical link between the two. Moreover, whereas Kautsky famously wrote that "social democracy is a revolutionary party, but it is not a party that makes revolution" (Kautsky quoted in Salvadori 1979, 40), Lenin argued that the party "would not sit [a]round waiting for the call to insurrection, but would carry out such regular activity that would guarantee the highest probability of success in the event of an insurrection" (Lenin quoted in Harman 1996, 31). And where Lenin does allow himself a utopian aside in *What is to be Done?*, it suggests he understood Marxism not as an abstract model imposed on the workers from the outside but as a critique of capitalism from the standpoint of tendencies immanent to it. Thus he famously followed the liberal democratic Pisarev to argue that whilst some "dreams" are disconnected from reality, others are rooted in reality and point to a concrete alternative to it. Lenin wrote that "of this kind of dreaming there is unfortunately too little in our movement" (Lenin 1961a, 509–510).

Although the gap between Lenin and Kautsky was only implicit before 1914, the shock of war and Lenin's subsequent reading of Hegel made his split with his former teacher explicit and, on this issue, absolute. In notes taken from a close reading of Hegel's *Science of Logic* he expressed his break with dualism thus: "The activity of man, who has made an objective picture of the world for himself, **changes** external actuality, abolishes its determinates (= alters some sides or other, qualities, of it), thus removes from it the features of semblance, externality and nullity, and makes it as being in and for itself (= objectively true)" (Lenin 1961b, 217–218). Commenting on these notebooks, Stathis Kouvelakis points out that it is "particularly significant that Lenin ended the section on 'philosophical materialism' with a reference to the notion of 'revolutionary practical activity.' " For Lenin understood that subjective practical activity lay at the center of the "objective" world, and consequently insisted that social scientific laws should not be "fetishized" as things distinct from conscious human activity but instead be recognized as necessarily "narrow, incomplete, [and] approximate" attempts to frame political intervention (Kouvelakis 2007, 174, 186). Consequently, whereas Second International theorists had interpreted Hegel's claim that to act freely meant to act in accordance with necessity in a reductive manner, for Lenin, as Day argues, "man's consciousness not only reflects the objective world but creates it" (Day quoted in Anderson 1995, 113). This is a far cry from John Holloway's claim that Lenin took Engels' "scientific" distortion of Marxism to its logical, undemocratic, conclusion when he posited the existence of a party of "knowers" who would impart their scientific knowledge from on high to the workers (Holloway 2002, 128). In fact, as Alex Callinicos argues, it was because Lenin was unsure about the future that he acted with the intention of influencing the course of history: his activism was rooted in his belief that "the very unpredictability of history requires that we intervene to help shape it" (Callinicos 2007b, 26). More generally, John Rees suggests that in his "Philosophical Notebooks," Lenin came to recognize that "practice overcomes the distinction between subjective and objective and the gap between essence and appearance" (Rees 1998, 191). By thus repositioning social practice at the core of Marxism, Lenin was able to recognize the affinity between Marxism and idealism: "Dialectical idealism is closer to intelligent [dialectical] materialism than metaphysical, undeveloped, dead, crude, rigid materialism" (Lenin 1961b, 274).

Commenting on Lenin's contribution to Marxism, Lukács argued that Lenin alone within the Second International held to "the original Marxist conception" against positivist and neo-Kantian alternatives (Lukács 1978, 162). This, in turn, informed his practical deepening of Marxist politics: "the development which Marxism thus underwent through Lenin consists merely—merely!—in its increasing grasp of the intimate, visible, and momentous connexion between individual actions and general destiny—the revolutionary destiny of the whole working class" (Lukács 1970, 13). If Lenin's praxis subsequently led him to a break with Kautskyism, it was in part because, as he argued, "practice is higher than (theoretical) knowledge" (Lenin 1961b, 213). Nevertheless, the break with the Second International had to be theorized, and while Lenin, in *State and Revolution*, went back to Marx and Engels' criticisms of the Gotha and Erfurt programmes to move beyond the limitations of Kautskyism (Lenin 1968, 335), Lukács' *History and Class Consciousness* magnificently expressed this break at a philosophical level.

Like Marx, Lenin insisted that freedom was the goal of the socialist workers' movement, and that, on the one hand, with the emergence of the proletariat came the potential to realize this freedom at a higher level then ever before, and, on the other hand, contra Kautsky, this could only be achieved through the "smashing" of the old capitalist state. Freedom was thus conceived as the self-determination of the "new fangled" social individuals through, first, the immense expansion of democracy characteristic of workers councils (soviets) as the institutional form of the dictatorship of the proletariat, and subsequently the withering away of even this ultra-democratic state form as classes themselves withered away in the wake of a successful revolution (Lenin, 1968, 324–5).

Although Lukács was not alone in extending this break with Second International Marxism—the German Communist Karl Korsch being the most prominent thinker to independently develop a similar philosophical perspective (Korsch 1970; Jay 1984, Ch. 3; Arato and Breines 1979, 170ff)—it remains the case that, as Martin Jay has written, *History and Class Consciousness* "can be seen as the most articulate expression on a theoretical level of the world-historical events of 1917" (Jay 1984, 103). More specifically, Arato and Breines point out that within this book Lukács developed a "powerful critique of Kantian ethics" (Arato and Breines 1979, 126). In a discussion of Kant's idea of the thing-in-itself, Lukács claimed not only that this concept underpinned the antinomies of Kant's philosophy, but that these antinomies—between, for instance, freedom and necessity, fact and value, form and content, and subject and object—were characteristic of theory elaborated from the standpoint of civil society, that is bourgeois social theory, more generally (Jay 1984, 110). These antinomies were reproduced within Second International Marxism, and they were overcome only with the rediscovery of the living concept of the totality associated with Lenin's return to Marx (Lukács 1970).

Concretely, Lukács insisted that whereas individuals within bourgeois society tend to misconceive their world as a ready-made thing which cannot be changed, when viewed from the perspective of working-class struggle it becomes apparent that capitalism is a product of human history that can be remade. Because "man in capitalist society confronts a reality 'made' by himself (as a class) which appears to him to be a natural phenomenon alien to him" (Lukács 1971, 135, 193), freedom cannot be understood as the ability to change the world, but only as freedom of consciousness or freedom within the world (Lukács 1971, 161). In this way the perspective of the individual within the modern world is one that is unable to grasp the world as a historical totality. This does not mean that an understanding of the social totality is inaccessible. Rather, Lukács insists that, when individuals come together as members of a class, "the positing subject" ceases to be an atomized individual but itself becomes "a totality" whose actions, by aiming at "changing reality" (Lukács 1971, 28, 129), uncover the historical character of capitalist society. Thus, it is only as part of a global subject that people are able to change the world, and it is only by changing the world that we are able to conceive of it as a product of human labour. Lukács goes on to argue that of the two central classes of modern capitalism, only the proletariat is able to conceive the totality as a historical form. Although the bourgeoisie is, like the proletariat, a global class, it is unable to conceive capitalism as a totality because of the structurally competitive relations between its individual members. Human liberation could only come from a global class, and the bourgeoisie, unlike the proletariat, is incapable of playing this role because, although it is global, it is also necessarily fragmented. Marxism, as the scientific understanding of capitalist society, emerged and could have only emerged from the standpoint of the practice of the proletariat. For while the working class is often fragmented, its sectional struggles have tended to spill over into more general confrontations rooted in a class-wide solidarity. So, whereas Kant had argued that the essence of the world, the thing-in-itself, remained shrouded in mystery, Lukács countered that capitalism is essentially a system of generalized commodity production within which, fundamentally, human labour-power was a commodity. The emergence of proletarian class-consciousness coincides with the growing self-consciousness of the capitalist mode of production as a totality: the proletariat could potentially become the "unmediated consciousness of the commodity" (Lukács 1971, 173). Marxism is therefore "the *self-knowledge of capitalist society*" (Lukács 1971, 229).

Lukács' deployed the concept of "imputed class consciousness" to describe the relationship of Marxism to the actual political consciousness of the working class. His critics have often pointed to this concept to suggest that while he aimed to overcome the dualism characteristic of

Second International theory, in practice he failed to conceptualize the movement toward class consciousness within the working class except as a consequence of a mythical final collapse of capitalism (Stedman Jones 1977, 42). Against this argument, John Rees shows that in both *History and Class Consciousness*, and in the recently discovered defence of that book, *Tailism and the Dialectic*, Lukács did point to the process by which workers could develop class consciousness (Rees 2000, 28ff). In fact, Lukács insisted that the emergence of socialist consciousness within the working class "does not lie outside the real process of history. It does not have to be introduced into the world by philosophers" (Lukács 1971, 77). More specifically, he argued that the revolutionary party should not be understood as an elite group of intellectuals, but should be thought of as "that part of the proletariat that spontaneously rebels against its leaders' behaviour" (Lukács 1971, 289). He suggested that "in no sense is it the party's role to impose any kind of abstract, cleverly devised tactics upon the masses. On the contrary, it must continuously learn from their struggle and their conduct of it. But it must remain active while it learns" (Lukács 1970, 36; 1971, 331, 334). Therefore, for Lukács, as Michael Löwy points out, " 'imputed' class consciousness is not a transcendental entity, an 'absolute value' floating in the world of ideas: on the contrary, it assumes an historical, concrete and revolutionary shape—the Communist Party" (Löwy 2003, 183; cf Rees 1998, 219–225; Lukács 2000, 63–86). This model of revolutionary leadership is therefore predicated upon the existence of a spontaneous socialist working-class movement from below, and by synthesizing revolutionary leadership and the movement from below Lukács confronted full square the dualism accepted by Bernstein, Kautsky and Bauer.

Commenting on Auer's famous letter to Bernstein which suggested a *de facto* reformist practice as a more efficient strategy for changing the party than Bernstein's frontal assault on the programme, Lukács claimed that Auer's proposed project had in practice been realized by Kautsky; for Kautsky deployed Marx's concepts, while simultaneously assuming a dualism between facts and values which effectively neutered Marxism by clinging to its vocabulary whilst jettisoning its practice (Lukács 1972, 133). More generally on the revisionist debate, Lukács claimed that Bernstein's embrace of Kantianism did not overcome Second International fatalism, but was merely its flipside: it "is the subjective side of the missing category of totality" (Lukács 1971, 38). While Lukács agreed with Kautsky's criticisms of the formalism of Kant's ethics, he insisted that it was not enough to conclude that any moral imperatives derived from this perspective were an inadequate basis for socialist strategic thought. Rather, Kant's ethical formalism pointed back to the methodological problem of his concept of the thing-in-itself, which acted in his system as a fundamental limit to human knowledge of the world (Lukács 1971, 124–5). Thus, the critique of Kant's ethical formalism should have led Kautsky back to the concept of the totality. That it did not reflected the way in which his dualism allowed him to talk revolution whilst abandoning the real practical leadership of the party to the reformists.

Lukács argued that whereas Kant naturalized contemporary social relations, by showing that these were a product of human history, Hegel pointed beyond this dualism, and by materializing Hegel's project Marx subsequently overcame it. To separate free human actions from a necessarily given social world, as was done by the neo-Kantians, implied losing sight of the fact that both freedom and necessity existed in a dynamic relationship such that both the social world and the kind of people that we are, are products of history: in Parkinson's paraphrase "we are both producer and product of the historical process" (Parkinson 1977, 43). A consequence of this methodological movement was to unfreeze the concepts through which we aim to understand the world. As Jay argues, "Being would then be understood as Becoming, things would dissolve into processes, and most important of all, the subjective origin of those processes would become apparent to the identical subject-object of history" (Jay 1984, 111). Lukács suggested that a key philosophical task "is to discover the principles by means of which it becomes possible in the first place for an 'ought' to modify existence. And it is just this that [Kant's] theory rules out from the start" (Lukács 1971, 161; Arato and Breines 1979, 127).

The aim of *History and Class Consciousness* was "to demonstrate methodologically that the organization and tactics of Bolshevism are the only possible consequence of Marxism" (Lukács 2000, p.47). Lukács argued that the structure of both the SPD specifically and the Second International more generally reflected their *de facto* reformism, while the Bolshevik Party, because it was built as a combat organization, became the organizational embodiment of the Marxist sublation of the dualism between freedom and necessity: Lenin's aim was not to comment upon objective developments within the world but to shape such processes through praxis (Lukács 1971, 295–342).

Lukács suggested that two works were of fundamental importance to the renewal of Marxism out of the degeneration of the Second International orthodoxy: Lenin's *State and Revolution* and Rosa Luxemburg's *The Accumulation of Capital* (Lukács 1971, 34–5). In these books Lenin completed his political break with Second International fatalism, while Luxemburg played a similar role in freeing Marx's economic theory from Second International Marxism.

Luxemburg's study was intended as an extension of her earlier critique of Bernstein's rejection of Marx's breakdown theory. Whereas Kautsky denied that Marx held to such a model, in her initial critique of Bernstein's revisionism, *Reform or Revolution*, Luxemburg argued that the contradictions of capitalism will progressively worsen "resulting inevitably, at some point, in its collapse" (Luxemburg 1989, 29). Similarly, in *The Accumulation of Capital*, she claimed that capitalism "must break down" and that at "a certain stage of development there will be no other way out than the application of socialist principles" (Luxemburg 1951, 467). Whatever the undoubted merits of this argument, it is open to the criticism that, through her embrace of a theory of breakdown, Luxemburg did not actually succeed in adequately theorizing a break with Second International positivism. The entire language of the inevitable breakdown of the capitalist system seems to connote the very fatalism which Lukács suggested was the Achilles' heel of Second International Marxism.

By contrast with this line of argument, Rick Kuhn has recently argued that the problem with Luxemburg's analysis of capitalism lay not in her embrace of a theory of breakdown, but the substantive arguments through which she defended this theory. Kuhn argues that it was to this problem that the early Frankfurt School Marxist, Henryk Grossman, applied himself in his classic *The Law of Accumulation and the Breakdown of the Capitalist System* (1929). Grossman claimed that Luxemburg's arguments failed because they were "not rooted in the immanent laws of the accumulation process, but in the transcendental fact of the absence of non-capitalist markets" (Grossman, quoted in Kuhn 2007, 126). In relation to Bernstein, Grossman insisted that he "was perfectly right in saying . . . 'if the triumph of socialism were truly an immanent economic necessity, then it would have to be grounded in a proof of the inevitable economic breakdown of the present order of society'" (Grossman 1992, 39). By denying that Marx held to a theory of breakdown, Kautsky, or so Grossman argued, fatally damaged his critique of Bernstein by accepting his basic assumptions about the nature of capitalism. He went on to say that it was Luxemburg's great contribution to the revisionist debate to return to Marx and defend the theory of breakdown. Unfortunately, because she shifted "the crucial problem of capitalism from the sphere of production to that of circulation" she undermined her own arguments. She tended to conceive of the breakdown as a "mechanical" process, which consequently opened her defence of the theory to the charge of "fatalism" (Grossman 1992, 41–2). So whereas Grossman has been criticized, for instance by Anton Pannekoek, for apparently reducing Marxism to a form of mechanical materialism (Pannekoek 1977, 62), in actual fact he followed Lenin's insistence that "there is no absolutely hopeless situation" for capital. He therefore believed that a defensible theory of economic breakdown must be integrated into an adequate theory of political revolution. His goal was thus to overcome the problems with Luxemburg's defense of the theory of breakdown such that it could be developed as a theoretical basis for political action. Against political fatalism, he insisted that capitalist breakdown was not an automatic, mechanical process. Conversely, against political voluntarism he pointed out that an adequate theory of political practice must be rooted in an understanding of the crisis-prone dynamic of the capitalist system. Consequently, as Kuhn explains, Grossman aimed to do for the Marxist approach to the critique of political economy what Lenin had done for politics and what Lukács had done for philosophy: to overcome Second International dualism through a dialectical approach to the relationship between freedom and necessity (Kuhn 2007, 125).

Grossman insisted that Second International theorists had departed from Marx's model of the falling rate of profit. It was this secular tendency, he argued, itself rooted in the capitalist accumulation process, which condemned capitalism to recurrent crises. Following Marx's method of moving from the abstract to the concrete, Grossman opened his book with an abstract model of capitalism's tendency toward crisis. He then shifted to examine the countervailing tendencies which mediated against breakdown. Finally, in a section that is unfortunately absent from the English edition of his book, he examined the interaction between crises and class struggle. Arguing that no crisis is irresolvable so long as workers are prepared to pay the price, he pointed out that the class struggle would itself "shape the actual course of the system's tendency to break down" (Kuhn 2007, 135). Kuhn points out that Grossman took the British miners' strike of 1926 as an example of the dialectical relationship between economics and politics in a period of crisis: economic crisis set the scene for the miners' lockout and the General Strike, but the actual outcome of these struggles and thus of the economic crisis itself was ultimately determined by the political struggle. Writing to Paul Mattick two years after the completion of his book, Grossman suggested that his aim had been to show how "objective revolutionary situations arise," which inform the intensification of the class struggle, but which neither mechanically guarantee the victory of either side in these struggles, nor determine the outcome of the crisis itself: "The purpose of my breakdown theory was not to exclude this active intervention, but rather to show when and under what circumstances such an objectively given revolutionary situation can and does arise" (Grossman quoted in Kuhn 2007, 144). Interestingly, Gramsci, who only managed to read a review of Grossman's book (Gramsci 2007, 190–1, 521), argued that Grossman had pointed to the political implications of Marx's theory of crisis, which did not imply the fatalism that Croce ascribed to it, but rather showed how "the economic contradiction becomes a political contradiction and is resolved politically by overthrowing praxis" (Gramsci 1995, 428–430).

Revolutionary Ethics

If Lenin, Lukács, and Grossman all added to the renewal of Marxism through a break with Second International dualism, it is unfortunate that none of them made more than tentative comments on the ethical dimension of socialism. Thus, whereas we have noted Lukács' critique of Kant's ethics, and while I have elsewhere commented upon the ethical dimension of Lenin's Marxism (Blackledge 2006a, 66), no Marxist associated with the Comintern wrote a study of ethics that could compete with the scope of Kautsky's small book. Nevertheless, three works were produced in this period which pointed toward a Marxist ethics: Evgeny Pashukanis's *Law and Marxism* (1924), Leon Trotsky's *Their Morals and Ours* (1938), and Ernst Bloch's *The Principle of Hope* (1938–1947). Additionally, Lukács' and Gramsci's comments on the need to root revolutionary politics in working-class struggle are highly suggestive of the practical shape of an ethical Marxism.

According to Pashukanis there exists an intimate and necessary relationship between the emergence of the idea of individual equality and the system of generalized commodity production: "For the products of human labour to be able to relate to each other as values," he wrote, "it is necessary for people to relate to each other as autonomous and equal personalities" (Pashukanis 1978, 151). Pashukanis insisted that three conditions must be satisfied for capital accumulation to become generalized: people must become "moral subjects," "legal subjects," and they must live their lives "egoistically." Corresponding to this situation, moral law, far from being a universal good, is best understood as the ideological form necessary to regulate the "intercourse between commodity owners." A consequence of the relationship between morality as the ideology of free action and capitalism as a system of social compulsion, Pashukanis argued that there is a necessary ambiguity in the moral law whereby, on the one hand, it presents itself as the rational basis for the actions of free individuals, while, on the other hand, it is a social law standing above individuals (Pashukanis 1978, 154). The only way to rid the moral law of this ambiguity, he claimed, is to eliminate capitalism through the creation of a planned economy. In so doing, the atomized nature of our present-day individuality would be overcome, and so would the basis for the ethical form itself (Pashukanis 1978, 158). Thus, just as the struggle for socialism involves a struggle against states and laws, it similarly involves the struggle against morality (Pashukanis 1978, p. 160; on Pashukanis see Miéville 2005, 75–115).

Trotsky's pamphlet, *Their Morals and Ours*, written in a more concrete register than Pashukanis' book, was produced as an explicit challenge to those for whom Marxism was a crude form of moral consequentialism according to which "the ends justified the means." In opposition to such interpretations of Marxism, Trotsky first insisted that any adequate ethical theory must have an eye to the ends of action, as the alternative most fully expressed by Kant could not survive without the idea of God, and thus represented a backward step after Darwin (Trotsky 1973, 16–7). While Trotsky therefore argued that "a means can only be justified by its end," he also pointed out that "the end in its turn needs to be justified." He subsequently proceeded to offer two Marxist justifications of the end of revolutionary socialist action: first, "if it leads to increasing the power of humanity over nature and to the abolition of the power of one person over another"; second, which is really a variation on the first, "that is permissible . . . which really leads to the liberation of humanity" (Trotsky 1973, 48). Whereas the distance between this formulation and Bernstein's neo-Kantianism is plain, it is less obvious that Trotsky's model escapes the charge of consequentialism. Nevertheless, Trotsky did insist that Marxism "does not know dualism between means and ends," and suggested a "dialectical interdependence" between the two. To this end he repeated Lassalle's suggestion that "a different path gives rise to a different goal." He claimed that "not all means are permissible," and because "the liberation of the workers can only come through the workers themselves" only those means are permissible "which unite the revolutionary proletariat." He argued that any means which lowers the "faith of the masses in themselves," by, for instance, "replacing it by a worship for the 'leaders,' " is not permissible (Trotsky 1973, 49–51).

Whatever the shortcomings of this short pamphlet, Trotsky's argument certainly does not fit easily with the claim that Marxism is a form of dualism which posits itself as the ideology of the leaders who use the working class as an instrument in their struggle for state power. Against the claim that Trotsky simply regurgitated a form of consequentialism, John Dewey pointed out that he had in fact made an implicit differentiation between two types of ends: final ends and those ends which are themselves means to the final end. While Trotsky did not make this differentiation explicit in *Their Morals and Ours*, Dewey suggested that it would be a simple matter so to do. If this were done then Trotsky could, quite rigorously, claim both to have maintained a position through which means and ends were interdependent, and to have provided an answer to those who argue that by positing only some distant end, consequentialism does not actually reflect on the observable short-term consequences of the means deployed to reach this end (Dewey 1973, 68–69). Nevertheless, despite these strengths, Dewey claimed that the force of Trotsky's position was weakened by what he perceived to be a dogmatic "deduction" of the claim that the agency of radical change would be the working class: "the selection of class struggle as a means," Dewey insisted, has itself "to be justified" (Dewey 1973, 70–1).

An outline to a solution to this gap in Trotsky's argument is obviously immanent to Lukács' suggestion that Marxism, by examining society from the standpoint of the proletariat, is able to overcome the antinomies of bourgeois thought. More concretely, Lukács extended Lenin's conception of soviet democracy to suggest a potential bridge between the "is" of existing society and the "ought" of socialism. Workers' councils or soviets, he argued, had since the Russian Revolution of 1905 spontaneously emerged in periods of heightened class struggle as "already essentially the weapons of the proletariat organising itself as a class" against the old state and the bourgeoisie (Lukács 1970, 63). As opposed to the institutions of bourgeois democracy which relate to voters as "abstract individuals," these structures organize workers as "concrete human beings who occupy specific positions within social production." Consequently, whereas bourgeois parliaments tend toward "disorganizing" the working class, soviets represent an organic attempt by the proletariat to "counteract this process" (Lukács 1970, 65–6). These spontaneous institutions of workers' struggle therefore provide a potential ethical basis from which to criticise the alienation of capitalist society. If "the form taken by the class consciousness of the proletariat is the Party," and "class consciousness is the 'ethics' of the proletariat" (Lukács 1971, 41–42), this ethical standpoint is itself rooted in and realized through the workers' spontaneous institutions of revolutionary struggle.

A similar argument was developed by Gramsci during Italy's *biennio rosso*—the two "red years" of 1919 and 1920. While Gramsci famously celebrated the Russian Revolution as a break with the last vestiges of political fatalism (Gramsci 1977, 34–7), he did not respond to it by embracing its obverse: political voluntarism. Rather, he set about fighting for an Italian revolution that would be organically rooted in the class struggle against capitalism. In an allusion to Marx's preface to the *Contribution to the Critique of Political Economy*, he wrote that "the scientific base for a morality of historical materialism is to be looked for, in my opinion, in the affirmation that 'society does not pose for itself tasks the conditions for whose resolution do not already exist.' Where these conditions exist 'the solution of the tasks becomes 'duty,' 'will' becomes free'" (Gramsci 1971, 409–10). More generally, through a critical engagement with the work of the idealist philosopher Benedetto Croce, Gramsci suggested that while Croce had played a pivotal role in the emergence of European revisionism in the 1890s, his attempt to articulate an "ethico-political history," through which he strove to place individual agency at the center of the historical process, was understandable as a reaction against Kautsky's mechanical materialism. Gramsci argued that authentic Marxism "does not exclude ethico-political history," and Lenin's revolutionary break with Second International Marxism consisted precisely in asserting the fundamental importance of this moment, the moment of hegemony, to the historical process (Gramsci 1995, 329, 345–6, 357, 360).

In the midst of the struggles of the Turin factory workers in 1919 and 1920, the group around Gramsci's newspaper *L'Ordine Nuovo* sought to provide an answer to the question of how "the dictatorship of the proletariat" might move from being an abstract slogan to a concrete end of action (Gramsci 1977, 68). In answer to the question "how are the immense social forces unleashed by the war to be harnessed?," Gramsci answered that "the socialist state exists potentially in the institutions of social life characteristic of the exploited working class" (Gramsci 1977, 65). These institutions were the factory councils, which had emerged out of existing representative bodies: the internal factory commissions (Molyneux 1986, 146). In a self-criticism of early issues of *L'Ordine Nuovo*, Gramsci wrote that these were "abstract": the journal did not read like it belonged to the local workers: "it was a review that could have come out in Naples, Caltanissetta, Brindisi," it was an example of "mediocre intellectualism" (Gramsci quoted in Williams 1975, 94). To overcome this Gramsci quickly reoriented *L'Ordine Nuovo* to address an issue that was central to the lives of the local working class, the "problem of the development" of factory councils. A consequence of this reorientation was that, in Gramsci's words, the workers came to "love" *L'Ordine Nuovo* (Gramsci quoted in Williams 1975, 94–5).

This approach grew out of Gramsci's project of critically learning from the Russian Revolution. He argued that socialists should aim to emulate Lenin because he had managed to "weld communist doctrine to the collective consciousness of the Russian People." By rooting his political activity within the real movement of workers, Gramsci intended to repeat that success in Italy (Gramsci quoted in Williams 1975, 100). He thus aimed at what Gwyn Williams has called the translation of "the Russian soviet experience into Italian," and he did this by relating his practice to those working-class institutions of struggle, which "arose directly out of the process of production itself" (Williams 1975, 102). In so rooting revolutionary politics within the real movement of workers, Gramsci's Marxism began to realize an ethics that went beyond the antinomies of bourgeois thought. Nevertheless, despite Gramsci's formal allegiance, first, to the Socialist Party, and, second, to the Communist Party after the split between the reformist and revolutionary wings of the Socialist Party, in these early years Williams points out that there was a complete absence in his work of "any discussion of how the organic culmination of this apparatus, the party, is going to act; how the 'state apparatus' is actually to get 'state power' in vulgar reality" (Williams 1975, 155). This lacuna in Gramsci's early Marxism meant that he became isolated from the struggle for leadership of the party in these decisive years (Gramsci 1978, 189). Over the next few years Gramsci worked to remedy this problem by struggling for the leadership of the Communist Party against tendencies within the party which tended to reduce communism to an abstract ideal. However, his was a hollow victory for it came after the triumph of fascism.

Whatever the concrete facts of Gramsci's embrace of "Leninism," many have argued that this process undermined the powerful ethical dimension of his earlier Marxism. Typically, Carl Boggs implies at least a tension between Gramsci's ethical Marxism and his Leninism, claiming that Lenin's "highly centralised conception of the party . . . contradicted all expectations of self-management and democratic participation" (Boggs 1976, 86). This paradox is of Boggs' own making; for he both mistakes Lenin's Party for Stalin's, and abstracts the rise of Stalinism from the debilitating material conditions which confronted Russian socialists in the wake of the Revolution. It was material scarcity at home, and failed revolutions abroad, as we shall see below, that gave rise to Stalinism; and it was from Stalin that the "Leninist" caricature of Lenin's politics issued. If we think beyond this caricature, then Gramsci's increased focus on the importance of the party after 1920 is explicable as a response to his realization that "important as workers' control was, it had of neces-sity to be supplemented by the physical dismantling of the capitalist state" (Gluckstein 1985, 187). As is apparent from Gramsci's last major publication before his imprisonment, *The Lyons Theses*, his stress on the need to build a party did not mean that he forgot the strengths of the *L'Ordine Nuovo* period. Thus he insisted that "the party organisation must be constructed on the basis of production and hence of work-place (cells)" (Gramsci 1978, 362). Concretely, these party cells were designed not merely to reflect the consciousness of the workers around them, but aimed at real leadership of the class struggle. This argument informed the claim, made in the *Prison Notebooks*, that while "parties are only the nomenclature for classes, it is also true that parties are not simply a mechanical and passive expression of those classes, but must react energetically upon them in order to develop, solidify and universalise them" (Gramsci 1971, 227). Importantly, this conception of leadership escapes the common conflation, originating with Weber, of leadership with domination. It did so because from the *L'Ordine Nuovo* period onward in applying "itself to real men" it was, in Gramsci's words, "not abstract." Consequently, 'the element of spontaneity was not neglected and even less despised. It was educated, directed, purged of extraneous contaminations, the aim was to bring it in line with modern theory [Marxism]—but in a living and historically effective manner" (Gramsci quoted in Molyneux 1986, 156). Commenting on this argument, Molyneux points out that Gramsci thus made a clear break with the dualistic formulation of the relationship of spontaneity to consciousness within Lenin's *What is to be Done?* (Molyneux 1986, 157). Gramsci made this break with the elitist residue of Second International Marxism without reverting to a crude dismissal of leadership *per se*. Rather he suggested that leaders could be divided into democratic and anti-democratic types: "In the formation of leaders, one premise is fundamental: is it the intention that there should always be rulers and ruled, or is the objective to create the conditions in which this division is no longer necessary?" (Gramsci 1971, 144; Molyneux 1986, 158).

There is an affinity between Gramsci's insistence that the Communist Party shake off its tendency toward abstract phrase-mongering to instead root itself in real workers' struggles and Ernst Bloch's elaboration of the distinction between abstract and concrete utopia. Bloch had been close enough to Lukács before the First World War to suggest that parts of *History and Class Consciousness* "really came from me" while elements of his own pre-Marxist essay, *Spirit of Utopia* (1918), "originated with Lukács" (Hudson 1982, 38). Though this may be true, it is also the case that within his book Lukács sought to distance his reinterpretation of Marxism from Bloch's thought. Specifically, he tended to dismiss utopianism as an abstract category which had been superseded by historical materialism (Lukács 1971, 160, 192–3). Commenting on this claim, Bloch argued that Lukács had one-sidedly reduced the idea of utopia to an abstract and unworldly caricature (Hudson 1982, 38–41). Against this approach, Bloch insisted, as Wayne Hudson points out, that "human consciousness is pervaded by a utopian dimension" (Hudson 1982, 108). He argued along similar lines to Lenin's comments on dreaming noted above that a distinction be drawn between abstract and concrete forms of utopia, and that Marxism, at its best, was a form of the latter (Geoghegan 1996, 148). Bloch developed this point at great length in his magnum opus *The Principle of Hope*—a work written in the decade from 1938 but first published in the mid-1950s. While this would seem to place Bloch's work in a period outside the scope of the creative moment discussed in this chapter, his work has widely been linked to that of Lukács and Korsch. Jose Merquior wrote that it was these "three wise men who broke with the unphilosophical quietism of the Second International and restored Marxism to the humanist wealth of its idealist origins" (Merquior 1986, 82). More concretely, Oskar Negt described Bloch as "the German philosopher of the October Revolution," whilst Martin Jay has claimed that even in his maturity Bloch remained a "fossilized remnant of Western Marxism's earliest years" (Jay 1984, 176, 195).

Substantively, Bloch sought to "rehabilitate the concept of utopia within Marxism" (Levitas 1990, 83). Accordingly, whereas earlier moral theories had imposed their ideas of justice abstractly from "the outside," Marxism criticized capitalist society concretely in "immanent dialectical terms." This form of critique was not merely critical of that which is, but simultaneously orientates toward the "Not Yet" which is growing within capitalism as a concrete alternative to it. Far from being unrealistic, this form of utopianism is the only adequate form of realism: "There is no realism worthy of the name if it abstracts from this strongest element in reality, as an unfinished reality" (Bloch 1986, Vol. II, 619–624). More specifically he insisted that rather than make a simplistic juxtaposition between Marxism and utopianism it is better to view Marxism as strengthening utopianism by providing it with a renewed concreteness: not only has Marxism not "extinguished the pillar of fire" in the dreams of the utopians, but it has "driven the cloud in our dreams further forward" (Bloch 1986, Vol. I, 146). To this end Bloch argued that Marx's claim that the working-class has no ideals to realize should not be understood mechanically as suggesting that Marxists have no vision of a better future, but that its ideals are "tendentially concrete goals" rather than "abstractly introduced goals" (Bloch 1986, Vol. I, 173, 199). In fact this is very close to Lukács' claim that while the ultimate end of socialism is "utopian in the sense that it transcends the economic, legal and social limits of contemporary society," because Marxism is rooted in the real movement of things it "changes the transcendent object into an immanent one"; that is, the "means" are not alien to the goal . . . instead they bring the goal closer to self-realisation" (Lukács 1972, 5; on the difference between immanence and transcendence see McCarney 2000, 39–48).

So, whereas Kant's categorical imperative "lacks all real practice," Marx "cultivates not a general and abstract but an *addressed* humanity" (Bloch 1986, Vol. II, 872; Vol. III, 1357). As against the formalism of Kant's morality, which Bloch nevertheless suggests anticipates the morality of a future classless society, Marx was able to see beyond the negative side of the present to the potential inherent in the revolt against capitalism (Bloch 1986, Vol. II, 874; Vol. III, 1357). This concrete morality went beyond Kant because it was addressed to real historical people. Bloch thus rewrote Kant's categorical imperative so that it called upon people to "overturn all circumstances in which man is a degraded, a subjected, a forsaken, a contemptible being" (Bloch 1986, Vol. III, 1358). Marxism in this sense was, as Andrew Feenberg suggests, the "secularisation of religious utopia" (Feenberg 1981, 252), because, as Bloch wrote, it was not satisfied with "mere wishing" but insists that we "want" in a way that "shows this wanting what can be done" (Bloch 1986, Vol. III, 1354).

While it is tragic that the author of these lines could become an apologist for Stalinism in the 1930s, 40s, and 50s, this is perhaps partially explicable by the massive defeats suffered by the workers' movement in this period. When the working class could not point toward a concrete alternative to capitalism in this period, Bloch, at least until 1961, substituted the Stalinist bureaucracy for it at the core of his vision for a better society.

If the first signs of a socialist alternative both to capitalism and Stalinism in the post-war period was signalled by the resistance of the East German working class in 1953, it was the events of 1956, particularly the brief reemergence of real soviets as institutions of workers' power in Hungary as workers defended themselves from Russian tanks that reignited the socialist vision of a better society (Harman 1988, 63–79, 119–186). It is from this moment, that Gramsci's project of an ethical Marxism could begin to be unpicked by the New Left from the counterrevolutionary distortions that Marxism endured at the hands of Stalin and his followers.

Stalinism and Marxism

As is evidenced by the discussion above, Perry Anderson papered over a number of cracks when he wrote of the "organic unity of theory and practice realized in the classical generation of Marxists before the First World War" (Anderson 1976, 29). Nevertheless, Anderson undoubtedly pointed to an important characteristic of classical Marxism that was entirely absent from its Stalinist caricature. For, if Second International orthodoxy involved a compromise between revolutionary rhetoric and reformist practice in a genuine, if ultimately flawed attempt to foster the maximum unity across the working class, Stalinism emerged as a crude attempt to represent the defeat of the workers' movement as its victory. The division between theory and practice institutionalized within the Second International was taken to a qualitatively higher level by the Stalinists, in whose hands Marxism was reduced to a tool which justified the actions of the Soviet bureaucracy.

The success of the Russian Revolution of October 1917 had been predicated on the success of similar revolutions across Europe: Russia in isolation was too backward to sustain socialist relations of production, but the war had shown that her economy was but a part of a broader international economy which was sufficiently developed to underpin the transition to socialism. Thus, in July 1918, Lenin argued that "we never harboured the illusion that the forces of the proletariat and the revolutionary people of one country, however heroic and however organised and disciplined they might be, could overthrow imperialism. That can be done only by the joint effort of the workers of the world" (quoted in Hallas 1985, 7). Unfortunately, while revolutionary upheavals did erupt outside Russia after 1917, these movements had, by the end of 1923, been defeated. In the wake of these defeats the Soviet Union became politically isolated, and the Soviet bureaucracy, which was already evolving as a distinct social layer during the civil war, became increasingly self-conscious of their own particular interests within society. This process initially took the form of the successful attempt by the then-leadership of the Communist Party (the "Troika" of Zinoviev, Kamenev, and Stalin) to stop Trotsky succeeding Lenin as Party leader on the latter's death (Deutscher 1959, 75–6). The conflict between Trotsky and the leadership opened when Trotsky, in his pamphlet *The New Course*, criticized the growing bureaucratization of the Party and the Soviet State. After this dispute had been suppressed, the conflict between Trotsky and the Troika moved on to a bitter exchange over Trotsky's criticism, in *The Lessons of October*, of Zinoviev's and Kamenev's roles in the October Revolution. It was in this context that, as Kamenev and Zinoviev were later to admit, the concept of "Trotskyism" was invented by members of the Troika as a stick with which to beat Trotsky (Cliff 1991, 88). Simultaneously, the myth of "Leninism," as a monolithic party which imparted science to the workers from the top down, was concocted with the short-term goal of curtailing any criticism, particularly Trotsky's, of the new leadership (Le Blanc 1990, 1–13).

Unfortunately for Lukács, all this occurred just as he published *History and Class Consciousness*. Whereas the earliest reviews of his book within the Communist movement were generally positive, very quickly an attack was mounted by both the Russian philosopher Abram Deborin and an ex-member of Lukács' group within the Hungarian Communist Party—the Moscow-based Lazslo Rudas. In two separate reviews, Rudas, from a mechanical materialist perspective, criticized, first, Lukács, and then Trotsky, for their supposed shared over-emphasis of the subjective factor in history. At the Fifth Congress of the Comintern in June–July 1924, Zinoviev picked up on the first of these essays to lambaste Lukács and Korsch for their supposed "revisionism" (Rees 2000, 25). Consequently, for what were initially at least merely conjunctural reasons, Lukács' book became an incidental casualty of the attack on Trotsky. Whatever its basis, the debate on *History and Class Consciousness* marked the moment at which the renewal of Marxism associated with the post-war revolutionary wave was sacrificed on the altar of political reaction. In place of Lukács' sophisticated philosophy, Deborin rehashed a variant of Plekhanov's caricatured Hegelianism (Halliday 1970, 17), whilst Rudas embraced a kind of crude mechanical materialism (Rees 2000, 23).

It was in this context that Stalin, in 1924, invented the concept of "socialism in one country." If classical Marxism had hoped to give theoretical expression to the real movement of the working class, the concept of socialism in one country was the ideological reflection of the emerging soviet bureaucracy. It was through this concept, as Trotsky argued, that the bureaucracy came to equate the victory of socialism with "their own victory" (Trotsky 1972, 32). The importance of this development is difficult to overstate. Stalin was no mere dictator who imposed his vision of the future on an unwilling Russia. He was the embodiment of the bureaucracy's project of building a strong Russia in a world of imperialist states. And within a few years the Stalinists had recognized that a strong Russia could only be built on the backs of the workers and peasants who had made the revolution in 1917. Therefore, while 1924 marked an important watershed in Soviet politics, Michal Reiman has convincingly argued that the key turning point was the period from 1927–29. For it was at this point, after a period of developing structural crisis throughout the 1920s, that Stalinism took final shape as the Stalinists created a sociopolitical system that was "dia-metrically opposed" to socialism (Reiman 1987, 119, 122). In contrast to Lenin and Trotsky's strategy of fostering world revolution, from the late 1920s onward Stalin sought to solve the problem of Russia's historical backwardness through a process of state-led industrialization (Haynes 1985, 110; Cliff 1974).

Despite the counterrevolutionary nature of Stalinism, Stalin continued to deploy the—bastardized—language of Marxism to legitimize the Soviet State by reference to the October Revolution whilst simultaneously robbing socialist opponents of the regime of the language of historical materialism. In so doing, Stalinism marked a fundamental transformation of Marxism. As Marcuse wrote, "during the Revolution, it became apparent to what degree Lenin had succeeded in basing his strategy on the actual class interests and aspirations of the workers and peasants." However, "from 1923 on, the decisions of the leadership have been increasingly dissociated from the class interests of the proletariat" (Marcuse 1958, 124). Soviet Marxism served not as a guide to working-class action, but as a justification for the actions already taken by the Soviet ruling class (Marcuse 1958, 17, 128; Harris 1968, 152). Similarly, Slavoj Žižek argues that to treat Stalinist "dialectical materialism" as a serious philosophical system would be to miss the point: "it was an instrument of power legitimation to be enacted ritualistically" (Žižek 2000, 155).

Concretely, Stalin's "philosophy" led to all manner of ridiculous pronouncements. Perhaps the most famous of these was his attempt to square Marx's argument that socialism would be characterized by the withering away of the state with a justification of the increasingly repressive nature of the Russian state: "We stand for the withering away of the State. At the same time, we stand for the strengthening of the dictatorship of the proletariat, which is the mightiest and strongest State power that has ever existed . . . Is this contradictory? Yes, it is contradictory. But this contradiction is bound up with life, and it fully reflects Marx's dialectics" (quoted in Harris 1968, 162). Nonsense like this led the historian Edward Thompson to suggest that Stalin had transformed Marx's historical and dialectical materialism into "hysterical and diabolic" materialism. The great virtue of the dialectic, thus conceived, was that it could be used to justify just about any policy because few understood what it meant.

More generally, Stalin repeated the dualism characteristic of bourgeois thought when he articulated a social theory that incoherently combined voluntarism with mechanical determinism. History was conceived as a mechanical story of the liberation of the forces of production from the fetters of increasingly regressive relations of production. Marx's revolutionary theory was subsequently reduced to a general evolutionary schema: "the productive forces of society change and develop, and then, *depending* on these changes and *in conformity with them*, men's relations of production, their economic relations, change" (Stalin 1938). Whereas Marx had understood the growing contradiction between forces and relations of production as the context within which struggles for freedom were fought out (Blackledge 2006a, Ch. 2), Stalin reduced the growth of human freedom to development of the forces of production. This allowed him to equate the industrialization of Russia with the liberation of the Russian people. He thus twisted Marx's critique of capital's tendency to accumulate for accumulation's sake into a justification of just that process in Russia. In the realm of moral theory the Stalinist counterrevolution was associated with the reemergence of what was both socially and sexually a conservative morality (Kamenka 1969, 60). This involved a "competitive work morality" whose highest principles were "Soviet patriotism and love for the motherland" and which served to completely endorse "work as the very content of the individual's whole life." Indeed, "the restoration of a rigid, disciplinary, authoritarian morality in the early thirties" acted to legitimize the "subordination of individual morality to the development of the productive forces" (Marcuse 1958, 191, 204).

While this model offered very little by way of a rationale for revolutionary practice, Stalin felt compelled to include an account of agency in his social theory if only to justify his own role in Russia. To his mechanical theory of historical evolution, he therefore added a model of bureaucratic activity. The ideology of "Leninism," invented by the Stalinists in the mid-1920s, served a useful purpose here (Le Blanc 1990, 1–13). "Theory," as embodied in the party and in practice in the pronouncements of Stalin, acted as the ghost in the machine guiding Russia to liberation. As Nigel Harris put it, as a social theory Stalinism contradictorily combined "determinism for the masses, voluntarism for the leadership" (Harris 1968, 156; Marcuse 1958, 121). Of course, it mattered little to Stalin that his theory was analytically useless: the point was to justify the actions of the Soviet state, not to explain them. Nonetheless, a key intellectual consequence of the rise of Stalinism was that the interpretation of Marxism which became hegemonic within the Communist movement was a positivistic caricature of Marx's thought, within which the normative aspect of Marxism was buried beneath rhetoric about the onward march of the forces of production.

Conclusion

Whereas Lenin, Lukács, Luxemburg, and Grossman amongst others, contributed to the theoretical break with Second International dualism, and while Lukács, Pashukanis, Trotsky, Bloch, and Gramsci pointed toward the ethical consequences of this break, nobody within the pre-Stalinist Comintern produced a fully worked out revolutionary ethics. Nevertheless, individuals did suggest the political implications of a renewed ethical Marxism. By contrast with Eagleton's claim that "an aesthetic society will be the fruit of the most resolutely instrumental political action" (Eagleton 1990, 206), Lukács argued that "class consciousness is the 'ethics' of the proletariat," and because "the party" is the "incarnation of the ethics of the fighting proletariat" its "true strength . . . is moral" (Lukács 1971, 42; cf Mészáros 1995, 313).

This argument, of course, presupposes the model of, on the one hand, the dialectical relationship between the class struggle of workers against the atomization and fragmentation of capitalist society, and, on the other, the emergence of socialism and a revolutionary party through which a vision of a cooperative, free society is embodied as the immanent critique of capitalism. While this, as I have argued, was the position of Lenin and Lukács, it is a tragedy that the revolutionary process which underpinned the intellectual revolution that gave rise to this argument was, by the mid-1920s, in full retreat, only to suffer a catastrophic defeat at the hands of Hitler and Stalin in the 1930s. From then on, the ideology of "Leninism," to the extent that it was more than a crude justification for the actions of the Stalinist bureaucracy, degenerated into the kind of dualism between leaders and led, or science and spontaneous movement, against which Lenin had earlier rebelled. Similarly, once divorced from its content as the expression of a revolutionary movement, Lukács' conception of the role of the party was distorted to justify support for the Stalinist bureaucracy. Nevertheless, whilst the Stalinist counterrevolution put an end to the revolutionary renewal of Marxism, as we shall see in Chapter 5, the crisis of Stalinism in the 1950s once again opened the door to a rebirth of revolutionary social and ethical theory. The small group of revolutionaries associated with the far-left of the New Left were, however, but a minority of those influenced by Lukács' thought, and the dominant tendency, as we shall discuss in the next chapter, was the much more pessimistic, and abstractly utopian, school of Critical Theory.

4

Western Marxism's Tragic Vision

Socialist Ethics in a Non-Revolutionary Age

> The existence of revolutionary ideas in a particular period presupposes
> the existence of a revolutionary class.
>
> —Marx and Engels 1976, 60

> The defining problem of Western Marxism has been the lack of a
> revolutionary subject.
>
> —Žižek 2009, 51

Introduction

In *The Hidden God* (1964), his magnificent study of the works of Pascal and Racine, Lucien Goldmann developed a theory of what, following Lukács, he called the "tragic vision." He deployed this concept to describe a series of similar worldviews characteristic of the perspective of certain social groups at certain historical junctures when, without a basis for hope, they could not but continue to hope. In religious terms this paradox emerged when, although the belief in God could no longer be assumed, people continued to act with His eye upon them. These actors consequently found themselves in a situation whereby they could neither succeed in, nor abandon, their divinely appointed tasks. Goldmann argues that variations on this vision emerged classically at three historical junctures: those of Sophocles, Shakespeare, and finally Pascal, Racine, and Kant. He argues that each of these writers expressed a specific tragic vision as a representative of a particular social group's experience of "a deep crisis in the relationship between [its vision of] man and his social

141

and spiritual world" (Goldmann 1964, 41). According to Goldmann, the characteristics of the tragic worldview in each of these periods included the belief that while we can "never give up hope," neither can we put "hope in this world" (Goldmann 1964, 56–7). Part of Pascal's contribution to the tragic vision of his age was his suggestion that the search for meaning in the world involved a wager on God's existence. Thus he wrote, "You wish to obtain faith, but do not know how to go about it; you want to cure yourself of your unbelief, and you ask for a remedy: *learn from those who have been tied as you are now tied, and who now wager all they have*" (Goldmann 1964, 285–6).

After each of the historical moments characterized by a tragic vision there emerged attempts by representatives of new social groups to move beyond this crisis by showing that "man is capable of achieving authentic values by his own thoughts and actions." These new worldviews were expressed in the works of Plato after Sophocles, "European rationalism and empiricism" after Shakespeare, and Hegel and Marx after Pascal, Racine, and Kant (Goldmann 1964, 46). In each of these periods the new vision pointed beyond the limits of the old situation through a wager on the possibilities for change anchored in the novel ways in which these new social groups engaged with external reality. Drawing critically on Pascal, Goldmann argued that, like the tragic vision, the dialectical approach to history took the form of a wager, but this wager is no longer on forces beyond the human world but on forces immanent to it: "man's life takes on the aspect of a wager on the success of his own action and, consequently, on the existence of a force which transcends the individual." From this perspective, Marxism involves not a deterministic prediction of the socialist future of humanity but rather a wager on the revolutionary potential of the proletariat (Goldmann 1964, 300–301). Precisely because it takes the form of such a wager, he suggests that the defeats experienced by the labour movement in the mid-twentieth century led some of the most honest thinkers of the period to recognize the existence of a "dichotomy . . . between man's hopes and the human predicament." They found themselves in a situation where the forces that had offered the potential to move beyond the tragic condition appeared no longer to exist (Goldmann 1964, pp. 60–61).

In this context, the wager on the revolutionary potential of the proletariat which had been at the heart of Lenin's orientation toward the "actuality of the revolution" (Lukács 1970, p. 11),—his wager that every cook could govern (Lenin 1964, p. 113)—increasingly seemed to be dissociated from reality. Thus, as we noted in the previous chapter, after the defeat of the German Revolution in October 1923 the intimate relationship that had once existed between Communist politics and the workers' movement was inverted by Stalin and Zinoviev, who turned Leninism into a crude ideological tool in their struggles for power. If this process opened with their attacks on Trotsky, it culminated with the expulsion of Bukharin from the leadership of the Russian Party. And just as the attack on Trotsky was the backdrop to the denunciation of Lukács' renewal of Marxist philosophy, the expulsion of Bukharin went hand-in-hand with a lurch toward a form of political ultra-leftism within the Comintern. One consequence of this political shift was the paralysis of the German Communist Party in the face of Hitler's rise to power and the subsequent defeat of the German workers' movement by the Nazis. It is hardly surprising that in this context the authentic revolutionary left became atomized and isolated.

Represented principally by Trotsky, whose critique of Stalinism provides the basis for all serious subsequent work on the subject (Blackledge 2006c; 2006d), the revolutionary left in the 1930s became, if anything, even more isolated than Lenin had been in 1914. Furthermore, because Stalinism was a product of the defeats of the workers' movement, and because Stalin's policies led to further defeats, as Trotsky himself recognized the grip of Stalinism over the left was reinforced by its own vices, defeats left socialists feeling isolated and more likely to look to Moscow as the one hope against Hitler. If, after Trotsky's death, the victory of Russia over the Wehrmacht reinforced the international left's faith in Stalinism, subsequent events conspired to further marginalize the authentic forces of revolutionary socialism. The stabilizing role played by the Stalinist parties during the wave of popular revolts which ushered in the end of the war (Birchall 1974) combined with the post-war boom to mediate against the emergence of the type of generalized class struggles that might underpin a renewed revolutionary workers' movement. If, therefore, in the 1930s and 1940s the objective opportunities for the reemergence of a revolutionary movement were squandered by the subjective factor of the Stalinized Comintern, subsequently the postwar boom ensured that those small revolutionary groups that had managed to survive the tests of the previous two decades were confronted with a situation which seemed to falsify their core beliefs (Anderson 1976, 24–5).

In this context, it is hardly surprising that socialist intellectuals became increasingly disassociated from revolutionary politics. An extreme example of this phenomenon was the trajectory taken by the key thinkers associated with the Frankfurt School (Wiggershaus 1994): principally, Max Horkheimer, Theodor Adorno, and Herbert Marcuse. Launched in 1924, in the wake of a meeting held a year earlier at which Lukács and Korsch amongst others gathered to discuss the philosophical implications of Lenin's renewal of Marxism, it was originally hoped that this School, funded by Felix Weil the Marxist son of a German businessman, would prefigure a larger undertaking in a soon to be realized German Soviet Republic. In the wake of the failure of the German workers' movement to stop Hitler, the leading figures associated with the School became increasingly pessimistic about the future prospects of socialism. It was against this backdrop that Adorno attempted to formulate a new categorical imperative that was adequate to the demands of the modern world.

Whereas the intellectuals associated with the Frankfurt School were first attracted to Marxism in the wake of 1917 only to move away from it after Hitler's rise to power, across the border in France Jean-Paul Sartre, who had little engagement with pre-Stalinist Communist politics, was drawn toward the Communist Party and Marxism through his experience within the *Résistance*. This moment set the scene for a lifelong engagement with Marxism and Stalinism out of which emerged a powerful attempt to renew both revolutionary politics and revolutionary ethics in the unfavourable conditions at the outbreak of the Cold War.

If Sartre and the members of the Frankfurt School represented alternative attempts to articulate an ethical basis from which to oppose modern capitalist society in the wake of, first, the rise of fascism and Stalinism and, second, the post-War boom, perhaps the dominant voice of Western Marxism in the 1960s was that of Louis Althusser, who famously dismissed socialist humanism and its corollary ethical Marxism (Althusser 1969, 219–247). By the 1970s, however, not only was Althusser's star on the wane, but so too was the hegemony of continental European thinkers within the academic Marxist milieu. From the late 1970s onward the center of gravity of Marxist theory shifted to the Anglophone world, where, in the wake of the publication of Jerry Cohen's *Karl Marx's Theory of History: A Defence* (1978), a tendency known as Analytical Marxism emerged to become the dominant voice of academic Marxism for the next two decades (Anderson 1983, 24). As we shall see, the political trajectory of this group was to move away from classical Marxism toward an ethical variant of utopian socialism whose themes overlapped with egalitarian liberalism. Nevertheless, if this was the dominant trajectory of this school, others influenced by these debates came to altogether more radical conclusions. Most important amongst these is Alex Callinicos who has attempted a synthesis between these debates and revolutionary socialism.

I conclude with the argument that while none of these approaches successfully escape the parameters of our emotivist culture, at their strongest, particularly in the Frankfurt School's immanent critique of capitalism, Callinicos's extrapolation of the revolutionary implications of egalitarian liberalism, and Sartre's conception of praxis, they do provide important resources that point forward toward such a transcendence.

Searching for an Anti-Capitalist Ethics: The Frankfurt School

Theodor Adorno's critical theory has often been presented as a critique not only of Marx and Marxism but also of the more general idea of the possibility of social emancipation. Against this caricature of his thought, Jean-Marie Vincent points out that Adorno's *oeuvre* was in fact "centred on a search for adequate means of emancipation and liberation following the historical failures of the workers' movement" (Vincent 2008, 489). While he was deeply influenced by the ideas of the young Lukács, the political failure of the socialist movement in the 1920s informed Adorno's rejection, as Susan Buck-Morss argues, of "Lukács' concept of the pro-letariat as the subject-object of history." Adorno was unhappy both with the gap between the real empirical consciousness of the working class and the consciousness that was imputed onto them by Lukács and the Communist Party, and with the way that truth came to be "manipulated" within the Communist movement for the sake of "Party strategy." The fact that Adorno matured as an intellectual in the 1920s and 1930s, in the period when Lukács denounced much of the substance of *History and Class Consciousness* as he attempted to maintain a formal loyalty to its concluding defence of membership of the Communist Party, was enough for Adorno to radically question Lukács' contribution to the renewal of Marxism (Buck-Morss 1977, 28–32), and undoubtedly informed his Kantian concern with maintaining the autonomy of the intellectual as a critic of society (Delanty 2007, 122). Lukács's capitulation to Stalinism in the 1920s was, of course, but a minor episode in the history of the defeats suffered by the socialist movement in that period (Löwy 1979, 193–213), and it was these defeats that fundamentally informed Adorno's pessimistic political theory. Writing toward the end of his life, he commented that in his youth he had experienced a time when "change really seemed close" (Adorno 2006, 181). However, as his collaborator Max Horkeimer argued, while proletarian revolutions might reasonably have been expected in the "first half of the [twentieth] century," and whereas it had seemed realistic to hope that a unified working class response to Hitler could have prevented the victory of the Nazis in Germany in the 1930s, in the wake of the Second World War "the proletariat has been integrated into society" (Horkheimer 1972, v–vi). Hitler's rise to power seemed to refute both the hopes of historical progress associated with Second International Marxism and Lenin's revolutionary alternative. Thus, as Espen Hammer argues, Adorno's Marxism was formulated in the context of the rise of fascism, and against what he labels both Kautsky's naive evolutionary hope for progress, and Lenin's, Trotsky's and Lukács' variations on "voluntarist vanguardism" (Hammer 2006, 26).

In the *Dialectic of Enlightenment* (1944), Adorno and Horkheimer argued, contra Marx's hopes for the proletariat, that in the modern world "progress becomes regression" such that alongside man's growing control over nature there occurs a disappearance of individuality as "the impotence and pliability of the masses grow with the qualitative increase in commodities allowed them" (Adorno and Horkheimer 1979, xiv–xv). Extending Lukács' discussion of the ways in which the commodification of all aspects of life in bourgeois society tend to make the dissimilar comparable by "reducing it to abstract quantities," Adorno and Horkheimer rejected Lukács' hope that the standpoint of the proletariat might offer an alternative to this system by insisting that "the actual working conditions in society compel conformism." They claimed that the "impotence of the worker is not merely a stratagem of the rulers, but the logical consequence of the industrial society" (Adorno and Horkheimer 1979, 7, 37). So, whereas Lukács had broken with the romantic anti-capitalism of Weber's "Heidelberg Circle," to which he had belonged in the decade before 1918 when he embraced Marxism that year (Löwy 1979, pp. 37ff), Adorno and Horkheimer appeared to reverse this trajectory. In a manner that owed more to the ideas of Tönnies, Weber, and Simmel than it did to Marx, they characterized modern bourgeois society by an emerging rationalization of the means of actions, and a consequent fragmentation of the social world (Therborn 1977, 92ff; Bernstein 2001, 7, 30; Callinicos 2007a, 255).

Interestingly, in a later work Lukács criticized Weber's belief that "the cardinal distinguishing feature of capitalism remained rationality, calculability" not because these were not characteristics of modern bourgeois society, but because they gave the impression of a "comprehension of the essence of capitalism without having to go into its real economic problems" (Lukács 1980b, 607). Weber's approach thus "obfuscated . . . the real sociohistorical dynamics" of capitalism (Mészáros 1995, 333). As noted in the previous chapter, Grossman, in *The Law of Accumulation*, attempted to extend Lukács' renewal of Marxism by providing it with a powerful reinterpretation of Marx's critique of political economy. In contradistinction to this project, and despite the fact that Grossman's book was published under the auspices of the Frankfurt School in 1929, by the early 1940s Horkheimer and Adorno increasingly disassociated themselves from Grossman's classical Marxist interpretation of capitalism (Kuhn 2007, 182–186). By developing the Weberian side of *History and Class Consciousness*, the critique of capitalism articulated by the theorists associated with the Frankfurt School suggested no internal contradictions which might potentially undermine the postwar stabilization of capitalism.

Perhaps the most influential work produced from this general perspective was Herbert Marcuse's *One-Dimensional Man* (1964). According to Marcuse, whereas Marx had envisaged a proletarian challenge to the bourgeoisie's control over the means of production with the intention of deploying those technologies for the universal good, "in advanced capitalism, technical rationality is embodied, in spite of its irrational use, in the productive apparatus," and this situation leads to a "change in the attitude and consciousness of the labourer, which becomes manifest in the widely discussed 'social and cultural integration' of the labouring class with capitalist society" (Marcuse 1968, 34, 39). If the logic of this claim informed the dominant theme of Marcuse's book—"that advanced industrial society is capable of containing qualitative change for the foreseeable future"—he also aimed to locate those tendencies "which may break this containment and explode the society" (Marcuse 1968, 13). The book concludes with the suggestion, not justified within the text, that "underneath the conservative popular base is the substratum of outcasts and outsiders, the exploited and persecuted of other races and other colours, the unemployed and unemployable" whose struggles might just act as a basis for a better world (Marcuse 1968, 200). In answer to the question of how such a world was to be judged superior to the *status quo*, Marcuse proposed, generally, that modern society might be measured against "its own historical alternatives," and more specifically that it might be judged against the standards that "human life is worth living" and that in this society there exist opportunities "for the amelioration of human life." He suggested that "critical analysis has to demonstrate the objective validity of these judgements" on "empirical grounds" (Marcuse 1968, 10).

Nonetheless, while Marcuse maintained an intransigent opposition to global capitalism, his belief that it had morphed into a form of what he labelled, following Rudolph Hilferding, "organised capitalism" (Kellner 1984, 233; Howard. & King 1989, 270–276) informed his acceptance of the argument, widespread in the 1960s, that "economic depressions could be controlled and conflicts stabilised" (Wilde 1998, 66). This perspective reinforced the dominant pessimistic theme of his book. So while Marcuse, like Marx, subjected capitalism to an "immanent critique" (a method ultimately derived by the Frankfurt School from Hegel's *Science of Logic* (McCarney 1990, 18; Kellner 1984, 118), unlike Marx, for whom "existing conditions . . . contain the basis for a critical perspective" (Sayers 1998, 9), he tended to follow Adorno for whom there seemed to be little basis within existing conditions for a critique of capitalism.

This pessimism is apparent in Adorno's comments on the Stalinist debasement of Lenin's call for the unity of theory and practice. Adorno argued that in the modern world "every important practice whose theory one tries to grasp has the unfortunate and even fatal tendency to compel us to think in a way that conflicts with our own real and immediate interests." Therefore, "true practice is only possible once you have passed through theory" (Adorno 2000, 5–6). In *Negative Dialectics* (1966) he argued that "[t]he call for unity of theory and practice has irresistibly degraded theory to a servant's role, removing the very traits it should have brought to that unity" (Adorno 1973, 143; 2000, 4). Whereas Adorno thereby resisted the Stalinist degradation of theory, he was more than aware that for it to be an adequate guide to action, moral philosophy must be rooted in the concreteness of practice. Consequently, while he was "indebted to Kant's moral philosophy," he insisted that moral principles must, contra Kant, be "bound with a unique historical and social constellation" (Schweppenhäuser 2004, 344). For instance, in *Problems of Moral Philosophy* he referred to the actions of Fabian von Schlabrendorff, a participant in the 1944 plot to kill Hitler. Criticizing rationalistic approaches to the study of ethics, Adorno wrote that while Schlabrendorff's actions could not adequately be understood except in relation to his knowledge both of what Hitler was doing and also that the plot would probably fail and that the consequences of this failure would be horrendous both for himself and for his family, his actions also involved an irredeemably "spontaneous" and "irrational" element. He wrote that Schlabrendorff had told him that "there are situations that are so intolerable that one just cannot continue to put up with them, no matter what may happen and no matter what may happen to oneself in the course of the attempt to change them." It was to the issue of the pain involved in such theoretically informed but also irredeemably spontaneous acts of "resistance" that Adorno addressed his analysis of moral theory (Adorno 2000, 6–11).

Developing the idea that practice in the modern world lends itself to false consciousness, Adorno suggested that we, as "citizens of the wrong world," are so "impaired" by our experience of the world that we "would find the right one unbearable" (Adorno 1973, 352). He claimed that because we live in a "socialised society" we are unable to live by those moral precepts which "would be a reality only in a free society" (Adorno 1973, 299; 2006, 203). Thus, to approve of Kant's categorical imperative would first imply that we are what socialisation prevents us from being, autonomous beings (Bernstein 2001, 24). As he pithily expressed in *Minima Moralia* (1951), "wrong life cannot be lived rightly" (Adorno 1974, 39; 2000, 1).

Nevertheless, while this analysis suggested the impossibility of formulating some positive maxim by which we might hope to live a moral life, Adorno insisted that Hitler had imposed a new categorical imperative upon mankind: "to arrange their thoughts and actions so that Auschwitz will not repeat itself, so that nothing similar will happen." Discussing the reasons behind his condemnation of this kind of act, Adorno claimed some basic human standpoint, an "unvarnished materialistic motive," by which even if we are unable to know the nature of the good society we can at least resist this "unbearable physical agony" (Adorno 1973, 365, cf 285). This perspective has been described by Hammer as Adorno's "ethics of resistance," and by Jay Bernstein as his "ethical modernism" (Hammer 2006, 102; Bernstein 2001, xii).

So, while Adorno rejected the classical Marxist attempt to base the ethical critique of capitalism on working-class practice, he did attempt to posit some basis, however minimal, for critical politics. Unfortunately, as Joseph McCarney has argued, Adorno's interpretation of immanent critique proved unable "to enforce conclusions hostile to the existing state of things." For, whereas those most susceptible to the arguments presented in an immanent critique are those with "fewest reservations" about the dominant ideology such that it is aptly summed up as "a method of bourgeois self-criticism," the very fact that this class have non-moral reasons for maintaining their existing practice implies that they are able to respond to immanent critique by simply rejecting the principles upon which the *status quo* is judged (McCarney 1990, 21). The gap between Adorno's analysis of social degradation in the modern world and his hope that that the human products of this process might act to stop the repetition of the Holocaust is nowhere successfully resolved. Indeed, certain of Adorno's formulations suggest that this problem cannot be overcome. For instance, in the lectures collected as *History and Freedom*, he argued that those who committed the atrocities at Auschwitz and the other death camps were "unfree" and thus they were, as they themselves claimed, "just carrying out orders": "if Auschwitz could happen in the first place this was probably because no real freedom existed, no freedom could be regarded as an existing reality" (Adorno 2006, 202). Criticizing the logic of a similar argument as presented in Marcuse's *One-Dimensional Man*, Alasdair MacIntyre asked, if the book's thesis was true, how could "it have been written at all" and how could it find a sympathetic readership? (MacIntyre 1970, 62)

Analytical Marxism

If, in the late 1960s and early 1970s, an upturn in class struggle underpinned a period of political and ideological ferment that ensured a mass readership not only for Marcuse's work but for socialist literature more generally, the subsequent defeats suffered by the workers' movement opened the door to neoliberalism. Characterized by increasing social inequalities, neoliberal capitalism fostered a general sense of social injustice at just the time when the left was becoming progressively more pessimistic about the possibilities of socialist advance. Nothing seemed more natural in such circumstances than for the left to embrace an increasingly abstract moral critique of capitalism. The most prominent Marxist variant of this trend was Analytical Marxism. According to Will Kymlicka, the widespread belief that Marxism died with the collapse of Soviet Communism is, at best, only partially true. For, alongside the demise of classical Marxism, the last two decades of the twentieth century saw something of a "rebirth" of "Analytical Marxism." In light of the falsification of Marx's supposed claims about the inevitability of both the collapse of capitalism and the triumph of socialism, classical Marxist attempts to provide scientific accounts of the dynamic structure of capitalism have been jettisoned in favor of a movement amongst a layer of socialist analytical philosophers to reshape Marxism as a normative political theory (Kymlicka 2002, 167–8; Mayer 1994, 20–22, 314–316). There is a seemingly irreproachable logic to this trajectory: if Marx is understood as perhaps the archetypical economic determinist and mechanical materialist who scorned moral theory's engagement with the values that motivate individuals to action, then it makes sense for those socialists who came to reject his explanatory models as an inadequate account of human action would tend toward a reengagement with normative theory.

Nonetheless, if the emergence of Analytical Marxism—which is associated most prominently with the works of Jerry Cohen, John Elster, Andrew Levine, Philippe Van Parijs, Adam Przeworski, John Roemer, and Eric Olin Wright amongst others (Wright 1995, 13; Bertram 2008, 124)—coincided with a general Marxist reengagement with ethical theory, it was heralded by the publication of the most sophisticated defense of so-called "orthodox historical materialism": Cohen's *Karl Marx's Theory of History: A Defence* (1978). The turn toward Analytical Marxism occurred in the context of the collapse of Althusserian Marxism in the mid-1970s. Alan Carling points out that Cohen produced his powerful analytical defence of Marx's theory of history just as Britain's foremost Althusserians, Paul Hirst and Barry Hindess, announced their "utter despair at systematic social thought in general and Marxist theory in particular" (Carling 1995, 31). As Althusser's project appeared to run out of steam, an alternative conveniently emerged to challenge its hegemony within the academic left (Levine 2003, 122–145).

Analytical Marxists accepted Althusser's "expulsion of Hegelian modes of thinking from Marxist theory" (Callinicos 1989, p. 3), while reversing his attempt to expunge ethical and moral concerns from Marxism. Their interest in the normative component of the socialist project had at least two roots. First, Anglophone philosophers had, from the 1960s onward, begun to reengage with issues of morality (Cohen et al. 1980, vii). Second, from the 1970s onward a layer of Marxists began

various projects of " 'rescu[ing]' Marx from the Althusserian interpretation," by probing "the normative element of his work" (Wilde 1998,
4–5). One consequence of this debate was that whereas the Althusserians had once contrasted Marx's scientific method positively with the
ungroundable propositions of moral discourse, by the early 1980s it
was generally accepted by academic Marxists that Marxism did include
an ethical dimension, and that this was a good thing. However, it was
also widely accepted that Marx's ethics were at best only implied, and
that therefore it was incumbent upon Marxists to overcome what Alex
Callinicos has since called Marxism's "ethical deficit" (Callinicos 2006,
220). In what was perhaps the seminal text of the 1980s debate on
Marxism and ethics, Norman Geras' "The Controversy about Marx and
Justice," Geras claimed, as we noted in the discussion of Marx above,
that "Marx did think that capitalism was unjust but he did not think
he thought so" (Geras 1989, 245; Cohen 1983, 444). Although it
was suggested that this lacuna was not problematic so long as socialism
was conceived as the inevitable telos of history, once this certainty was
removed then the implications of this problem became glaringly apparent: socialism must be fought for, and therefore it was essential that
the left formulate both a powerful normative critique of capitalism and
a compelling moral case for socialism.

One person who certainly accepted this general proposition was
Jerry Cohen, who was perhaps the most important representative of the
general trajectory noted by Kymlicka. In the wake of the publication of
his *Karl Marx's Theory of History* Cohen's research increasingly moved
to focus upon issues of normative theory. He explained his own shift in
perspective as a direct response both to major theoretical problems within
classical Marxism and to changes in the world capitalist system. Central
to the problems with classical Marxism, or so Cohen contended, is its
embrace of what he calls "an obstetric conception of political practice."
As we noted in the introduction to this volume, Cohen claimed that
in this model, because society only asks of itself the kinds of questions
which it is capable of answering, revolutionary politics is reduced, as it
were, to an act of midwifery: it is not the role of socialists to consider
the "ideals" they want to realize but rather more prosaically to "deliver
the form that develops *within* reality." He commented that both because
of its "inevitabilitarian" structure and its denial of the role of ideals in
history this conception of politics is "patently false" (Cohen 2000b, 43,
50, 54; 75, 105).

Developing this point, he related a conversation he had with his "uncle Norman" in 1964. Cohen enquired of his uncle, who was then domiciled in Czechoslovakia as an editor of the Stalinist *World Marxist Review*, his opinion on the relationship between Marxism and morality, and was quite shocked by the response he elicited. Morality, Norman suggested (rather moralistically!), "is ideological eyewash; it has nothing to do with the struggle between capitalism and socialism." Unfortunately, Cohen saw in this reply not the arid response of a Stalinist apparatchik, but a "faithful" rendering of the viewpoint of "classical Marxism" (Cohen 1995, 133). He thus characterized his own shift from a defense of Marx's theory of history to an articulation of a socialist morality as a break with classical Marxism: "To the extent that Marxism is still alive . . . it presents itself as a set of values and a set of designs for realising those values." Insofar as Marxism continues to be a vibrant tradition, it has morphed from an explanatory to a moral theory; thus becoming a variant of what Marx labelled "utopian socialism" (Cohen 2000b, 101–103).

As we noted in Chapter 2, at the center of Marxism's explanatory account of the capitalist mode of production is his interpretation of the labour theory of value. In a powerful rearticulation and defense of this theory, John Weeks has argued that Marx's labour theory of value "is not an aspect of the analysis of capitalism, but the theoretical core from which all other analysis unfolds." It is "the key to unlocking the inner nature of capitalism" (Weeks 1981, 4, 6; cf Marx 1981, 957). As opposed to the central position of the labour theory of value within classical Marxism, Analytical Marxists have almost unanimously accepted the power of the attack on this theory mounted by the neo-Ricardians in the 1970s (Roberts 1996, 155). One consequence of this development is that, in their discussions of the injustices of modern capitalist societies, the Analytical Marxists have discarded Marx's theory of exploitation (Roberts 1996, 157). John Roemer suggested that "the classical concept of exploitation should . . . be abandoned, and replaced by a definition of exploitation phrased directly in terms of an unjust distribution of property in the means of production" (Roemer 1986a, p. 6; 1986b, 262–263). Commenting on this reduction of exploitation to inequality, Michael Lebowitz argues that an obvious implication of this theoretical movement is the conclusion that inequality is not unjust "if the original inequality in property endowment itself was not unjust" (Lebowitz 1988, 210). Lebowitz points out that this was exactly the point made by John Elster, who argued that exploitation has been typically judged unjust because historically it "has almost always had a thoroughly unclean causal origin, in violence, coercion, or unequal opportunities." Lebowitz asked, "but, what if there were a 'clean path' of original accumulation?" (Lebowitz 2009, 59).

Prefiguring an answer to this question, Cohen argued in a series of essays written over two decades from the mid-1970s to the mid-1990s and collected as *Self-Ownership, Freedom and Equality* (1995), that capitalism generates unjust inequalities even assuming an initially just distribution of resources. Against those right-wing libertarians such as Robert Nozick who articulated a moral defense of the traditional libertarian claim that the demand for equality leads to the suppression of freedom, Cohen suggested that while it is conceivable that a conflict may exist between freedom and equality, "there is no conflict between equality and what the libertarian Right *calls* freedom," whereas the real nature of libertarian capitalism is that it "erodes the liberty of a large class of people" (Cohen 1995, 36, 111). While this argument informed Cohen's negative anti-capitalism, he tended to dismiss Marx's positive alternative. "Classical Marxists," he suggested, "believed that economic equality was both historically inevitable and morally right." Further, they believed that two "irrepressible historical trends" had worked together to ensure this inevitability: the "rise of an organised working class" and "the development of the productive forces" (Cohen 1995, 6). In contradiction to these predictions, the process of economic growth has culminated in the "disintegration of the proletariat" and in a potentially catastrophic environmental crisis. Consequently, Marx's optimism for the future of humanity could no longer be assumed. Socialists, he suggested, "must therefore settle for a less dramatic scenario" of social transformation than was envisaged by Marx, and "they must engage in more moral advocacy than used to be fashionable" (Cohen 1995, 9).

Commenting on these and similar arguments articulated by Roemer, Marcus Roberts points out that by disassociating the concept of exploitation from Marx's critique of political economy, Analytical Marxists have explicitly divorced "moral advocacy from any concerted attempt at the identification of the class agency of social transformation" (Roberts 1996, 179). So, whereas Cohen remained a firm critic of capitalism, his criticisms of historical materialism when combined with his diagnosis of the collapse of the Soviet Union informed his pessimistic prognosis of the possibilities for socialism (Cohen 1995,

245–265; 2000a, 389–395). Taken together with his move toward moral advocacy, the trajectory taken by Cohen is typical of the move amongst Analytical Marxists away from Marx's programme toward a variant of egalitarian "liberal theories of justice" (Roberts 1996, 203). Consequently, Cohen could write, in a short booklet published just prior to his untimely death in 2009, that his vision of socialism was one which "all people of goodwill would welcome" (Cohen 2009, 51). Pronouncements such as this informed Chris Bertram's claim that "it is now impossible to say clearly who counts as a socialist, who is an egalitarian liberal etc. These ideological camps have fused and inter-penetrated" (Bertram 2008, 137; cf Levine 2003, 123).

Interestingly, the same cannot be said of Alex Callinicos, who is amongst the most prominent contemporary defenders of classical Marx-ism both as a theoretical and a political tendency. He reacted positively to the Analytical Marxist engagement with egalitarian liberalism, and criticized Cohen less for the normative aspect of his work than for his interpretation of Marx's theory of history. Callinicos argues that the dichotomy suggested by Cohen between Marxism as an explanatory social science and Marxism as morality is a false one, and that there is no good reason why one should not, as it were, "have your cake and eat it" (Callinicos 2001, 170; 2006, 220). This argument is predicated upon Callinicos's rejection of the conflation of classical Marxism with the obstetric conception of politics. He points out that while there exist passages in Marx that can be interpreted along the lines suggested by Cohen, there are many others that need not be, and that, in fact, the "canonical" obstetric interpretation of Marx's theory of history was articulated not by Marx, or by any other classical Marxist, but by Cohen himself in his *Karl Marx's Theory of History* (Callinicos 2001, 174).

In Cohen's *Karl Marx's Theory of History*, historical materialism is characterized by two key propositions. First, "the forces of production tend to develop throughout history (the developmental thesis)," and second, "the nature of the production relations of a society is explained by the level of development of its productive forces (the primacy thesis)" (Cohen 2000a, 134). He deployed a functionalist model to account for historical transformations, which is underpinned in turn by his assumption that human agents find it rational to develop those forces of production over time. "Men are . . . somewhat rational. The historical situation of men is one of scarcity. Men possess intelligence of a kind and degree which enables them to improve their situation (Cohen 2000a, 152).

Consequently, Cohen committed himself to accepting what Wright et al. call a "transhistorical" model of human rationality (Wright et al. 1992, 24). This model not only bypassed Marx's search for specific dynamics of particular modes of production (Callinicos 2004, 83), but also, by suggesting that the transition from capitalism to socialism would occur with a functional necessity, and despite his own arguments to the contrary (Cohen 1988, 51–82), it sits uneasily with his political activism.

Callinicos's critique of Analytical Marxism includes a devastating counter to the inevitablist structure of Cohen's reinterpretation of historical materialism. Indeed, he suggests that this "is almost a *reductio*" of historical materialism (Callinicos 2004, 69). Nevertheless, it is precisely because Callinicos recognizes the need for an interpretation of historical materialism that has the power, as Marx intended it, to act as a guide to socialist practice that he has followed the Analytical Marxists' engagement with egalitarian liberalism: "my aim here is not to water down the Marxist critique, but rather to make it more effective" (Callinicos 2006, 221). Substantively, he suggests that Hegel's positive claims for the method of immanent critique are limited because it depends upon his "speculative conception of determinate negation." This implies the need for a more positive approach from which to conceive transcendence (Callinicos 2006, 1, 243, 296). It is from this perspective that he suggests a dialogue between Marxism and egalitarian liberalism, from which the former might appropriate the resources necessary to escape the limitations of Marx's incoherent rejection of morality, while the latter might recognize the revolutionary implications of their moral judgements (Callinicos 2006, 221).

Underpinning this dialogue is the shared concept of equality, which as Andrew Levine points out, is "the principle point of contact" between Rawlsian liberalism and Analytical Marxism (Levine 2003, 140). Callinicos argues that by focusing on the issue of "Equality of What?" (Sen 1982, 353–369), the debate about equality within normative theory has highlighted the way in which libertarians such as Nozick limit equality to equality of individual freedom, while egalitarian liberals have debated the relative merits of equality of resources, capabilities, and advantage, etc. as a reasonable alternative to libertarianism. Commenting on this debate in his *Resources of Critique* (2006), Callinicos suggests that in each case egalitarian liberalism is forced to engage with objective models of human well-being which "cuts across" the liberal claim that individuals must be allowed to "pursue their own conceptions of the good" (Callinicos 2006, 223–7). Although the concept of well-being is ultimately Aristotelian in derivation, Callinicos follows James Griffin's "padded out utilitarian" defense of its relevance to contemporary society. For his part, Griffin aims to avoid the usual utilitarian conflation of the good with what is desired through the notion of "informed desire"; by which he means those desires that individuals would have if "they appreciated the true nature of their objects" (Griffin 1986, 11–16; Callinicos 2006, 227–9). Such an objective model of the good is, of course, dependent upon "a causal theory of human nature" by which general needs can be established, and which might therefore act as a universal and transhistorical principle of justice (Callinicos 2000, 28). In his defense of classical revolutionary politics, Callinicos thus commits himself to an ethical theory which draws not only on Marx's critique of capitalism, but also on both Kantian discussions of equality and autonomy and consequentialist interpretations of the Aristotelian concept of well-being.

In so doing, Callinicos criticizes Marx's formal hostility to normative concepts by references to what he suggests is a tacit appeal in Marx to a "universal" and "transhistorical principle of justice" (Callinicos 2000, 28): the needs principle. According to this standard each person should receive a slice of the social product according to their needs. He argues that such a principle implies some objective model of human well-being against which existing societies can be measured (Callinicos 2000, p. 63). Indeed he has defended egalitarian liberals from a common Marxist criticism of their work—that they are unduly abstract—by reference to Adorno's analysis of the works of Beckett and Schoenberg. Like these, Callinicos claims that it is precisely because of their "stark abstraction" that egalitarian liberals expose "the cruelty and injustice of the late capitalist world" (Callinicos 2006, 222). Elsewhere he develops Noberto Bobbio's suggestion that "the criterion most frequently used to distinguish between the left and right is the attitude of real people in society to the ideal of equality." Extending this point, Callinicos, first, locates the emergence of the concept of equality in the epoch of the bourgeois revolutions, before, secondly, engaging with egalitarian liberal criticisms of modern society, and, finally, drawing what he suggests are the revolutionary implications of this body of work by explicating the links between existing patterns of inequality and the "economic structures of capitalism" (Callinicos 2000, 15–16).

Sartre's Revolutionary Ethics

Although Callinicos successfully points to the revolutionary political implications of egalitarian liberalism's moral claims, these claims, like those of the Frankfurt School, remain open to the critique that they are but one voice amongst many in the contemporary moral cacophony. Amongst postwar Marxists, it was perhaps Sartre who pushed hardest at the limits of this nihilist culture without successfully overcoming its limitations.

Whereas the socialists associated both with the Frankfurt School and Analytical Marxism moved toward moral theory as they distanced themselves from classical Marxism, Sartre was drawn toward Marx through an engagement with the contradictions of bourgeois morality generally and the issue of oppression more specifically (Birchall 2004, 80–84). Thus, in his study of anti-Semitism published just after the War, Sartre contrasted the struggle for individual authenticity with the racism of the anti-Semite, arguing that whereas the former involves the struggle for humanity, anti-Semitism involves "a fear of the human condition" (Sartre 1995, 54). Interestingly, in contrast to Adorno's characterization of modern man as essentially unfree, for Sartre anti-Semitism was freely chosen (Sartre 1995, 17). Indeed, in his existential ontology he "define[d] man through action" and consequently he embraced a "morality of action and commitment" (Sartre quoted in Mészáros 1979, 156). Mészáros wrote that for Sartre freedom was "the most fundamental dimension of human existence passionately striving to realise itself" (Mészáros 1979, 160–1, 14). Superficially this perspective placed his thought radically at odds with Marx's social theory. In *Being and Nothingness* (1943), he characterized Marx as the author of the "original dogma of the serious when he asserted the priority of the object over the subject" (Sartre 1958, 580). According to Sartre, to be "serious" involved, in Levy's words, attributing "more reality to the world than to human agency and which holds that the values and meanings to be found in the world are simply there, a part of the in-itself, independently of our choosing them" (Levy 2002, 120). Marxism, for the early Sartre, was therefore an example of "bad faith"—an attempt to disclaim responsibility for our actions (Levy 2002, 75, 121). By contrast with any such maneuver, Sartre insisted that because humans were inalienably free they were completely responsible for their behavior. This quasi-Kantian argument (Jopling 1992, 105; Mészáros 1979, 169) was rooted in his dualist ontology, according to which the objective world—being, the in-itself—can only be known from the perspective of a situated conscious human actor—the for-itself—who necessarily imposes value upon the world. So whereas Marx had claimed that being determines consciousness, Sartre countered that because consciousness imposes meaning on the world it determines being. More concretely, whatever our situation within the world, we are able to choose how to act in that situation. Against bad faith generally and Marxism more specifically, Sartre, in *Being and Nothingness*, asserted that we act "authentically" when we "willingly and deliberately assume the burden of choice" (Levy 2002, 66).

Although this argument flies in the face of crude interpretations of Marx's thought, given Lenin's claim that "dialectical idealism is closer to intelligent [dialectical] materialism than metaphysical, undeveloped, dead, crude, rigid materialism" we might expect that if the opportunity for a serious engagement with Marx arose, the affinity between existentialism and authentic Marxism might become apparent. This opportunity was afforded, first, through Sartre's wartime experience with the *Résistance* and subsequently through his engagement with socialist politics (Birchall 2004). Sartre had studied Marx before the War and was therefore in a position, once his experiences opened him up to it, to make sense of the gap between Marx's thought and Stalinism: "I had read and re-read Marx, but that is nothing: you really only begin to understand something in context within the world. To understand Marxism meant above all to understand the class struggle—and that I only understood after 1945" (Sartre quoted in Dobson 1993, 9). This was facilitated in post-War France which witnessed a general and "intense ferment in the world of ideas" with a specific revolutionary edge: Birchall comments that the subtitle of Camus' paper *Combat* summed up the general mood of the period: "Resistance to Revolution" (Birchall 2007, 194).

The shift in Sartre's thinking is apparent in his posthumously published *Notebooks for an Ethics* (1947). In these notebooks he aimed to realize the promise, famously made in the final sentence of *Being and Nothingness*, that he would devote a future work to the ethical implications of his ontology (Sartre 1958, 628). Against the implied Kantianism of his earlier work, in these notebooks he suggested that "ethics must be historical: it must find the universal in History and must grasp it in History" (Sartre 1992, 6). Interestingly, in a discussion of Trotsky's *Their Morals and Ours*, whilst praising the "power" of this "short book" Sartre criticized Trotsky for his use of "bourgeois criteria." Specifically, he asked what bourgeois democrat would demur from Trotsky's praise of an individual for his lifelong devotion to the cause of the "oppressed." According to Sartre, whereas Trotsky argued that Marxism held to the dialectical unity of means and ends in practice he did not provide an ethical justification for the class struggle as the means to the end of socialism, and by suggesting "an absolute end" as a goal for his activity he implicitly reverted back to a form of Kantianism (Sartre 1992, 159–161). This Kantianism was also apparent in the reality of Trotskyism in France in 1947. In a situation in which the PCF was hegemonic within the working class, and where, at a global level, the fundamental question posed of any political activist was in what relation did they stand vis-à-vis the conflict between Washington and Moscow, Sartre suggested that the "Trotskyist deprives himself of the possibility of preventing war or of attaching himself to one or other of the two camps. He refuses *realistic* politics in the name of an imperative that appears to have no connection with the facts." Somewhat ironically given the ontology of *Being and Nothingness*, he criticized this perspective for its "*idealis[m].*" And while this idealistic attitude may have been "commendable," because it was divorced from the real workers' movement it was a "*moral* and abstract" perspective (Sartre 1992, 163). Thus Sartre concluded that Trotsky, despite his valiant attempt to formulate a socialist ethics, had failed to move beyond a typically bourgeois moral standpoint.

Against Trotsky's abstract morality Sartre comments that Lenin had a greater intuitive sense of the dialectic of means and ends when, for instance in *Left-Wing Communism an Infantile Disorder*, he recognized (in a way which Sartre suggests is reminiscent of Spinoza's tool forging itself in forging) that in building the organizations necessary for the negative task of smashing capitalism the proletariat simultaneously re-forges itself as a positive alternative to capitalism: "the proletariat transforms itself into its own ends." Because, therefore, "the negativity becomes an internal positivity," Marxist ethics transcends the limitations of bourgeois moral theory in which the "abstract will towards positivity turns into absolute negativity." By contrast with bourgeois morality, as it organizes "*against* the oppressive class, the proletariat becomes conscious of being its own end for itself. It assimilates its cause to that of man" (Sartre 1992, 166–7).

If Sartre criticized Trotsky's idealism, elsewhere he argued that the Stalinists had reduced Marxism to a crude form of materialism. As opposed to his dismissive treatment of Marx in *Being and Nothingness*, just three years later he was to argue that Marx should be disassociated from those crude Marxists who failed to ground their strategic pronouncements in detailed studies of concrete historical processes but tended instead to impose abstract Platonic ideals onto reality. This is the thrust of his "Materialism and Revolution" (1946), in which he drew a distinction between Marx and his epigones: "Marx had a much deeper and richer conception of objectivity" than did the Stalinists. He claimed that his criticisms of Marxism in the essay were "not directed against" Marx, but against "Neo-Stalinist Marxism" (Sartre 1955, 188, 185).[1]

For Sartre, the materialist pretensions of Stalinist Marxism acted to negate its revolutionary intent as materialism tended toward "the elimination of human subjectivity" from history. This was important because if the revolutionary is defined by transcendence, her "going beyond the situation" in which she finds herself, then revolutionary politics demands that the revolutionary evolve a total comprehension of her "situation" within society. Consequently, "revolutionary thinking is thinking within a situation; it is the thinking of the oppressed in so far as they rebel together against oppression; it cannot be reconstructed from the outside." Revolutionary thought is therefore, first and foremost, thinking from the standpoint of revolutionary activists, and cannot be equated with Stalin's contemplative materialism (Sartre 1955, 188, 210–12, 237).

Sartre believed that his activist-centered approach to politics had much in common with Marx's attempt to overcome the opposition between materialism and idealism, but that, in reverting to simple materialism, intellectuals within the Communist Party had retreated back from Marx's revolutionary theoretical breakthrough to a variant of the position from which he had broken in his *Theses on Feuerbach* (Sartre 1955, 203). Against Stalinist materialism, Sartre insisted that "the superiority of revolutionary thinking consists in its first proclaiming its active nature" (Sartre 1955, 213). He argued that it was the role of the revolutionary to show that any "collective order" is not the necessary product of either God or History, that those values which suggest otherwise are not universal truths but in fact reflect and tend to preserve the status quo, and contra these values any society can be transcended: "The revolutionary philosopher has, above all, to explain the possibility

---

1. This section draws upon the discussion of Sartre's contribution to the Marxist theory of history in Blackledge 2006a, 154–161.

of this movement of transcendence" (Sartre 1955, 219–220). The idea of freedom was central to this project, because it was only through an act of free will that the revolutionary is able to "rise above" her situation (Sartre 1955, 220, 228–9).

Despite the tension between these arguments and the ontology of *Being and Nothingness*, Sartre's engagement with Marxism did not lead him to make a fundamental break with his earlier phenomenology. In part this was because, despite the distinction he drew between Marx and Stalinism, he continued to believe that Stalinism, through the medium of the PCF, was the real practical manifestation of both the workers' movement and of Marxism in modern France. If this position was made most explicit in *The Communists and Peace* (1952–54), it was implicit to his writings of the 1940s where, for instance, he considered it an adequate riposte to Henri Lefebvre's reassertion of Marx's claim to have transcended the opposition between materialism and idealism to refer negatively to the crude critique of idealism articulated by the PCF's Roger Garaudy (Sartre 1955, 203).

This theoretical ambiguity was highlighted by Marcuse in a discussion of "Materialism and Revolution." Marcuse claimed that Sartre's existentialism offered two "apparently contradictory aspects": on the one hand it suggested "the transcendental stabilization of human freedom in the face of actual enslavement," while, on the other hand, it posits a "revolutionary theory which implies the negation of this entire ideology" (Marcuse 1972, 162). Marcuse argued, contra Sartre's claim that "freedom is the very structure of human being and cannot be annihilated even by the most adverse conditions," that although this aspect of consciousness is "one of the preconditions for the possibility of freedom—it is not freedom itself" (Marcuse 1972, 162, 183). By conflating these two aspects of freedom, Marcuse noted that Sartre immunized his thought against the "tribulations to which man is subjected in the empirical reality" (Marcuse 1972, 176–7).

If Sartre's early conception of freedom is therefore "at most a freedom of consciousness, not the concrete freedom of a situated human being" (Anderson 1993, 24), in the wake of the publication of "Materialism and Revolution" he increasingly confronted the realities of the objective context of action. Marcuse commented that in the two decades following the publication of *Being and Nothingness*, in Sartre's "concept pure ontology and phenomenology recede before the invasion of real history" (Marcuse 1972, 189). This process was informed by Sartre's political engagement. Unfortunately, while the idea of revolution was very much alive in the immediate postwar period when millions of French workers were involved in a strike wave, once this movement subsided there was a gap of two decades before the events of 1968 once again revived hopes for revolution (Birchall 1974, 62–66). The difficulties faced by the French left became apparent when, in the late 1940s, Sartre attempted to build a socialist organization that was independent of but also able to bring together both Communists and social democrats, the *Rassemblement Démocratique Révolutionnaire* (RDR). Ian Birchall points out that this project failed, in part, because, in the absence of a revolutionary workers' movement, Sartre was unable to articulate a positive political goal that offered an alternative to both the East and the West in the Cold War: "The RDR was against Washington and Moscow, against the PCF and the SFIO; what was it for?" (Birchall 2004, 104). Sartre's radicalization through the 1940s subsequently broke against the problem of how to articulate a revolutionary political programme in the absence of a revolutionary movement.

In response to the failures both of Trotskyism and of his own revolutionary alternative to Communism and Social Democracy, in *The Communists and Peace* he attempted to justify a policy of fellow-travelling with the PCF. He did so by extending his criticism of contemporary Trotskysim for juxtaposing an "ideal" class struggle to the "real" struggles of the French masses (Sartre 1968, 105–6). Against this method, Sartre maintained that "I don't concern myself with what would be desirable nor with the ideal relationship which the party-in-itself sustains with the Eternal Proletariat; I seek to understand what is happening in France today before our very eyes" (Sartre 1968, 120). Concretely, he argued that the proletariat needed a party through which it could be constituted as a class: "it is the party which demands of the masses that they come together into a class under its direction" (Sartre 1968, 128–9). He went so far as to suggest that "without the CP the French proletariat would not have an empirical history" (Sartre 1968, 134). To criticize the bureaucratization of the CP, as did the Trotskyists, was therefore anachronistic: "Will you speak after that of 'communist betrayal?' Come off it! This 'bureaucratisation' is a necessity in the period of scientific management" (Sartre 1968, 213). The politics of the PCF merely reflected the real needs and aspirations of the French workers, rather than the needs and aspirations ascribed to them by Trotskyism.

While this argument aimed to inform realistic revolutionary politics by escaping from the unreal abstractions of orthodox Trotskyism, it ran the risk of providing an apology for the politics of the PCF. If both

the Trotskyists and the Stalinists could be faulted for the methodological sin of dissolving real history in a generalizing bath of "sulphuric
acid" (Sartre 1963, 44), at least the Stalinists could claim a degree
of real political support for their project whereas the Trotskyists were
confined to the sectarian wilderness. If this reality informed Sartre's
rapprochement with the PCF in the early 1950s, his argument that
revolutionary thought could advance only if it aimed at the scientific
analysis of the "projects" of free individuals to move from one concrete
situation to another meant that he could never wholly commit to the
Stalinist project (Sartre 1963, 91; 1955, 220; 1976, 36). In fact, the
anti-Stalinist political implications of his understanding of revolutionary
practice became apparent in the wake of the Soviet invasion of Hungary
in 1956. So whereas Sartre had responded to the Cold War in the early
1950s by moving to occupy a position of intellectual fellow-travelling
with the PCF, the news of Khrushchev's invasion of Hungary and of
the PCF's support for that policy forced him to rethink this stance.
The most important consequence of this rethink was his break with
the PCF, which he described as "monstrous" for its defence of Russia's
intervention. He described the Soviet attack on Hungary as a moment
when "the concrete struggle of the masses [was] drowned in blood in
the name of a pure abstraction" (Sartre 1969, 87, 104).

Partly as a response to these events, over the next decade Sartre
continued to deepen his conception of practice through an extension
of his understanding of the historical conditioning of freedom. While
this trajectory took him closer to Marx, there remained an important
tension between his thought and Marx's. For while he aimed to affirm
the "specificity of the historical event," he introduced two transhistorical
concepts into the heart of his theory of history—*scarcity* and *the practico-
inert*—which seemed to imply not simply that Trotskyism was an unreal
utopia but also that socialism itself was an unattainable goal. In his *Critique of Dialectical Reason* (1960) Sartre suggested that scarcity is the
"fundamental relation of our history." This starting point had dramatic
consequences for his Marxism. He argued that because scarcity "produces
everyone in a multiplicity as a mortal danger for the Other," its existence
implies that reciprocal relations of solidarity between individuals must,
of necessity, be transient (Sartre 1976, 735). Consequently, while social
atomization might be challenged through revolutionary struggles, the
"fused groups" thus created could hope only to reproduce themselves
for short periods of time before becoming "institutionalised" (Poster
1979, 81–111). Once institutionalized those groups would break down,

to be replaced by reemerging antagonistic relations between individuals. Sartre labelled this type of relationship "seriality," and suggested that this condition was the basis for the formation of states. Accordingly, he dismissed as "absurd" the Marxist concept of dictatorship by the proletariat, because the proletariat could not possibly rule collectively (Sartre 1976, 662). The pessimistic implications of this ahistorical conception of scarcity were reinforced by his concept of the practico-inert. By this notion, Sartre meant to explain the "equivalence between alienated praxis and worked inertia" (Sartre 1976, 67). The practico-inert, in Poster's words, is "matter which has absorbed the past actions and meanings of human beings" (Poster 1979, 60). It is therefore much more than the human created world around us: it is an alienated context, the product of our praxis, the "unintended consequences" of which constantly "thwart" and "confound" our intentions. Following the logic of these claims, in the unfinished and posthumously published second volume of the *Critique of Dialectical Reason*, he argued that Stalinism, or at least something very much like it, was "inevitable" in the conditions existent in postrevolutionary Russia (Aronson 1980, 280; McBride 1991, 8).

These conclusions suggest a degree of continuity across Sartre's *oeuvre* from *Being and Nothingness* to *Critique of Dialectical Reason*. In both cases, freedom appears as something to which humans are condemned, rather than something that we can fight for and deepen through struggle. Whilst Sartre rejected Stalinism after 1956, his claim that something like it was an inevitable consequence not simply of the Russian Revolution but of any revolution seemed to fly in the face of his own commitment to an anti-Stalinist socialism.

Nonetheless, elsewhere in the *Critique of Dialectical Reason* Sartre suggested a very different and much more historical conceptualization of scarcity. For instance, he wrote that "Man is violent . . . until the elimination of scarcity" (Sartre 1976, 736). Commenting on this ambiguity, Thomas Anderson points out that by thus historicizing the concept of scarcity, Sartre suggests a "much more hopeful reading of human history than most of the *Critique* offers" (Anderson 1993, 109). Interestingly, it appears that it is this optimistic element to his thought that underpinned his attempt to formulate a second ethics in the 1960s that went beyond what Sartre himself characterized as the abstract idealism of his earlier *Notebooks for an Ethics* (Anderson 1993, 111).

He signalled his belief that revolutionary practice demanded an ethical component in a brief comment on the question of ethics in the *Critique of Dialectical Reason*. Here Sartre argued that moral values are "bound up with the existence of the practico-inert field, in other words with hell as the negation of its negation." While such values are born as a reaction to exploitation and oppression, insofar as they are realized in some system or another they subsequently contribute to exploitation and oppression, even where such systems are "constructed by oppressed classes." It was Marxism's strength, he suggested, that it grasped this aspect of morality—the way in which it functioned as part of the ideological superstructure by helping reproduce systems of exploitation and oppression. However, Sartre suggested that while the base-superstructure metaphor thus contributed to the critique of existing moral categories, it unfortunately lent itself to a myopic rejection of morality tout court (Sartre 1976, 247–250; cf 132ff).

It was to help overcome this lacuna in Marxism that Sartre embarked upon his second ethics in the 1960s. In a lecture presented at the *Instituto Gramsci* in Rome in 1964, part of which was published as "Determinism and Freedom," and another series of lectures that were to be presented at Cornell University in 1965, but which were cancelled by Sartre in protest at America's involvement in the Vietnam War, Sartre suggested an ethics which went beyond the limitations both of Marxism and of his own earlier thought (Anderson 1993, Ch. 7; Stonet and Bowman 1991; 1986).

The Rome notes opened with the claim that "[t]he historical moment has come for socialism to rediscover its ethical structure, or rather, to unveil it" (Anderson 1993, 112; Stone and Bowman "Dialectical Ethics," 196). To this end, Sartre first rejected "all ethics by edict," examples of which included, or so he argued, the work both of Kant and Nietzsche (Stone and Bowman 1986, 197; Sartre 1974, 241). Such ethics, he suggested, represent the domination of the practico-inert, the alienated consequences of earlier human praxis, over new praxis. According to Stone and Bowman, by contrast with Marx, Sartre characterized history "not as class struggle . . . but as the struggle between praxis, which is always creative, and the practico-inert which always appears as repetition" (Stone and Bowman 1986, 200). Concretely, he argued that needs sit at the core of human praxis, for we must satisfy them if we are to survive. Consequently, praxis comes from "the future that has been projected by need" (Stone and Bowman 1986, 207). Nevertheless, so long as people are isolated and serialized they remain trapped within the alienated system of the practico-inert. Conversely, it is only when they come together in revolutionary groups that their praxes are capable of becoming autonomous, for it is only in such groups that they are able to "submit the world to the fulfilment of needs" (Sartre quoted in Stone and Bowman 1986, 210). Therefore, while Sartre followed Kant's insistence that for a person to become moral she must become an autonomous agent, against Kant he argued that we are able to do so only when united in groups acting in revolutionary praxis. As William McBride argues, Sartre's ethical goal in this essay involves a synthesis of "autonomy and need satisfaction"—the first reminiscent . . . of the Kantian ethic as well as of Sartre's career-long emphasis on freedom, the second crucial in the Marxist understanding of human beings as material entities" (McBride 1991, p. 179). This was not the only parallel with Marx, for Sartre also argued that because the bourgeoisie benefited from the capitalist system they fought to reproduce this alienated world: they are "products of the capitalist system, but they unceasingly uphold it and perpetuate it—not from inertia but by choice." By contrast, the proletariat, as a class, has at least two futures: passive object with the system or transcended subject. "One appears imperiously and restrictively within the system: find work, feed your family, save your pay, etc. The other is manifested as pure and total future through the rejection of the system and the production of a different system" (Sartre 1974, 251). In the words of Anderson, while the "oppressed proletariat also support that system in order to survive in it, . . . at the same time, and more deeply, they contest it" (Anderson 1993, 116). Specifically, insofar as proletarian praxis challenges capitalism it aims at autonomy in a way that is not true of the bourgeoisie. Following Marx, Sartre suggested that in struggling more or less consciously against capitalism the workers aim for a "pure future beyond the system" (Sartre 1974, 251). Through this example Sartre aimed to illuminate his attempted synthesis of moralism and materialism. While the materialists robbed humans of their conscious will, he had previously underestimated the material moment of human action: "the agent determines his behaviour as a synthetic unity" of external causes and internal "imperative or value" (Sartre 1974, 244). Thus Sartre aimed at developing Engels' claim that people make "history on the basis of prior circumstances" (Sartre 1974, 250).

The overall intent of these arguments was to outline a dialectical synthesis of materialism and idealism which deepened Sartre's attempted justification for the claim, made in "Materialism and Revolution" that "the declaration that 'we too are men' is at the bottom of any revolution" (Sartre 1955, 217, 219). So, whereas Sartre, in the 1940s, had insisted that to act authentically "involves at once recognizing the ultimate gratuitousness of all human projects and yet devoting oneself to one's freely-chosen project with full reflectiveness" (McBride 1991, 63), by the early 1960s he pointed toward a humanistic justification for taking the side of the proletariat in its struggle against capital. Unfortunately, as Stone and Bowman point out, Sartre's discussion of these issues is "disappointingly abstract" (Stone and Bowman 1986, 211). This is true most especially of his tentative statements on agency. Anderson notes that Sartre, by positing the future-oriented and needs-satisfying character of praxis, asked how one might judge the moral code of the existing society by the morality of a different future society (Anderson 1993, 113). And while, as we have seen, Sartre had, in 1947, pointed to an answer to this problem in his claim that proletarian praxis was simultaneously the means and ends of socialist morality, he did not explore how the proletariat might move from even a revolutionary state of dissatisfaction with the existing capitalist society toward the more positive goal of creating a future socialist society. For instance, whereas Sartre claimed that ethical systems represent "the totality of imperatives, values, and axiological judgements constituting the commonplaces of a class, a social milieu, or an entire society," he did not develop these themes and their implications therefore remain vague. Moreover, when Sartre moved to discuss the practical consequences of his theory, he reinforced the sense that he had come to an impasse. Thus in an interview given in 1969, he argued that whereas the working class needed a revolutionary party to fully realize the anti-capitalist potential of its practice which he suggested would proceed "more on the basis of 'alienation' than on 'needs,'" he confessed that he could not envisage "how the problems which confront any stabilised structure could be resolved" (Sartre 1970, 242, 245).

Conclusion

In the wake of their rejection of Lukács' immanent critique of capitalism from the standpoint of the proletariat, the leading members of the Frankfurt School were left, on the one hand, with a model of immanent critique which could not escape the parameters of bourgeois thought, such that, on the other hand, they were compelled to grasp at a starkly abstract conceptualization of the categorical imperative as the negative rudder by which they would aim at avoiding another Auschwitz, even if socialism itself was no longer feasible. This pessimism was reflected, despite other profound differences, in the conclusions drawn by the Analytical Marxists. Cohen, like Adorno before him, could not but oppose capitalism from a perspective informed by the stark abstractions of egalitarian liberalism, even if his criticisms of Marx's predictions for the working class meant that he believed there was little hope of an alternative to capitalism. Although Callinicos does not share this pessimistic analysis of the modern working class, because he agrees about the limits of immanent critique, he does see the sense in following Cohen through an engagement with egalitarian liberalism. The strengths of his endeavors are plain to see: first, it involves a powerful counter to Cohen's almost caricatured "obstetric" reworking of Marx's theory of history; second, it points to the anti-capitalist implications of much egalitarian liberalism; and, third, it is alive to the need for Marxists to be explicit and coherent about the moral aspect of their critique of capitalism. Unfortunately, if his deployment of Griffin's concept of "informed desire" is intended as a mechanism to escape the problem of moral relativism, it is not clear how it does not simply push this problem backward to the equally contested discourse on human nature. Interestingly, Callinicos suggests a solution to this problem by reference to Lukács' defense of the standpoint of the proletariat as the basis for grasping the truth of society as a totality (Callinicos 2006, 247–252). However, because he does not link the standpoint of workers' struggles to his preferred concept of human nature through a historically emergent conception of desire, his argument is open to precisely the charge it is intended to escape: that of relativism. In stark contrast to these various approaches, Sartre, at least in places, pointed toward an engagement with Lukács' Hegelian ethics through his analysis of the way workers' struggles simultaneously act as the means to and ends of the ethical alternative to capitalism. Nonetheless, despite these powerful insights, whereas Marx powerfully historicized the concept of scarcity (Harvey 1996, 139–149), Sartre never adequately disarticulated his understanding of this idea from its reification in liberal theory so as to provide a coherent historical and structural account of a long-term socialist alternative to seriality.

So, whereas Callinicos' perspective provides a basis for historical optimism it is less clear that he escapes the emotivist parameters of modern moral discourse, while Sartre points beyond this emotivist culture even if he was unable to provide a coherent model of a socialist alternative to it. If the problem for Marxism is to synthesize insights from both of these perspective, in the following chapter I argue that such a synthesis was suggested by Alasdair MacIntyre in the 1950s and 1960s.

5

Alasdair MacIntyre's Contribution to an Ethical Marxism

Two images have been with me throughout the writing of this essay.
Between them they seem to show the alternative paths for the intellectual. The one is of J. M. Keynes, the other of Leon Trotsky. Both
were obviously men of attractive personality and great natural gifts. The
one the intellectual guardian of the established order, providing new
policies and theories of manipulation to keep society in what he took
to be economic trim, and making a personal fortune in the process.
The other, outcast as a revolutionary from Russia both under the Tsar
and under Stalin, providing throughout his life a defence of human
activity, of the powers of conscious and rational human effort. I think
of them at the end, Keynes with his peerage, Trotsky with an icepick
in his skull. These are the twin lives between which intellectual choice
in our society lies.

—MacIntyre 2008f, 166

In his magnum opus, *After Virtue* (1981), Alasdair MacIntyre wrote
that a "provisional conclusion about the good life for man . . . is a
life spent seeking for the good life for man," and that we must aim to
construct "local forms of community within which civility and intellectual and moral life can be sustained through the new dark ages which
are already upon us" (MacIntyre 1985, 219, 263). If the "pessimism"
of this conclusion is, as MacIntyre rightly argues, "alien to the Marxist
tradition," why discuss his ideas in this book? The simple answer is that
prior to writing *After Virtue* MacIntyre made an important contribution
to Marxist ethical theory which pointed beyond the limitations of those
writers discussed in Chapter 4 of this study and toward a realization

of the renewal of Marxism begun by the writers discussed in Chapter 3. This chapter aims to rescue this contribution to Marxism[1] from the "enormous condescension of posterity."

As noted in the introduction, Althusser rejected the idea that Marxism was a form of humanism, and criticized the socialist humanists for contaminating Marxist materialism with bourgeois, idealist moral theory. The logic of the socialist humanist "turn to ethics" included, or so he insisted, a retreat from Marxism toward liberalism. If, as Perry Anderson has pointed out, there was evidence aplenty in the 1960s of ex-Marxists who had passed through the socialist humanist milieu before breaking with Marxism (Anderson 1980, 108), and while the more recent convergence between Analytical Marxism and egalitarian liberalism seems to confirm this prognosis, it is nonetheless far too simplistic to claim that this trajectory necessarily followed from the humanistic critique of Stalinism. Edward Thompson was also undoubtedly right when he wrote that, whatever else it was, "1956 was a year of hope" (Thompson 1978b, 304). We might add that this was a hope for, amongst other things, a renewal of Marxism. Against both too uncritical and too dismissive approaches to socialist humanism, I argue that the socialist humanism of the generation of 1956 is best understood, in Chris Harman's words, as an "intellectual staging post" (Harman 1983, 61): it marked a fork in the road through which a generation of radicals passed on their way to more coherent, if sometimes less savoury, political conclusions. If many took the road to Cold War liberalism, for a small minority of the left, socialist humanism pointed beyond the morass of Stalinism toward Marx's humanist critique of capitalism. In the decade after 1956, Alasdair MacIntyre took this turn and made an important contribution to the revitalization of Marxism. Extending the New Left's critique of Stalinism, he argued that Marx's concept of practice suggested a standpoint from which to overcome the division between science and morality characteristic of mechanical materialism. This contribution not only

---

1. It is a weakness of much of the academic literature on the British New Left that they tend to stress in a one-sided fashion the ways in which it acted as a conduit through which a number of important intellectuals bade their farewell to Marxism. (See, for instance, Chun 1993, 191; Kenny 1995, 200–206; Foote 1997, 296.) Interestingly, in their eagerness to portray the New Left as a way out of Marxism, all of these studies downplay Alasdair MacIntyre's important contribution to its debate on socialist humanism.

complements the renewal of Marxism associated with the revolutionary break with Second International Marxism discussed in Chapter 3, it also provides the most powerful materials from which to construct a counter to the claim that Marx was a nihilist whose rejection of moral discourse reflected his inadequate model of social transformation.

The New Left's Socialist Humanism

In 1956 four events came together to create a political space to the left of the two faces of the Cold War. First, in February, the Soviet leader Nikita Khrushchev made the so-called "Secret Speech" at the Twentieth Congress of the Soviet Communist Party in which he detailed some of the crimes committed by Stalin before his death in 1953. Second, over the summer and autumn of that year there occurred a rapid polarization and radicalization in Poland and Hungary which culminated, in October and November, in the emergence of a revolutionary workers' movement in the latter country: for the first time since the 1920s workers' councils emerged as a potential alternative form of rule to bureaucratic dictatorship (Eley 2002, 334; Anderson 1964, 66–72, Lomax 1976, and James 1992, 265; Fryer 1997; Harman 1988, 88–186). Third, in November Soviet troops intervened to crush the Hungarian Revolution. While, fourth, on the very same weekend, British and French troops in cooperation with Israel invaded Egypt with a view to seizing the Suez Canal.

As a response to these events, a New Left emerged out of dissident groups within the Communist Party, alongside student radicals, left labourites and members of the tiny revolutionary left (Sedgwick 1976, 143; Blackledge 2004b; 2006b; 2007a). While the New Left had neither fixed political positions, nor an agreed agenda, it did aim at making socialism a living force in Britain. New Leftists articulated this message in a number of journals, including *Universities and Left Review* edited by students in Oxford and *The Reasoner/New Reasoner* edited by the historians and (ex-)Communist activists Edward Thompson and John Saville in Yorkshire. Published initially as a dissident magazine within the Communist Party, and subsequently as an independent journal of socialist theory and practice after its editors refused the Party leadership's demand to stop publishing, *The Reasoner/New Reasoner* made its name as the foremost British voice of socialist humanism. It was in this journal that Edward Thompson opened an important debate on the socialist humanist alternative to Stalinism, through which he aimed to rescue Marxism from its mechanical bastardization at the hands of Stalin.

Thompson was perhaps the most prominent English representative of an international milieu which emerged in response to developments in Russia in the wake of Stalin's death. At its core, socialist humanism involved a call to "revise" Marxism-Leninism through a return to the humanist values of the young Marx (Satterwhite 1992, 3–11). Amongst the most influential of those to articulate a variant of this position was the Polish academic Leszek Kolakowski. In his "Responsibility and History" (1956–58), he suggested that moral crimes were moral crimes whether or not Stalin proclaimed that they were inevitable: "no one can be absolved of moral responsibility for supporting crime on the grounds that he was intellectually convinced of its inevitable victory" (Kolakowski 1971, 132). Developing this point, he argued that socialists must retain the concept of "moral responsibility," and further that they must liberate it from that interpretation of Marxism by which it had become "a tool of history," and which in turn was a "pretext for villainy" (Kolakowski 1971, 149, 157). By contrast with this Stalinist perversion of Marxism, Kolakowski insisted that "social involvement is moral involvement" and moral involvement is premised upon our "power to choose freely" (Kolakowski 1971, 159–160).

The first major theoretical contribution to the British New Left's engagement with Marx's humanism was Thompson's "Socialist Humanism: An Epistle to the Philistines" (1957). Published in the launch issue of *The New Reasoner* this essay was a brilliant and original contribution both to the analysis of Stalinism and to Marxist moral theory more generally. At the heart of Thompson's essay, as Kate Soper has argued, there was a reaffirmation of "moral autonomy and the powers of historical agency" within historical materialism (Soper 1990, 89). Stalinism, Thompson wrote, was an ideology whose characteristic procedure involved the imposition of abstract ideas upon reality. Moreover, this ideology represented the world-view of a "revolutionary elite which, within a particular historical context, degenerated into a bureaucracy." The Stalinist bureaucracy had acted to block the struggle for socialism, and thus the human revolt which underpinned the struggle for socialism had evolved to include a revolt against Stalinism. Negatively, this revolt was a revolt against ideology and inhumanity. Positively, it involved a "return to man," in the social sense understood by Marx. It was thus a socialist humanism: humanist, because it "places once again real men and women at the centre of socialist theory and aspiration"; socialist, because it "reaffirms the revolutionary perspectives of Communism" (Thompson 1957, 107–9).

Thompson's argument opened with the claim that one-quarter of the earth's surface was controlled by a new society, which, despite its many abhorrent features, represented a qualitative break with capitalism: "The instruments of production in the Soviet Union are socialised. The bureaucracy is not a class, but is parasitic upon that society. Despite its parasitism, the wave of human energy unleashed by the first socialist revolution has multiplied the wealth of society, and vastly enlarged the cultural horizons of the people" (Thompson 1957, 105, 138). In contrast to this characterization of the soviet system as at once socialist while yet morally unpalatable, elsewhere, he insisted that "the 'end' of Communism is not a 'political' end, but a human end" (Thompson 1957, 125). This formulation suggested a tremendous gap between the human ends of the Soviet experiment and the inhuman means through which these ends were, at least partially, being realized. Consequently, though Thompson implied that a plurality of means could be utilized to achieve the end of communism, he was aware that these means were not morally equivalent. In the Soviet case, he argued, the flaws of the Stalinist system could best be understood as a consequence of the Bolsheviks' inadequate model of Marxism. They had embraced a mechanical interpretation of Marx's base-superstructure metaphor according to which agency in the form of conscious activity is reduced to structure, only to reappear through the monolithic party which became the guardian of true socialist consciousness. The Bolsheviks subsequently, and "immorally," replaced the actions of real individuals with those of cardboard abstractions; abstractions which became "embodied in institutional form in the rigid forms of 'democratic centralism'" (Thompson 1957, 121). Thompson's moral critique of Stalinism therefore concluded not only with a call for a more flexible interpretation of Marx's theory of history, but also with a rejection of the Leninist form of political organization.

For all the undoubted power of Thompson's reaffirmation of moral agency at the core of the socialist project, his thesis was susceptible to a number of distinct, but related, criticisms. First, could a mechanical version of Marxism as embodied in a democratic centralist organization adequately explain the rise of Stalinism? Second, what, if any, were the relations between socialism and Communism in his model, and if the latter was a human "end," then what could be said of the abhorrent means through which the Stalinists had at least gone some way to achieving this end? Third, if the base-superstructure metaphor had contributed to the emergence of Stalinism, then was not Marxism damned by this failure? Finally, was not Thompson's rejection of the base-superstructure metaphor open to the criticism that it informed a political voluntarism, which rather than correcting the errors of mechanical fatalism merely inverted them.

Thompson's implicit answers to these questions suggested that he had not broken with as much of the common sense of his age as he imagined. Thus, traditional consequentialist ethics, which included for the little they were worth the ethical justifications of their actions deployed by the Stalinists, suggest that good ends could come from bad means; while the dominant liberal and Stalinist histories of the Soviet system were agreed on one point at least, that Leninism led to Stalinism. In tacitly accepting both of these positions, Thompson opened his moral critique of Stalinism to an immanent critique from those who saw a contradiction between his humanist claim that socialism represented the realization of historically (self) created human potentialities, and the suggestion that the Stalinist system might represent, in an albeit distorted form, a progressive break with capitalism. This is more or less the form of the critique formulated by Harry Hanson in the next issue of *The New Reasoner*.

Hanson argued that "Communism, in the modern world, is not the creed of the proletariat. First and foremost, it is a technique, operated by a revolutionary elite, for pushing forward the economic development of an underdeveloped country at the fastest possible rate . . . [which] is a very painful process" (Hanson 1957, 88). He insisted that, for all of Thompson's rhetoric and his indisputable honesty, his was an untenable critique of Stalinism, as it shared with the Stalinists, and Marxism more generally, a consequentialist moral framework which, despite fine talk of the interdependence of means and ends, tended to subordinate the former to the latter, thus offering an unsatisfactory basis from which to criticize Stalinist immorality. Though this negative criticism of Thompson was convincing, Hanson's own positive critique of Stalinism was less than satisfactory. He argued that there was no alternative to something like Stalinism in Russian conditions—forced industrialization could not succeed in a democracy—but that he could not embrace Stalin's methods. His morality was thus cut adrift from any practical political anchorage in contemporary conditions: it was abstract and utopian in the negative sense of those words (Hanson 1957; cf Kolakowski 1971, 161).

If Hanson criticized Thompson's moral consequentialism without providing a viable alternative to it, Charles Taylor argued that Thompson's attempt to retrieve a vibrant Marx from the Stalinist distortion of his theory elided over deep problems within Marxism itself. For Marx's understandable impatience with abstract moral criticisms of capitalism, and his juxtaposition of proletarian virtue to bourgeois morality, could easily slip into a justification for the type of revolutionary elitism that had morphed into Stalinism. The party, according to Taylor, could imagine itself as the embodiment of proletarian virtue against the real inadequacies of the proletariat (Taylor 1957a; 1957b).

Beyond these theoretical issues, Thompson's model of socialist agency also informed the New Left's political orientation. In his introduction to the New Left collection *Out of Apathy* (1960), he addressed what he believed was the key political issue of the day: mass apathy. Defining apathy as the search for "private solutions to public evils," he explained its contemporary prevalence, principally, as a function of a lack of real political alternatives for the electorate (Thompson 1960, 5, 8). Developing this theme, he suggested that a solution to the problem of apathy should begin by presenting the electorate with a real, viable political alternative to what in 1954 the *Economist* labelled "Butskellism": the consensus between the policies of the Labour and Tory chancellors Hugh Gaitskell and Rab Butler. Concretely, Thompson aimed to win over the Labour Party to the New Left's vision of socialism. Thus in 1960 he suggested that the transformation of Labour into a socialist party was not only possible, but also that this potential was being realized as he wrote: "Labour is ceasing to offer an alternative way of governing existing society, and is beginning to look for an alternative society" (Thompson 1960, 19). He argued that the New Left's role should be to encourage this process, while remaining aware that if his more optimistic perspective for the transformation of the Labour Party were frustrated "then new organisations will have to be created" (Thompson 1960, 29).

With hindsight the problems with this argument are manifest. Thompson, alongside the majority of the New Left, underestimated the power of the right wing within the Labour Party machine whilst simultaneously overestimating the contemporary British working class's

receptiveness to radical socialist ideas (Blackledge 2006b). These weaknesses meant that the New Left was ill-equipped to deal with defeat. And
when they experienced defeat at the 1961 Labour Party conference, the
New Left's response was abrupt demoralization (Williams 1979, 365).

In this context, the more pessimistic voices within the New Left
milieu became increasingly prominent. In contrast to the political optimism evident in Thompson's analysis of the prospects for the New
Left in the late 1950s, Stuart Hall had argued that there had been a
deeper structural transformation of the working class which undermined
old class loyalties and replaced them with a new sense of fragmented
lifestyles (Hall 1958, 27). Prefiguring much of what he was to write
on the pages of *Marxism Today* in the 1980s (Sparks 1996, 78), Hall
argued that there had been a "major shift in the patterns of social
life" in Britain, such that those factors which shaped the formation of
socialist class consciousness in the past were no longer dominant. By
contrast with nineteenth-century capitalism, changes in the economic
structure of society meant that the worker in the 1950s "knows himself
much more as consumer than as producer." Whereas in the nineteenth
century there had been a workers' way of life as collective producer,
this had recently been fragmented into many competing lifestyles. Hall
contended that these multifarious ways of life meant that while Britain
remained a capitalist country, the working class had become entrapped
in "new and more subtle forms of enslavement" (Hall 1958). Apathy,
or the privatization of wants, was seen to be endemic to this situation.

Hall's essay brought forth two powerful responses on the pages of
the next issue of *Universities and Left Review*. Raphael Samuel argued
that Hall had mythologized the conditions of the nineteenth-century
working class and so created a straw man against which he compared
the situation of modern workers: "the working-class community was
formed against pressures markedly similar to those upon which attention is focused today" (Samuel 1958, p. 44). If Samuel pointed out
that Hall's misunderstanding of the past informed his mistaken analysis
of the present, Thompson powerfully argued that Hall's model of the
present situation of workers was far too static. Anticipating criticisms he
would later make of Raymond Williams, Thompson insisted that cultures
were best understood not as static "ways of life," but rather as active
"ways of struggle" (Thompson 1959, 52; 1961; cf Hall 1959).

Despite the obvious power of these rebuttals, the point remained
that class struggle in 1950s and early 1960s Britain had not given rise

to a widespread socialist consciousness within the working class. For their part the second generation of the British New Left who gravitated around Perry Anderson in the wake of the collapse of the First New Left in 1961–62 explained this situation by reference to the corporatism of the British working class. Developing the more idealist themes of New Left thinking through a proto-Eurocommunist reading of Gramsci, Anderson argued that English working-class life was characterized by "an unmovable corporate class consciousness and almost no hegemonic ideology" (Anderson 1992, 33; Blackledge 2004a, Ch. 2).

If Thompson's comments on the weaknesses of Hall's static model of working-class consumerism undoubtedly scored a point, this criticism was, as Thompson made abundantly clear, doubly true of Anderson's thesis (Thompson 1978a). Nevertheless, though Thompson outlined powerful criticisms of first Hall's and then Anderson's impressionistic interpretations of contemporary working-class life, he nowhere offered a viable alternative to their account of the deep roots of contemporary apathy. Consequently, although their models of Britain's class structure were unable to point beyond the existing apathy to the widespread radicalization of the British working class that occurred in the late 1960s and early 1970s (Kelly 1988; Harman 1998), his account was unable to explain the apathy itself. An adequate socialist humanism was needed to address both of these phenomena.

Beyond Thompsonian Marxism: Alasdair MacIntyre's Marxist Ethics

MacIntyre's key contribution to the New Left debates of the 1950s, "Notes from the Moral Wilderness," was written as a critical defense of Thompson's general perspective and against the more or less explicit Kantianism of both Kolokowski and Hanson. MacIntyre suggested that "[t]he ex-Communist turned moral critic of Communism is often a figure of genuine pathos . . . They repudiate Stalinist crimes in the name of moral principle; but the fragility of their appeal to moral principles lies in the apparently arbitrary nature of that appeal" (MacIntyre 2008a, 46). This statement should not be read as implying that MacIntyre was in any way an apologist for Stalinism. He agreed with Kolakowski that Western supporters of Stalin abandoned socialism's moral core amidst a mechanical theory of historical progress. And as to Stalin's theory of history, although MacIntyre acknowledged that it was understood by many on both sides of the Cold War to be authentically Marxist, he could not accept that it could truthfully be read into either Marx's younger or his more mature writings (MacIntyre 2008a, p. 51). In place of the orthodox interpretation of historical materialism, MacIntyre insisted that if the moral core of Marxist political theory was to be retrieved and reconstructed from the fragments that Marx had written on the subject then it must be carried out alongside a similar reconstruction of Marx's theory of history.

MacIntyre argued that the Stalinists, through the medium of a teleological vision of historical progress, identified "what is morally right with what is actually going to be the outcome of historical develop-ment," such that the " 'ought' of principle is swallowed up in the 'is' of history" (MacIntyre 2008a, 47). It was not enough to add something like Kant's ethics to this existing Stalinist theory of historical develop-ment if one wished to reinsert moral principle into Marxism, for the Stalinist theory of history negated moral choice. Neither was it right to reject, as immoral, any historical event from some supposed higher standpoint, as "there is no set of common, public standards to which [one] can appeal." In fact, any such maneuver would tend to gravitate to an existing tradition of morality which, because these had generally evolved to serve some particular dominant class interests, would "play into the hands of the defenders of the established order" (MacIntyre 2008a, 50). For these reasons the arguments of apologists for both the East and the West in the Cold War were inadequate to their stated aims of providing a rationally justifiable guide to action. MacIntyre insisted that a "third moral position" was necessary, and believed that such a perspective could be constructed by "replacing a misconceived but prevalent view of what Marxism is by a more correct view" (MacIntyre 2008a, 52).

The Stalinist claim that the course of history was predictable, and that the victory of socialism was inevitable, rested, or so MacIntyre insisted, on a distortion of the role of the base-superstructure meta-phor in Marxist theory. What Marx suggested when he deployed this metaphor was neither a mechanical nor a causal relationship. Rather, he utilized Hegelian concepts to denote the process through which society's economic base provides "a framework within which super-structures arise, a set of relations around which the human relations can entwine themselves, a kernel of human relationships from which all else

grows." As against the claim that Marx believed that the reorganiza-
tion of political superstructures would follow necessarily upon changes
in economic bases, MacIntytre insisted that in "creating the basis, you
create the superstructure. These are not two activities but one." Thus,
Stalin's mechanical materialist model of historical progress, according
to which political developments followed automatically from economic
causes, could not be further from Marx's model. For, in Marx's view,
"the crucial character of the transition to socialism is not that it is a
change in the economic base but that it is a revolutionary change in
the relation of base to superstructure" (MacIntyre 2008a, 55).

The concrete form taken by the universal human essence of freedom
is always mediated by our practical engagement with nature to meet
our needs. It is because this practice has a historical dimension that
our essence tends to develop in a dialectical relationship with changes
in both our needs and the productivity of labour. And as labour is a
purposeful activity, these changes are registered through our ordering
of changing desires. Labour, therefore, necessarily has an ethical dimension, and because it acts as the key medium between the universal and
the specific in human history it provides a powerful basis from which
to criticize both abstract universalist and simple historicist ethics. What
universal moralities, which are abstracted from the concrete historical
form of production, and historicist moralities, which are abstracted
from the universal human essence, have in common is an inadequate,
one-sided, model of human history. This characteristic of these theories
undermines their competing claims to guide human practice. Neither
abstract universalism nor historical relativism are able to provide satisfactory accounts of practice as human behavior, and consequently both fail
as accounts of ethical life. It follows from this, as MacIntyre argued in
his critique of Stalinism and Stalin's liberal critics, that we should look
for an ethical "theory which treats what emerges in history as providing
us with a basis for our standards, without making the historical process
morally sovereign or its progress automatic" (MacIntyre 2008a, 57).

To this end MacIntyre claimed that Marxists should follow Aristotle
specifically, and the Greeks more generally, by linking ethics to human
desires: "we make both individual deeds and social practices intelligible
as human actions by showing how they connect with characteristically
human desires, needs and the like" (MacIntyre 2008a, 58). He thus
proposed to relate morality to needs and desires in a way that was radically at odds with Kant. For whereas, in Kant, "the 'ought' of morality

is utterly divorced from the 'is' of desire," MacIntyre insisted that to divorce ethics from activities which aim to satisfy needs and desires in this way "is to make it unintelligible as a form of human action" (MacIntyre 2008a, 58). MacIntyre therefore sought to relate morality to human desires and needs in a way that radically historicized human nature without losing sight of its biological basis (MacIntyre 2008a, 63). The power of Marx's theory of history, or so he claimed, was rooted in his historicization of the human essence: for he refused to follow either Hobbes into a melancholic model of human needs and desires, or Diderot into a utopian counterposition of the state of nature against contemporary social structures. Instead, Marx comprehended the limited historical truth of Hobbes's insight, but juxtaposed to it, not an abstract utopia, but the real collective movement of workers in struggle through which they realize that solidarity is a fundamental human desire.

Marx, according to MacIntyre, understood both the deep historical and sociological content to this question when he suggested that "the emergence of human nature is something to be comprehended only in terms of the history of class-struggle. Each age reveals a development of human potentiality which is specific to that form of social life and which is specifically limited by the class-structure of that society." In particular, under advanced capitalism "the growth of production makes it possible [for man] to reappropriate his own nature." This is true in two ways: first, the increasing productivity of labour produces the potential for us all to lead much richer lives, both morally and materially; while, second, capitalism creates an agency—the proletariat—whose struggles for freedom begin to embody a new democratic spirit, through which individuals come to understand both that their needs and desires can best be satisfied through collective channels, and that they do in fact need and desire solidarity (MacIntyre 2008a, p. 64). Consequently, the proletariat, created objectively by the development of the forces of production, could begin in its struggles against capital to match the potential inherent in its objective structure to create the conditions for the solution of the contemporary problems of morality: it begins to embody the practice which could overcome the "rift between our conception of morality and our conception of desire" (MacIntyre 2008a, p. 63). By acting in this way members of the proletariat come to realize that solidarity is not simply a useful means through which they struggle to meet their needs, but is in fact what they naturally desire (MacIntyre 2008a, 66). The political practice of socialists, who aim in the first instance to win majorities over to their view, is rooted in these new needs and desires. MacIntyre therefore understood the history of morality to be "the history of men ceasing to see moral rules as the repression of desire and as something that men have made and accepted for themselves." This process culminates in the socialist struggles of the proletariat against its alienation, and against reified ways of perceiving the world. Conversely, "both the autonomy of ethics and utilitarianism are aspects of the consciousness of capitalism; both are forms of alienation rather than moral guides" (MacIntyre 2008a, 68). So, once the political left has rid itself of both the myth of the inevitable triumph of socialism, and of the reification of socialism as some indefinite end which justifies any action taken in its name, then socialists will truly comprehend the interpenetration of means and ends through the history of class struggle, and will understand Marxist morality to be, as against the Stalinists, "an assertion of moral absolutes," and "as against the liberal critic of Stalinism it is an assertion of desire and history" (MacIntyre 2008a, 66).

In extending Thompson's humanist reinterpretation of Marx, MacIntyre suggested an absolute rupture with Stalinism that went beyond Thompson's position. For whereas Thompson insisted that "the October Revolution and its aftermath in East Europe and the Chinese Revolution have effected a fundamental revolution in property relations, and have vastly increased the real potential for intellectual, cultural and democratic advance within these societies," MacIntyre argued that Marx's model of socialism as proletarian self-emancipation "marks a decisive opposition to Fabianism and all other doctrines of 'socialism from above'" (Thompson 1958, 93; MacIntyre 2008i, 297). By rejecting the socialist credentials of the Stalinist states, MacIntyre consequently could not accept the assumption, common across the New Left, that peaceful transitions to socialism had been realized by Russian tanks in Eastern Europe. This argument saw him come under the influence of Trotskyism—as did, to a certain degree, Thompson, who, at the time, was influenced by Trotsky's characterization of the Soviet social formation as a degenerated workers' state; at least as this concept had been developed by Isaac Deutscher (Thompson 1957, 102). However, for MacIntyre the appeal of Trotskyism was much deeper, and in 1959 he joined the Trotskyist Socialist Labour League (SLL).

MacIntyre's response to Thompson's general dismissal of what he called the "cardboard abstractions" characteristic of democratic centralist organizations, not only involved a defence of Lenin's relevance to the modern world but was also part of an attempt to win the SLL over from the abstract and undemocratic perspectives of its leadership (Callaghan 1984, 78). In "Breaking the Chains of Reason," MacIntyre insisted that freedom could not be won by telling the masses to do what the elite desires it do, but only by helping "them move where they desire. The goal is not happiness, or satisfaction, but freedom. And freedom has to be both means and ends. The mechanical separation of means and ends is suitable enough for human manipulation, not human liberation" (MacIntyre 2008f, 163).

More concretely, in "Freedom and Revolution" he argued that "to assert oneself at the expense of the organisation in order to be free is to miss the point that only within *some* organisational form can human freedom be embodied." Moreover, because capitalism emasculates freedom, to be free means to involve oneself in some organization that challenges capitalist relations of production: "The topic of freedom is also the topic of revolution" (MacIntyre 2008e, 130). At this point, he introduced a crucial mediating clause into his argument: although working-class struggles against capital had spontaneously generated emancipatory movements, on their own these struggles had proved inadequate to the task of realizing the potential for socialism. Assuming, with Marx, that freedom cannot be handed to the working class from above, how then might it be realized from such unpromising material? MacIntyre answered that socialists must join revolutionary parties, whose goal should be to act in such a way as to aid the proletariat to achieve freedom: "the path to freedom must be by means of an organisation which is dedicated not to building freedom but to moving the working class to build it. The necessity for this is the necessity for a vanguard party" (MacIntyre 2008e, 132). MacIntyre suggested that socialists who rejected the project of building a party suffered from "the illusion that one can as an isolated individual escape from the moulding and the subtle enslavement of the status quo." He insisted that "the individual who tries most to live as an individual, to have a mind entirely of his own, will in fact make himself more and more likely to become in his thinking a passive reflection of the socially dominant ideas; while the individual who recognizes his dependence on others has taken a path which can lead to an authentic independence of mind." He concluded that given the existence of a capitalist state and the hegemony of reform-ist bureaucracies within the working class, "the road to socialism and democratic centralism are . . . inseparable" (MacIntyre 2008e, 133;

2008d). More specifically, MacIntyre argued, because it was at the "point of production" that people in "our society . . . begin to act and think for themselves," it was the duty of socialists to orientate their activity toward the workers' struggles. And because the New Left did not focus its activities on these struggles it tended to "dissipate socialist energy and lead nowhere" (MacIntyre 2008b, 89).

Unfortunately, the SLL's leadership embraced a dualistic and school-masterly approach to political practice. Against this method, MacIntyre concluded that "the only intellectual who can hope to aid the working class by theoretical work is the one who is willing to live in the working-class movement and learn from it, revising his concepts all the time in light of his and its experience" (MacIntyre 2008c, 100).

This model of socialist leadership was very different from the top-down imposition of "cardboard abstractions" which Thompson claimed was characteristic of democratic centralist organizations. MacIntyre's implication was that, in this regard at least, it was Thompson who was far too abstract. By generalizing from the undoubtedly inadequate leadership styles of the Communist Party and, as MacIntyre was becoming increasingly aware, the SLL, Thompson too quickly concluded that these were necessary features of democratic centralist organizations as such. Nevertheless, the fact that Thompson was right about the SLL, forced MacIntyre to engage with the degeneration of orthodox Trotskyism, and it was this process that brought him into the orbit of the *International Socialism* (*IS*) group.

International Socialism, led by Tony Cliff and Michael Kidron, was one of a number of groupings to emerge out of the postwar crisis and subsequent degeneration of "orthodox" Trotskyism. Trotsky predicted that the War would culminate with the collapse of Stalinism, the final crisis of capitalism, and a mushrooming of the revolutionary workers' movement. If orthodox Trotskyism maintained a dogmatic allegiance to these falsified perspectives, the more vibrant sections of international Trotskyism asked if Trotsky's predictions could be unpicked from the hard core of historical materialism (Hallas 1979, Ch. 5; Callinicos 1990, 25–6, 55–89). Importantly, a number of these groups deployed Marx's claim that socialism would come through the self-emancipation of the working-class as a tool from which to criticize Trotsky's suggestion that Russia had become a "degenerated workers' state." These heterodox Trotskyists criticized Trotsky's argument both for underestimating the resilience of the Soviet Union and for conflating workers' power with the juridical relations characteristic of a statist economy. Beyond making these points, the most coherent of these groupings came to argue that the Stalinist states were (like their Western competitors, though to a higher degree) forms of state capitalism, and that military competition between Eastern and Western state capitalist economies acted to stabilise the postwar world system by means of a permanent arms economy (Kidron 1961; 1968). Alongside *IS*, the American Johnson-Forrest Tendency led by Raya Dunayevskaya and CLR James, and the French journal *Socialisme ou Barbarie* edited by Cornelius Castoriadis, developed variations of the state capitalist analysis of the Soviet Union (Van der Linden 1997). Interestingly, by placing Marx's concept of proletarian self-emancipation at the center of their criticisms of orthodox Trotskyism, all three of these groups were drawn from their criticisms of orthodox Trotskyism to question the claim, repeated by Lenin in *What is to be Done?*, that socialism would have to be introduced to the working class from "without" (Cliff 2001a; 2001b; James 1992b; Dunayevskay 1988; Castoriadis 1988).

If this process led both the Johnson-Forrest Tendency and *Socialisme ou Barbarie* to reject Leninism, *IS*'s position was somewhat more nuanced. In two essays published at about the same time as MacIntyre's discussions of Lenin, Cliff argued that "for Marxists, in advanced industrial countries, Lenin's original [1902–1904—PB] position can serve much less as a guide than Rosa Luxemburg's, notwithstanding her overstatements on the question of spontaneity" (Cliff 2001a, 113). Nevertheless, he insisted that the need to build revolutionary parties followed from the "unevenness in the level of culture and consciousness of different sections and groups of workers." Against crude forms of Leninism, Cliff suggested that it was the function of a revolutionary socialist party to engage in workers' day-to-day struggles with the aim of generalizing the lessons of those struggles and so winning a majority of workers over to the idea of socialism (Cliff 2001b, 126). Extending this point, he insisted that revolutionary leadership should not be conflated with the top-down practice of either the Communist Party or the SLL.

> One can visualise three kinds of leadership that for lack of better names we shall call those of the teacher, the foreman and the companion in struggle. The first kind of leadership shown by small sects is "blackboard socialism" . . . in which didactic methods take the place of participation in struggle.

The second kind, with foreman-worker or officer-soldier relations, characterises all bureaucratic reformist and Stalinist parties: the leadership sits in a caucus and decides what they will tell the workers to do, without the workers actively participating. What characterises both these kinds of leadership is the fact that directives go only one way: the leaders conduct a monologue with the masses. The third kind of leadership is analogous to that between a strike committee and the workers on strike, or a shop steward and his mates. The revolutionary party must conduct a dialogue with the workers outside it. The party, in consequence, should not invent tactics out of thin air, but put as its first duty to learn from the experience of the mass movement and then generalise from it. (Cliff 2001b, 129)

Given the general convergence of this argument with those put forward in "Breaking the Chains of Reason" and "Freedom and Revolution" it is unsurprising that MacIntyre's break with the SLL coincided with his decision to join the IS. On the pages of IS, it was argued that the problem with both the Communist Party and orthodox Trotskyism was not their shared democratic centralist structure—in fact neither group was organized along lines that were very much like the Bolsheviks (Cliff 2001b, 122). Rather, their key failing was that neither had developed an adequate assessment of postwar realities. There were two distinct reasons for this: for the Communists it was because the party line originated in Moscow and was intended, primarily, to serve the foreign policy directions of the Soviet Union (Hallas 1985; cf Claudin 1975). Alternatively, orthodox Trotskyism's sectarianism was a product of its reification of Trotsky's falsified perspectives from 1938 (Hallas 1969).

Though MacIntyre agreed with the essence of this argument in 1960, within a decade he had left IS, arguing that Cliff had been mistaken to believe that Marxists could escape top-down models of leadership (MacIntyre 1973, 340–2; 1995, 99–101). Interestingly, the roots of this shift in MacIntyre's perspectives can be traced back to the period when he was co-editor of *International Socialism*. As I have shown elsewhere, in the early 1960s MacIntyre substantiated his claim that socialists should orientate toward workers' struggles at the point of production through the medium of an exchange on the pages of *International Socialism* with his co-editor Michael Kidron and the labour historian Henry Collins

(Blackledge 2007b; Collins 1961; Kidron 1961; MacIntyre 2008g). In his reply to Collins' defense of a militant form of left reformist practice, MacIntyre suggested that because it was at the point of production that workers' experience of alienation was most acute this locus was most likely to foster rebellion against capitalism and reformism. Whatever its merits, this argument did not fit the experience of British working-class struggle at the turn of the 1960s, which tended not to be explicitly against capitalism and reformism but more prosaically for higher wages.

If this fact informed MacIntyre's eventual break with Marxism (Blackledge 2005), Kidron's contribution to the debate with Collins illuminated two problems with MacIntyre's comments on the concrete shape of contemporary class struggles. Kidron suggested that even when workers' struggles at the point of production seemed limited to wage militancy, it was one-sided to dismiss them as mere sectional manifestations of a utilitarian logic. Because these struggles involved a shift in the locus of reformism from the leadership of the Labour and Trade Union movements down to the shop floor, and because they tacitly challenged the right of managers to manage, they created a space that could never be wholly incorporated into the capitalist worldview. Kidron argued that it was by engaging in and fostering these struggles that revolutionaries could make the first tentative steps toward winning a mass audience for their ideas.

However, the potential inherent in these struggles could only be realized if the apathy noted by Thompson was overcome. By the mid-1960s MacIntyre had come to the conclusion that this was unlikely as the Western ruling class had, through the use of Keynesian demand management techniques, overcome those tendencies toward economic crisis which might act to unify the various sectional struggles of the working class into a more general socialist movement (MacIntyre 2008i). Conversely, Kidron insisted that although MacIntyre was right about the contemporary political consequences of economic expansion, he had underestimated the contradictory nature of the postwar boom and thus overestimated the abilities of the Keynesians to manage the economy. Kidron predicted that the economy would eventually move into a general crisis, and at that moment the possibilities for socialist advance would expand dramatically (Kidron 1961; 1968). If this perspective allowed Kidron to recognize the partial truth expressed in Anderson's and Hall's pessimistic analyses of the situation of labour without succumbing to their pessimism, it also pointed beyond the limitations of Thompson's naive political voluntarism.

By rejecting these arguments, MacIntyre, first, disarticulated his interpretation of Marxism from an account of tendencies operating within society's base that were creating the conditions for generalized class struggle, while, second, dismissing the socialist potential of the more proximate aspects of the class struggle. He therefore unhinged his own conception of desire from one of the most important characteristics of the British working-class experience in the 1960s: the struggle for higher wages. If, in the short term, he attempted to square this circle by means of an increasingly voluntaristic political rhetoric, as the decade progressed he came to the conclusion that the fragmented desire of the sectional struggles of workers for higher wages bore little or no relation to his youthful conception of workers' solidarity as the practical manifestation of their ethical desire for socialism (Blackledge 2005). He thus concluded that the conception of desire he had begun to articulate in the 1950s was just as abstract as any Kantian "ought." Thus began his search for forms of agency that might do what he now believed the working class, as a class, could not: underpin a virtuous opposition to capitalism and the state through the practical embodiment of a social and ethical conception of informed desire (MacIntyre 1998; 2011).

Beyond Pessimism

If true, MacIntyre's mature analysis of working-class militancy would be damning of the Marxist project of socialism from below. By contrast, Kidron's approach both explained the widespread nature of contemporary apathy whilst pointing toward a deepening of the dialogical model of the relationship between socialist political leadership and the real movement of workers in struggle suggested by Cliff. Tacitly at least (Kidron was a political economist and did not express his arguments in these philosophical terms), desire in his model was the contested ideological terrain through which the class struggle was refracted. In this model workers' collective struggles within capitalism were best understood neither as a simple spontaneist socialist explosion against alienation as the youthful MacIntyre suggested, nor as an irredeemably corrupted expression of alienation as he later came to argue. Rather, Kidron suggested that these struggles create a terrain in which it is possible to start talking about and fighting for the transcendence of capitalism through a conception of informed desire.

Interestingly, on the few occasions where MacIntyre has alluded to the issue of class struggle in his mature work, the examples he cites are perhaps better understood in Kidron's terms rather than his own more pessimistic formulations.

If the conclusion of *After Virtue* recalls the pessimism of Adorno and Horkeimer's *Dialectic of Enlightenment* and Marcuse's *One-Dimensional Man*, MacIntyre's call to construct and defend local communities of resistance points beyond the absolute bleakness of their conclusions. Commenting on the difference between his post-Marxism and that of the Frankfurt School he has recently written:

> To Adorno my inclination is to respond by quoting Dr. Johnson's friend, Oliver Edwards, who said that he too had tried to be a philosopher, but "cheerfulness was always breaking in," perhaps a philistine, but also an appropriate response. What grounds then are there for cheerfulness in any social order such as our own about which some of Adorno's central claims still hold true? Those grounds derive surely from the continuing resistance to deprivations, frustrations, and evils that informs so many everyday lives in so many parts of the world, as well as much of the best thinking about those deprivations, frustrations, and evils, including Adorno's and Geuss's. To be good, to live rightly, and to think rightly, it may be said in reply to Adorno, is to be engaged in struggle and a perfected life is one perfected in key part in and through conflicts. (MacIntyre 2006b)

MacIntyre goes on to include amongst the struggles through which the good life might be lived the resistance mounted by some "rank and file trade union movements." On a similar note, in *Dependent Rational Animals* he suggests that nineteenth- and twentieth-century "Welsh mining communities" should be numbered amongst those local communities where practices survived in resistance to the market, and which were sustained by amongst other "virtues" those of "trade union struggle" (MacIntyre 1999, 143; 2006a, 180). Unfortunately, these comments on Welsh mining communities are tentative to say the least. In just a few lines he writes that these communities were informed by "the ethics of work at the coal face, by a passion for the goods of choral singing and of rugby football and by the virtues of trade union struggle against first coal-owners and then the state" (MacIntyre 1999, 143).

While empirical studies of the Welsh mining communities cohere with MacIntyre's general comments on these communities as important foci of virtuous resistance to capitalism, the actual content of this resistance tends to challenge the pessimism of his more general analysis of working-class life under capitalism. Thus, in their classic account of the South Wales Miners' Federation (SWMF), *The Fed* (1980), Hywel Francis and Dai Smith point to the intimate links between trade-union struggles and the sustenance of these local communities. They argue that it was "primarily" through the trade union that such "communities" were constructed from what would otherwise have been mere "aggregations of work-people." They claim that "the totality of commitment to the miners' cause was a form of class consciousness which translated itself into a community consciousness" (Francis & Smith 1980, 55). Their book perhaps also includes lessons for radicals active in the modern global economy. For they show how socialist activists within the SWMF led struggles which overcame divisions within a workforce that sprang not only from across the British Isles, but from many parts of Europe as well: Portuguese, Germans, French, Belgians, and Spaniards were brought together in the union alongside English and Welsh speakers with a multiplicity of local dialects and accents (Francis & Smith 1980, 11, 34). The role of these activists was central to the process whereby communities were formed out of these disparate materials. What is more, there was an important revolutionary voice within both the miners' union and the local communities. Thus Francis and Smith point out that South Wales was "one of the few areas in Britain where the Communist Party of Great Britain . . . had substantial roots" (Francis & Smith 1980, 28). And the Communist Party in South Wales drew on strong local traditions of Marxism and syndicalism which stressed, classically in the 1912 pamphlet *The Miners' Next Step*, that the official leadership of the trade unions could not be trusted and that control of the union should be kept as close as possible to the rank-and-file workers (Darlington 2008, 219–232). The militants organized in various revolutionary groups before 1920 and the Communist Party thereafter acted, despite the hegemony of (a left-wing variant of) Labourism in the valleys, in the words of one commentator as "a contagious minority which charged the south Wales labour movement with power, internationalism, and colour" (Williams 1998, 58). The class-struggle ideology of these activists meant that these communities were built in opposition to the ideology of "community" which the militants saw as a cover for the subordination of the workers' needs to the needs of capital. In place of the idea of community, the militants proposed workers' solidarity against both the coal owners and the state as their rallying cry (Francis & Smith 1980, 16). And far from being parochial localists, the militants fought for an internationalist interpretation of the concept of workers' solidarity. They acted, one might argue, as Gramscian organic intellectuals, drawing workers together through the ideology of "proletarian internationalism" in opposition to the attempts of the mine-owners and the state to divide and rule over them (Francis & Smith 1980, 31, 351, Ch. 10). If this ideology was framed by local and national class struggles, it was also fought for by organized militants of the Second and Third Internationals. And while there was no automatic relationship between the trade-union struggles in the pits and the formation of the broader mining communities, neither was there, as MacIntyre's mature critique of Marxism seems to suggest, an unbridgeable gulf between these two processes. The struggle at the coal-face was the backdrop against which local activists played leading roles educating and ordering desires to build the communities which MacIntyre claims fostered the virtues. Moreover, many of these communities paraded their internationalism by proudly embracing the pejorative name of "Little Moscow" which had been applied to them by a hostile press (Francis & Smith 1980, 53).

This example suggests that the trade-union struggles, which underpinned the formation of local communities of resistance to capitalism, also informed and reinforced within the Welsh working-class the emergence of an internationalist and socialist class consciousness which transcended the limits of sectional and utilitarian wage struggles. At a more general level John Kelly has suggested that this process was not peculiar to the South Wales valleys. Through the medium of an analysis of the history of the class struggle in Britain throughout the twentieth century he illuminates a relationship between industrial militancy and the emergence of socialist class-consciousness. At the close of a detailed comparison of the strike waves of 1915–22, 1968–74, and 1977–79 he concludes that, although there did not exist a simple causal relationship from economistic militancy to class consciousness, nonetheless there was some relationship between the former and the latter (Kelly 1988a, 127; 1988b; Robertson 1988).

These examples suggest that the self-activity of workers through industrial militancy informs a tendency, at specific moments of crisis, for more or less substantial minorities of workers to recognize their need for community. More concretely, this need tends to be felt as a desire for solidarity against the atomizing forces of capital and the state. And this desire suggests that Kidron was right in his rider to MacIntyre's youthful analysis of the social basis for socialism to point to a tension between wage militancy and bourgeois hegemony that could deepen in periods of (predictable) crisis. Moreover, the example of the South Wales coalfields suggests that one of the most important mediating factors between the day-to-day experience of class struggle and the formation of communities, which prized and reproduced the virtues of solidarity, were the leading local activists (many of whom considered themselves revolutionary socialists) organized together in political parties. MacIntyre's comments on Welsh mining communities of the nineteenth and twentieth centuries (implicitly) suggest that revolutionaries need not lead like managers, and that in fact they are successful (as revolutionaries) only when they do not. In stark contrast to Weber's conflation of leadership with domination and manipulation, these examples imply that an ability to give voice to real movements from below is the key to successful progressive revolutionary leadership (Barker et al. 2001, 7–8).

Conclusion

As I have argued elsewhere, it is minor intellectual tragedy that MacIntyre's contribution to the renewal of revolutionary Marxism in the 1950s and 1960s eventually floundered (Blackledge 2005). Nevertheless, in this period he showed, contra Althusser, that the logic of the humanist critique of Stalinism need not lead to a rejection of Marxism, but could grow into a reengagement with genuine revolutionary socialism. In so doing, he exploded the myth that Marx was a nihilist who had embraced a fatalist theory of historical progress. He also challenged the conflation of democratic centralism with the Stalinism of the Communist Party or the sectarianism of the SLL. Conversely, he suggested that the humanistic concept of practice was the basis for both Marx's scientific and ethical work, and that it was through the idea of practice that duty and desire might be synthesized. Far from negating the idea of socialism from below, Lenin's politics in fact flowed from this idea: socialist leaders could only be successful as socialist leaders by giving voice to and helping to shape the self-education of the desires of ordinary men and women as they struggled against one or other aspect of capitalist alienation. The key problem with both the Communist Party and the SLL was not the form of organization they (nominally) defended, but the abstract perspectives to which they clung. It was because these perspectives did not fit organically with the needs and desires of working-class struggle that these organizations necessarily degenerated into undemocratic caricatures of Leninism. In the 1950s and early 1960s MacIntyre argued that the solution to this problem was not to dismiss the idea of building a socialist party but to ensure that the politics of such an organization was rooted in the needs and desires of the real day-to-day struggles of the working class against capitalism. His mature rejection of Marxist politics flows from his belief that this project was no longer viable as working-class struggles had become trapped within the parameters of bourgeois instrumentalism. This argument highlights the fact that an attachment to Marxism continues to depend upon the wager that workers' struggles are able to generalize beyond their local parameters in a way that points toward a systemic alternative to the barbaric world in which we live, and that such a wager is also a call to action. If, more recently, he has mediated his claim that workers' collective struggles are necessarily trapped within the parameters of bourgeois instrumentalism by arguing that that some rank-and-file trade-union movements have helped reproduce virtues of solidarity against capitalism, this conclusion suggests that the prospects for socialism are not as bleak has he had once thought. To the extent that these struggles, despite their weaknesses, point to a political alternative to capitalism, I suggest MacIntyre's youthful politics retain their salience. In a context in which his youthful faith in the ability of Keynesians to manage away capitalism's crisis-prone tendencies has been long since falsified, we ought to orientate toward these struggles with the aim of strengthening them in the hope that they will realize their potential of overcoming the system of alienation.

Conclusion

From Ethics to Politics

History does nothing, it possesses *no* immense wealth, it wages no battles. It is man, real living man who does all that, who possesses and fights, "history" is not, as it were, a person apart, using man as a means to achieve *its own* aims; history is nothing but the activity of man pursuing his aims.

—Marx and Engels 1975, 93

Marx was not a nihilist but neither was he a moralist. In the *Theses on Feuerbach* he argued that because modern moral theory (idealism) was articulated from the standpoint of civil society it could not imagine, except as an impotent and abstract imperative, life beyond the egoistic individualism characteristic of that perspective. Consequently, like materialism, idealism was unable to grasp the full richness of "sensuous human activity, practice." Marx believed his "new materialism" was able to go beyond the limits of these outlooks to provide a justifiable basis for individual agency because it took as its standpoint the "social humanity" represented principally by collective working-class struggles against their alienation (Mészáros 1986, 105).

This historically constituted practice was the hinge linking Marx's politics, his scientific analysis of capitalism, his understanding of human history, and his ethics. The problem with so many who have found intractable contradictions in Marx's comments on ethics and morality is that their criticisms tend to rely on an assumption that he held to a positivist understanding of science, which necessarily excluded value judgements (Cohen 2000a, 46). This simply is not true. As we noted

195

above, Marx was no positivist, and neither, despite the clamour of many of his critics, was Engels (O'Neill 1996). John O'Neill suggests that the oft-repeated story of the degeneration of Marxism from an early and inspiring humanism into a dogmatic scientism (in which Engels plays the role of villain), involves a massive distortion not only of Engels' views on science but also of later, classical Marxist, contributions to the subject. In sharp contrast to positivism, because scientific socialism is self-consciously rooted in human practice, it necessarily includes an ethical dimension. O'Neill compares this humanist conception of scientific socialism with what he calls the "scientistic" Marxism of Althusser and others which "presents the case for socialism as relying on no ethical commitment" (O'Neill 1996, 64). If this "scientistic" framework is "indefensible," as we noted in Chapters 2 and 3, it also bears little relation to the approach articulated by Marx and later classical Marxists.

Classical Marxism not only presupposes the existence of workers' struggles against capitalism, it also includes a wager on the potential unification of these struggles into a movement capable of overthrowing capitalism. And because Marx challenges the reified separation between knowers and known, this wager involves the dialectical unity of an objective prediction and a subjective call to action: he would have agreed with James Connolly that "the only true prophets are they who carve out the future which they announce" (Connolly 1983, 263). This approach is ethical in a way that overcomes the impotence of moral advocacy because it is rooted in historically emergent needs and desires. At its core Marxism generalizes from the existence of the struggle over the working day to show that capitalism is in essence a system of alienation rather than, as is the dominant view of the modern market economy, the concrete embodiment of human freedom. Specifically, the mediation of consumption through the market necessarily obscures both the social aspect of our humanity and the productive essence of our relationship with nature. This mediation also underpins a form of individual rationality which, by its innocence of any conception of the common good, generates social irrationalities (Ramsay 1997, 14). These irrationalities—one thinks of the contemporary environmental and economic crises—are examples of broader social constraints which appear naturalized from the modern moral (liberal) standpoint of civil society. Workers' struggles not only point to a potential solution to these problems but this solution also has a universal significance (Harman 2009, part 4). For the workers' movement represents a historically specific attempt, however subdued at particular moments, to regain collective democratic control of our universal productive engagement with nature; and this is our best hope of avoiding economic and environmental catastrophe (Neale 2008). The contempt with which this idea is held even in leftist circles was recently highlighted by Slavoj Žižek, who rightly points to the paradox between the ease with which Fukuyama's "End of History" thesis has been ridiculed in intellectual circles, and the fact that "the majority today is Fukuyamaist" (Žižek 2009b, p. 53). What these tacit Fukuyamians miss is that socialism is liberalism's necessary "Other." For, regardless of liberalism's ignorance of its own historical specificity, modern liberal conceptions of freedom and equality emerged in the context of the growing commodification of labour, and socialism is the political expression of the rebellion of "free" wage labour against this dehumanizing process. Free wage labour therefore underpins both liberal ideas of freedom and equality and an immanent critique of the formalism of these concepts as they operate within liberal ideology. And by suggesting a concrete means of overcoming the limits of this ideology, workers' solidarity points to the possibility of reappropriating our (universal) nature as it is (historically) realized in the modern context.

Whereas the formal conceptions of freedom and equality, which sit at the core of modern liberalism, militate against it embracing a concept of human essence, the repressed nevertheless returns through a tendency to reduce essence to egoism: we can be anything we want to be so long as we are egoistic! If this contradiction reflects liberalism's weak conception of society, the existence of workers' struggles cannot satisfactorily be explained in terms of this model of egoistic behavior: for these struggles point to the irreducibly social, cultural (and consequently historical) nature of human individuality in a way that suggests a rich conception of human nature and freedom (see Rose et al. 1984; Lewontin & Levin 2007; Rose 1997). It is this historical model of human essence which is the concrete content of Marx's ethical critique of capitalism. Whatever else human nature includes, the solidarity expressed in workers' collective struggles illuminates the fact that community, in a much deeper sense than a mere collection of egoistic atoms, has become both a real human need and also a potentially realizable desire of specific historical agents. This standpoint also suggests that human freedom could be conceptualized not simply as (moral) freedom within the parameters of civil society but more profoundly as the need and desire to overcome that situation (Žižek 2001, 121).

So whilst modern moral theory, preeminently Kantianism, confronts egoism with an abstract call to duty against desire, workers' struggles in the nineteenth century began to act as a concrete and potentially systemic counter to alienated egoism, suggesting an immanent convergence of duty and desire through the idea of working-class solidarity as a bridge to socialism. This is the meaning of Marx's claim that communists do not preach morality because communism is the "real movement of things." Far from being an assertion either about the historical inevitability of communism or a sign (in a strong sense of flagrant contradiction) of Marxism's "ethical deficit," this argument merely illuminates the fundamental difference between his and Kant's standpoints. Whereas the conflict between desire and duty in Kant reflects the tragic nature of egoistic individualism, because Marx's vision of an alternative to civil society is rooted in the real movement of workers from below, it is concrete and explicitly interested. Marx's politics is best understood, therefore, not crudely in opposition to morality but as an expression of a practice that overcomes the opposition between materialism and idealism. Working-class solidarity points to a need and desire for association through which social duty, initially as class solidarity and eventually as human solidarity, can cease to be an abstract moral imperative. Because Marxist *revolutionary* politics is thus rooted in the emergence from below of new classes with new modes of association it cannot be reduced to the kind of top-down *insurrectionary* politics that merely reproduces traditional political hierarchies in a different form. If there is, nevertheless (in a weak sense), an "ethical deficit" in Marx, it is not the result of an attempt to sidestep the necessarily normative side of his thought, but rather a consequence of his failure to make explicit the difference between the concrete utopia which Ruth Lister argues is "fundamental" to his thought and which at least implicitly guides his practice, and the abstract models of the utopian socialists who preceded him (Levitas 1997, 79; 1990, 58).

Because working-class solidarity, which is the concrete form taken by freedom as self-determination, must be fought for as both the means to and ends of the struggle for socialism, the emergence of the working class as a potential agent of universal emancipation should not be confused with the claim that workers will inevitably succeed in this task. As we noted in Chapter 2, in contrast to positivistic readings of some of his work Marx does not make inevitabilist claims in his theory of history. Rather, he locates two broad historical tendencies: first, for the productivity of labour to increase as people collectively and purposefully strive to meet their needs; and, second, for conflicts to emerge over the control of the social surplus thereby created. Thus the famous lines of the *Communist Manifesto*:

> The history of all hitherto existing society is the history of class struggles. Freeman and slave, patrician and plebeian, lord and serf, guild-master and journeyman, in a word, oppressor and oppressed, stood in constant opposition to one another, carried on an uninterrupted, now hidden, now open fight, a fight that each time ended, either in a revolutionary reconstitution of society at large, or in the common ruin of the contending classes.

It is a caricature of this argument to suggest that Marx and Engels deny the existence of non-class forms of struggle. Their point is rather that the essence of each mode of production is characterized by a fundamental struggle over the control of our productive mediation with nature, which influences and shapes all other social conflicts (Barker and Dale 1999). Given the open-endedness of the paragraph quoted above, it is also absurd to claim that Marx and Engels held to a mechanical and reductive model of social change (Callinicos 1995, 160ff). Michael Löwy points out that "Marx characterised as 'reactionary' the 'so-called objective historiography' which treats 'historical relations separate from activity' and shows that, on the contrary, the conditions of activity 'are produced by this self-activity' " (Löwy 2003, 111). For Marx, the results of social struggles are determined only in the sense that the level of the development of the forces of production sets the parameters of possible outcomes, while the nature of the relations of production shape the characteristics of the key social actors involved. It should not need repeating that this is a negative claim, which in no way implies that the course taken by history is predictable in a strong Popperian sense.

Indeed, the whole thrust of Marx's detailed analysis of the capitalist division of labour is not intended as a basis for predicting the inevitable outcome of the struggle between the bourgeoisie and the proletariat. Rather it is an attempt to explore the contradiction between the fragmenting and unifying economic processes which operate on the working class with a view to intervening in that process to help transform the proletariat from a fragmented group into an independent political actor. What Marx does predict, and this is evident in the 1859 preface to *A Contribution to the Critique of Political Economy* (Marx 1970, 20), is that sooner or later workers' movements will be forced to confront the power of the state. It was to the practical consequences of both of these aspects of the class struggle that Lenin made such an important contribution to Marxism.

As Marxism points to the general shape and coloration of social struggles in specific modes of production without supplying "iron laws of history," which fatalistically predict the outcomes of these struggles, it is best understood as a theory of revolutionary practice. If Marxist science suggests the possibilities open at any specific conjuncture, it is real men and women who fight for and against these possibilities. In these struggles, the Marxist vision of the future is concrete because it extrapolates from the real social bonds that have emerged: first, throughout the history of capitalism as workers' and other groups have repeatedly come together in struggle to build collective organizations (unions, parties, etc.) to defend their interests within the system; and, second, from those collective organizations created by workers over the last century and a half which have gone further than this to pose more or less explicit challenges to the rule of capital. From the Paris Commune, through the factory councils in Europe after the First World War and the Russian and Western soviets of the same period, on to the workers' councils in Hungary, the shoras in Iran, the cordones in Chile, the inter-factory strike committee in Poland, and more recently to the local and communal organizations that were the backbone of the Bolivian insurrections of 2003 and 2005 (see Sturmthal 1964; Barker ed. 1987; Pannekoek 2003; Gluckstein 1985; Wrigley ed. 1993; Ginsberg 2008, 15–21; Gonzalez 2005; Hylton & Thomson 2005). To a greater or lesser degree, these organizational forms began to overcome the capitalist separation between politics and economics and to provide, at least in embryo, a concrete potential alternative to existing relations of production (Gluckstein 1985, 242).

Because the Marxist image of socialism is, in the first instance, generalized from these highpoints of workers' struggles against capitalism, it is best understood as a concrete utopia immanent to these struggles rather than a transcendent ideal that is to be handed to the working class from "without" (Collier 2009, 100–101). If this model illuminates the prefigurative dimension to Marxist politics, because, as Marx and (especially) Lenin and Gramsci insisted, solidarity is not an automatic fact but must be fought for both within the working class and against bourgeois states, Marxist politics cannot be reduced to this prefigurative aspect. Moreover, merely pointing to such historical examples does not overcome the problem of the ideal becoming reified into an abstract utopia. Marxists must also, as Gramsci insisted, be open to new forms of social organization that reflect the organic emergence of solidarity against egoism and be rooted in the more mundane day-to-day struggles of workers and other oppressed groups against capitalism. The creative problems of socialist leadership in these contexts include the need to recognize such organizations when they emerge and to marry the general goal of socialism with the more specific goals of these day-to-day struggles. If this latter task is easier when those struggles are at a higher pitch, that is, when workers can feel their collective strength against the power of capital, it is also necessary when these struggles are, as they have been in recent decades, at a lower ebb. Such situations generate a further problem: how to judge if the wager on the working class retains its validity. As we noted in the introduction, a key reason why the bulk of radical theorists have embraced the turn to ethics over recent decades is precisely because they no longer believe that this wager is defensible.

Revolutionary Politics

Beyond a context marked by defeats for the left and the rise of neo-liberalism (Eagleton 2003, 43; Callinicos 1989), the tendency amongst radical theorists to reject Marx's class-based politics has been informed by at least two arguments: first, Althusser's one-sided interpretation of Marx's focus on relations of production was generally accepted both to be true to Marx's materialism and inadequate to the task of understanding the purposeful (moral) aspect of human agency; while, second, it has been generally agreed that class divisions and patterns of struggle no longer fit with Marx's predictions (cf Wood 1986). Actually, these two arguments are two sides of the same caricature. As we have noted, Marx was keenly aware that although the modern division of labour created the working class as an objective entity, it simultaneously acted as a centrifugal force dividing it internally and thus mediating against it becoming a unified social actor. This was why he was, in Engels' words, "above all else a revolutionist": he was a political actor who built parties and other organizations. These organizations operated in the tension between the unifying and centrifugal forces that operate on the working class with the aim of winning a majority to the idea of socialism. Because this project is rooted in real collective struggles, which in turn reveal real collective interests, it cannot reasonably be classified as a moral perspective. Nonetheless, because it necessarily involves purposeful human agency, neither can it be dismissed as a variety of mechanical materialism. What is clear is that this model implies not only that the struggle will ebb and flow, but also that this movement will inform a similar ebb and flow in both class consciousness and in class awareness. Consequently, because they each follow from Marx's theory of revolution, Marxism cannot be falsified by simplistic empiricist reference to divisions in the working class, defeats of working-class struggles, or even a period of low level of such struggles. The real issue is to judge whether or not these tendencies add up to a qualitative break with the past.

To this end, we should begin by noting that no serious Marxist has suggested that there have been no important changes to the class structure attendant to the rise of neoliberal capitalism. The question is not have there been changes, but rather have these changes been so profound as to negate the Marxist wager on the proletariat (Callinicos 2008, 158ff). The beginning of an answer to Jerry Cohen's comments (repeated in the introduction) on this issue is relatively straightforward. As Alex Callinicos points out, Marx did not argue that the proletariat was the majority in society, and neither did he believe it to be the only exploited wealth producer nor the neediest group in society (Callinicos 2001, 175). More concretely, Hal Draper powerfully responded to an earlier elaboration of the myth, repeated by Simon Critchley, that Marx held to a model of increasing social simplification between the bourgeoisie and the proletariat. Draper shows, first, that the lines from the *Communist Manifesto*, which are generally deployed to support this interpretation of Marx, involve a slightly misleading translation of his claim that there would occur a decline of the *old* middle classes to a decline of the middle classes *per se*; second, Marx was in any case talking about a tendency which would be mediated by other countervailing tendencies; and, third, Marx explicitly criticized Ricardo for forgetting that the development of capitalism would include an expansion in the size of the new middle class (Draper 1978, 613–627). Nonetheless, while this is a powerful counter to the accusation that Marx embraced a simple model of social polarization, it does not answer the charge that the working class has ceased to be a revolutionary class, and that other more fragmented social actors have taken its place at the forefront of anti-capitalist struggles. As we shall see, while the trajectory of post-1968 politics would seem to leave no doubt that the time of classical Marxism has passed, this interpretation of events is much more problematic than a simplistic rehearsal of the facts of the emergence of "new social movements" and defeats suffered by the workers' movement in the 1970s and 1980s would suggest (Blackledge 2002).

In the first instance, it is important to recognize that the absolute number of wage-labourers has increased dramatically across the globe over the last few decades (Harman 2002, 38). This fact suggests that the problem with the working class is primarily political: how, if at all, is it possible for the "heterogeneous categories of wage-labourers . . . [to] succeed in forging themselves into a collective actor" (Callinicos 2003, 98). On this issue, Néstor Kohan argues that postmodernists have tended to confuse two quite distinct processes: the contingent defeats of the workers' movements in this period, which laid the ground for the subsequent fragmentation of new social movements, and the claim that "postmodern" society is necessarily characterized by such a fragmentation of movements. He argues that postmodernists have ascribed "a universal character to a social reality in which fragmentary political discourses prevail, social movements become dispersed, and the old subjectivities become schizophrenic. Yet in fact these are the characteristics of one specific stage in the course of capitalist development" (Kohan 2005, 141). Similarly, according to Alex Callinicos, the claim that class is fast losing its salience as contemporary society becomes increasingly individualized is a one-sided description of recent trends which is unable to make sense, for instance, of the upsurge in class agency in the French public sector strikes of 1995 (Callinicos 2007, 301–309).

In a more general survey of the literature on the situation of workers in a number of key sectors of the world economy—automobiles, construction, semiconductors, and finance—Bill Dunn provides evidence to support the argument that class continues to be relevant in the modern world. He points out that while certain social processes have increased the tendencies toward the fragmentation of the working class over the last two or three decades, other processes have tended in the opposite direction, and this situation sets part of the context for class struggles without mechanically determining the outcome of those struggles. In fact, against the simplistic view that changes in the labour process weakened the power of workers, he points out that, in the car industry for example, "decisive defeats for labour preceded substantial restructuring and may have provided the basis for it, rather than simply being its consequence" (Dunn 2004, 202).

Kevin Doogan has recently articulated parallel arguments which challenge the widespread belief that we have entered a period of "new capitalism" characterized by a shift to more flexible patterns of work which have fundamentally weakened the position of workers relative to capital. In opposition to this discourse, Doogan points to a mass of statistical evidence with which he highlights the contradiction between the reality that in the West "job stability has not declined" in the 1990s alongside a growing discourse, both within the academy and in popular culture, which emphasizes exactly the opposite: the growth of job insecurity. He suggests that this contradiction is rooted more in a fear of the consequences of job losses rather than of the likelihood of such losses, and this discourse has played an important role over the last couple of decades of ideologically disarming workers in face of a continued neoliberal assault. This attack on the working class has been aided by the deployment of the language of globalization to frighten workers into submission before any fightbacks break out (Doogan 2009). If this ideological process, especially prevalent in America, is evidence of what Ralph Miliband once called the "class struggle from above" (Miliband 1985, p. 16), the continued existence of a working class, albeit one that has experienced restructuring, and of class struggle, notwithstanding the fact that it is mainly (but not exclusively) from the top down, suggests that Marx isn't quite the dead dog he is often portrayed within the academy.

In an argument which dovetails these analyses of contemporary trends, Colin Barker and Gareth Dale have challenged the methodology of much of the literature on new social movements precisely because of its blindness to the continued salience of class. Just as Geoffrey de Ste. Croix criticized Weber's concept of status as "*static*," insisting that it "hardly helps us to *understand* or *explain* anything" (de Ste. Croix 1983, 90), Barker and Dale argue that Weber's approach informs a superficial and descriptive method which tends to overestimate the novelty of these movements when compared to traditional labour movements, and consequently to underestimate the relevance of Marxism to the modern world. In a defence of the power of Marx's claim that class struggle is the key defining characteristic of capitalism and not simply an episodic feature, Barker and Dale suggest that Marx supplies the materials necessary to analyze new social movements as concrete rebellions against alienation. Against the dominant trend within the literature on new social movements, Barker and Dale point out that because Marx refuses to reify the concepts of politics, economics, ideology, etc., he does not reduce the class struggle to economic struggles at the point of production. And since he analyzed capitalism as a system of alienation, he recognized that alongside the alienation of workers from the product of their labour and from control over the labour process, we are all alienated from the social bonds that constitute our humanity. One consequence of this system of alienation is that it tends to generate a plurality of different struggles against its dehumanizing effects. From this perspective, Barker and Dale argue not only that new social movements are not that new, but also that they do not reflect "a weakening of class struggle within capitalism, but an alteration of its form of appearance." This conclusion flows from their rejection of the all too typically caricatured juxtaposition of old labour movement struggles against new social movements. By contrast with this caricature, Barker and Dale argue that struggles against oppression are constitutive of labour movement struggles, and that such movements emerged in the 1960s and 1970s in conjunction with rising workers' struggles. And while these "were often seen . . . as critical" of existing labour movement practices, it was not until the downturn in workers' struggles from the late 1970s onward that these two forms of struggle came to be seen as "antithetical." Finally, although it was against the backdrop of workers' movement defeats that socialist politics lost its allure for many activists who were subsequently drawn toward identity politics, Barker and Dale conclude that this process could potentially be reversed with a shift in the fortunes of the labour movement. Given the continued salience of exploitation such a renewal in labour movement struggles is not only assured in the Gramscian sense that "one can 'scientifically' foresee only the struggle, but not the concrete moments of the struggle" (Gramsci 1971, 438) but could also potentially act as a unifying force for the myriad of others struggles against alienation (Barker & Dale 1998).

Draper's deconstruction of the myth that Marx believed that social divisions were becoming increasingly simplified, alongside Kohan's criticisms of the claim that the postmodern world is uniquely fragmented, Dunn's and Doogan's querying of the empirical evidence used to support the claim that the working class can no longer play a fundamental role in the anti-capitalist movement, Barker and Dale's reconceptualization of the relationship between new social movements and the traditional labour movement, and Callinicos's criticisms of the one-sidedness of the contemporary literature on the process of individualization, together suggest that a sophisticated interpretation of Marxism is well able to account for the defeats of the 1970s and 1980s and the emergence of "new social movements" whilst also pointing to the potential reemergence of workers' struggles against capital (Harman 1998). Indeed, Dunn comments that recent transformations in the situation of labour "do not require new conceptualisations nor do political strategies have to be re-imagined from scratch" (Dunn 2009, 225).

Although there is a good deal of truth to this statement, it is also the case that classical Marxism must be unpicked from the bastardized Stalinist caricature which has, regrettably, framed academic discussions of it for far too long. If the bulk of academic commentary on Marxism is not worth the paper it's written on, even sophisticated reinterpretations of Marx's ideas tend, for instance in the writing of Jerry Cohen, to reduce Marxism to a positivist account of historical progress. Given the hegemony of this reading of historical materialism within the academy, it is hardly surprising that Marxism is considered within these circles both politically and ethically deficient. And to the extent that the experience of Stalinism has had a devastating effect on Marxism as a living tradition within the labour movement, its academic image tends to reinforce a more widespread scepticism about its relevance to contemporary anti-capitalism.

As I have tried to show above, this is an unfortunate tendency which serves to obscure the real contribution that the classical Marxist tradition might make to contemporary radical politics. For Marx's vision of "socialism from below" acts not only as an immanent critique of the socialist pretensions of Stalinism (Thomas 1980, 122), it also points toward a democratic model of revolutionary-socialist political practice. When read alongside the argument that Leninism, properly disassociated from its Stalinist caricature, is a necessary complement to the idea that socialism can only come through the self-emancipation of the working class, classical Marxism points to an ethically compelling and politically powerful critique of capitalism. First, Marxism illuminates the necessary link between the contemporary emotivist culture and the standpoint of civil society. Second, it shows how workers' struggles against alienation provide the basis from which to understand the historical origins of this debased moral culture while simultaneously pointing beyond it. Third, in so doing, these struggles illuminate the historical character of our human essence. Fourth, they point to the specific way in which freedom as communal self-determination can be realized in the modern world. This, finally, is the concrete utopia through reference to which Marxist political practice generally, and individual participation in that practice, can be rationally justified.

By contrast with the liberal myth that we first judge a situation before acting upon it, Marx illuminated the assumed forms of practice that underpin this ideological way of conceiving the problem of choice and agency. Marx's self-awareness of the historical standpoint which informed his perspective on the world overcomes this contradiction. It does so by reinterpreting "is" and "ought" as two sides to the same practice. From this perspective the socialist movement justifies itself by providing an immanent critique of the unfreedoms of capitalist society while simultaneously pointing to a free, democratic alternative to that society.

Because the movements from below which give rise to this perspective necessarily emerge as uneven and fragmented struggles, they consequently generate "vanguards" of one form or another. In this context Marxist parties differentiate themselves from other groups by looking to the interests of the movement as a whole (Marx & Engels 1973, 79, 98) and aiming to create the conditions for their own dissolution through winning majorities to the revolutionary project of the real democratization of society. Against capital's alienated imperative to accumulate for accumulation's sake (Marx 1976, 742), Marxist politics is rooted in those struggles which, as Terry Eagleton suggests, prefigure the structures through which our emergent need and desire for solidarity might be realized (Eagleton 2009, 293). Amongst the revolutionary *phronesis* (practical wisdom) (Eagleton 2007a, 44) required of such activists is an ability to cast a critical eye at the dominant moral discourse, looking behind the superficial cacophony of opinion and, as we noted of Milton Fisk's discussion of debates on abortion rights (Fisk 1989, 278–281), examining the underlying (ideological) issues of control. In this context we should, as Geuss reminds us, always bear in mind Lenin's famous question "who whom?," or "who does what to whom for whose benefit," whenever we confront abstract moral debates (Geuss 2008, 23–30). In this way we can begin to move beyond a morality of subjective preferences to an objective ethics of the social struggle of the modern working-class to overcome the conditions of alienation.

This standpoint informs Lenin's famous argument that the model of revolutionary socialist practice "should not be the trade union secretary, but the tribune of the people" (Lenin 1961a, 423). This claim is best understood not as an abstract moral imperative, but rather as the elementary political corollary of the universal content of the modern class struggle for freedom against alienation. Beyond this day-to-day imperative, the longer-term political implication of Marx's ethics of liberation is the goal of freedom understood as the real democratization of society: workers' power.

References

Abendroth, Wolfgang. 1972. *A Short History of the European Working Class.* New York: Monthly Review Press.

Adler, Max. 1978. "The Relation of Marxism to Classical German Philosophy." In Tom Bottomore and Patrick Goode, eds., 1978, *Austro-Marxism.* Oxford: Oxford University Press: 62–68.

Adorno, Theodor. 1973. *Negative Dialectics.* New York: Continuum.

———. 1974. *Minima Moralia.* London: Verso.

———. 2000. *Problems of Moral Philosophy.* Cambridge: Polity.

———. 2006. *History and Freedom.* Cambridge: Polity.

———, and Horkheimer, Max. 1979. *Dialectics of Enlightenment.* London: Verso.

Anderson, Andy. 1964. *Hungary '56.* London: Solidarity.

Anderson, Kevin. 1995. *Lenin, Hegel and Western Marxism.* Chicago: University of Illinois Press.

———. 2007. "The Rediscovery and Persistence of the Dialectic in Philosophy and in World Politics." In Sebastian Budgen, et al. eds., *Lenin Reloaded: Towards a Politics of Truth.* London: Duke University Press: 120–147.

Anderson, Perry. 1974. *Passages from Antiquity to Feudalism.* London: Verso.

———. 1976. *Considerations on Western Marxism.* London: Verso.

———. 1980, *Arguments within English Marxism.* London: Verso.

———. 1983, *In the Tracks of Historical Materialism.* London: Verso.

———. 1992, *English Questions.* London: Verso.

Anderson, Thomas. 1993. *Sartre's Two Ethics.* Open Court: Chicago.

Anscombe, G. E. M. 1981 [1958]. "Modern Moral Philosophy." *The Collected Philosophical Papers of G. E. M. Anscombe, Vol. 3: Ethics, Religion and Politics.* Oxford: Basil Blackwell: 26–42.

Althusser, Louis. 1969. *For Marx.* London: New Left Books.

———. 1971. *Lenin and Philosophy and Other Essays.* London: New Left Books.

———. 1976. *Essays on Ideology.* London: New Left Books.

Arato, Andrew, and Paul Breines. 1979. *The Young Lukács and the Origins of Western Marxism.* London: Pluto.

Archibald, Peter. 1993. *Marx and the Missing Link: Human Nature*. Atlantic Highlands: Humanities Press.

Aristotle. 1976. *Ethics*. London: Penguin (Introduction by Jonathan Barnes, 1953 translation by J. A. K. Thomson, revised translation 1975 Hugh Tredennick).

Aronson, Ronald. 1980. *Jean Paul Sartre*, London: Verso.

———. 1987. *Sartre's Second Critique*. Chicago: University of Chicago Press.

Arthur, Chris. 1985. *The Dialectics of Labour*. Oxford: Blackwell.

Badiou, Alain. 2001. *Ethics*. London: Verso.

———. 2007. "One Divides Itself Into Two." In Sebastian Budgen, et al. eds., *Lenin Reloaded: Towards a Politics of Truth*. London: Duke University Press: 7–17.

Barker, Colin, ed. 1987. *Revolutionary Rehearsals*. London: Bookmarks.

———. 1991. "A Note on the Theory of the Capitalist State." In Simon Clarke, ed., *The State Debate*. London: MacMillan: 204–213.

———, and Gareth Dale. 1998. "Protest Waves in Western Europe: A Critique of 'New Social Movement' Theory." *Critical Sociology* 24: 1/2: 65–104.

Barker, Colin et al. 2001. "Leadership Matters." In Colin Barker, et al. eds., 2001, *Leadership and Social Movements*. Manchester: Manchester University Press: 1–23.

Baron, Samuel. 1963. *Plekhanov: The Father of Russian Marxism*. Stanford: Stanford University Press.

Bauer, Otto. 1978. "Marxism and Ethics." In Tom Bottomore and Patrick Goode, eds., 1978, *Austro-Marxism*. Oxford: Oxford University Press: 78–84.

Beamish, Rob. 1992. *Marx, Method, and the Division of Labour*. Chicago: University of Illinois Press.

Bentham, Jeremy. 1990. "Of the Principle of Utility." In Jonathan Glover, ed., 1990, *Utilitarianism and its Critics*. London: Macmillan: 9–14.

Berlin, Isaiah. 1997. "Two Concepts of Liberty." In *The Proper Study of Mankind*. London: Pimlico: 191–242, 204.

Berman, Marshall, 1999, *Adventures in Marxism*, London: Verso,

Bernstein, Eduard, 1988, "The Realistic and the Ideological Moments in Socialism." In Tudor and Tudor, eds., *Marxism and Social Democracy*: 229–243.

———. 1993. *The Preconditions of Socialism*. Cambridge: Cambridge University Press.

———. 1996. 'How is Scientific Socialism Possible?,' In Manfred Steger, ed., *Selected Writings of Eduard Bernstein*: 89–104.

Bernstein, Jay. 1991. "Rights, Revolution and Community." In Peter Osborne, ed., *Socialism and the Limits of Liberalism*. London: Verso, 91–119.

———. 2001. *Adorno: Disenchantment and Ethics*. Cambridge: Cambridge University Press.

Bertram, Christopher. 2008. "Analytical Marxism." In Jacques Bidet and Eustache Kouvelakis, eds., 2008, *Critical Companion to Contemporary Marxism.* Leiden: Brill: 123–141.

Birchall, Ian. 1974. *Workers against the Monolith.* London: Pluto.

———. 2004. *Sartre against Stalinism.* Oxford: Berghahn.

———. 2007. "Review of Michel Surya's *La Révolution rêvée.*" *Historical Materialism* Vol. 15, No. 2: 194–201.

Blackburn, Robin. 1977. "Marxism: Theory of Proletarian Revolution." In Robin Blackburn, ed., *Revolution and Class Struggle.* London: Fontana: 25–68.

Blackledge, Paul. 2002. "Marxist Interpretations of Thatcherism." In Mark Cowling and James Martin, eds., *The Eighteenth Brumaire: (Post) Modern Interpretations.* London: Pluto Press: 211–227.

———. 2004a. *Perry Anderson, Marxism and the New Left.* London: Merlin.

———. 2004b. "Reform, Revolution and the Question of Organisation in the First New Left." *Contemporary Politics* Vol. 10, No. 1: 21–36.

———. 2005. "Freedom, Desire and Revolution: Alasdair MacIntyre's Early Marxist Ethics." *History of Political Thought.* Vol. XXVI, No. 4: 696–720.

———. 2006a. *Reflection on the Marxist Theory of History.* Manchester: Manchester University Press.

———. 2006b. "The New Left's Renewal of Marxism." *International Socialism* 2/112: 125–153.

———. 2006c. "Leon Trotsky's Contribution to the Marxist Theory of History," *Studies in East European Thought.* Vol. 58, No. 1: 1–31.

———. 2006d. "Results and Prospects: Trotsky and his Critics." In Bill Dunn and Hugo Radice, eds., *Permanent Revolution—Results and Prospects 100 Years On.* London: Pluto Press: 48–60.

———. 2006e, "What was Done: Lenin Rediscovered." *International Socialism* 2/111: 111–126.

———. 2006f. "Karl Kautsky and Marxist Historiography." *Science and Society* Vol. 70 No. 3: 337–359.

———. 2007a. "Morality and Revolution: Ethical Debates in the British New Left." *Critique* Vol. 35, No. 2: 203–220.

———. 2007b. "Alasdair MacIntyre: Marxism and Politics." *Studies in Marxism* 11: 95–116.

———. 2008. "Alasdair MacIntyre's Contribution to Marxism: A Road not Taken." *Analyse and Kritik* Vol. 30, No. 1: 215–227.

———. 2009a. "Alasdair MacIntyre: Social Practices, Marxism and Ethical Anti-Capitalism." *Political Studies* Vol. 57, No. 4: 866–884.

———. 2009b. "History, Ethics and Politics." *Science and Society* Vol. 73, No. 1: 77–84.

———. 2010a. "Marxism and Anarchism." *International Socialism* 2/125: 53–80.

———. 2010b. "Marxism, Nihilism and the Problem of Ethical Politics Today." *Socialism and Democracy* Vol. 24, No. 2: 101–123.

Bloch, Ernst. 1986. *The Principle of Hope*, Vols. I-III. Oxford: Blackwell.

———. 1987. *Natural Law and Human Dignity*. MIT Press.

Bobbio Noberto. 1997. *Left and Right*. Cambridge: Polity.

Boggs, Carl. 1976. *Gramsci's Marxism*. London: Pluto.

Bourg, Julian. 2007. *From Revolution to Ethics*. Montreal: McGill-Queen's University Press.

Braverman, Harry. 1974. *Labour and Monopoly Capitalism*. New York: Monthly Review.

Brenkert, George. 1983. *Marx's Ethics of Freedom*, London: Routledge.

Brudney, Daniel. 1998. *Marx's Attempt to Leave Philosophy*. Cambridge: Harvard University Press.

Buck-Morss, Susan. 1977. *The Origin of Negative Dialectics*. London: Harvester.

Burns, Tony. 2001. "Karl Kautsky: Ethics and Marxism." In Lawrence Wilde, ed., 2001, *Marxism's Ethical Thinkers*. London: Palgrave: 15–50.

Callaghan, John. 1984. *British Trotskyism: Theory and Practice*. Oxford: Blackwell.

Callinicos, Alex. 1990. *Trotskyism*. Open University Press.

———. 1982. *Is There a Future for Marxism?*. London: Macmillan.

———. 1983. *Marxism and Philosophy*. Oxford: Oxford University Press.

———. 1989a. "Introduction: Analytical Marxism." In Alex Callinicos, ed., 1989, *Analytical Marxism*. Oxford: Oxford University Press: 1–16.

———. 1989b. "Bourgeois Revolutions and Historical Materialism." *International Socialism* 2/43: 113–171.

———. 1989c. *Against Postmodernism*. Cambridge: Polity.

———. 1995. *Theories and Narratives*. Cambridge: Polity.

———. 2000. *Equality*. Cambridge: Polity.

———. 2001. "Having Your Cake and Eating it." *Historical Materialism* 9: 169–195.

———. 2003. *An Anti-Capitalist Manifesto*. Cambridge: Polity.

———. 2004. *Making History*. Leiden: Brill.

———. Alex 2006. *Resources of Critique*. Cambridge: Polity.

———. 2007a. *Social Theory*. Cambridge: Polity.

———. 2007b. "Leninism in the Twenty-first Century?." In Sebastian Budgen, et al. eds., *Lenin Reloaded: Towards a Politics of Truth*. London: Duke University Press: 18–41.

———. 2008. "What does revolution mean in the twenty-first century?." In John Foran, *et al.* eds., 2008, *Revolution in the Making of the Modern World*. London: Routledge: 151–164.

Camfield, David. 2007. "The Multitude and the Kangaroo." *Historical Materialism* 15.2: 21–52.

Carling, Alan. 1995. "Rational Choice Marxism." In Carver and Thomas, eds., *Rational Choice Marxism*: 31–78.

Casarino, Cesare, and Antonio Negri. 2008. *In Praise of the Common*. Minneapolis: University of Minnesota Press.

Castoriadis, Cornelius. [1959] 1988. "Proletariat and Organisation, 1." In David Ames Curtis, 1988, *Cornelius Castoriadis: Political and Social Writings II*. Minneapolis: University of Minnesota Press: 193–222.

Chun, Lin. 1993. *The British New Left*. Edinburgh: Edinburgh University Press.

Claudin, Fernando. 1975. *The Communist Movement*. London: Penguin.

Cliff, Tony. 1974. *State Capitalism in Russia*. London: Pluto.

———. 1976. *Lenin: All Power to the Soviets*. London: Pluto.

———. 1986. *Lenin: Building the Party*. London: Bookmarks.

———. 1991. *Trotsky: Fighting the Rising Stalinist Bureaucracy*. London: Bookmarks.

———. 2001a. "Rosa Luxemburg." In Tony Cliff, *International Struggles and the Marxist Tradition*. London: Bookmarks: 59-116.

———. 2001b. "Trotsky on Substitutionism." In Tony Cliff, *International Struggles and the Marxist Tradition*. London: Bookmarks: 117–132.

Cohen, Marshall et al. 1980. "Introduction." In Marshall Cohen et al., eds., *Marx, Justice, History*. Princeton: Princeton University Press: vii–xiv.

Cohen, G. A. 1983. "Review of *Karl Marx* by Allen Wood." *Mind* Vol. 92, No. 367: 440–445.

———. 1988. *History, Labour and Freedom*. Oxford: Oxford University Press.

———. 1995. *Self-Ownership, Freedom and Equality*. Cambridge: Cambridge University Press.

———. 2000a. *Karl Marx's Theory of History: A Defence*. Oxford: Oxford University Press.

———. 2000b. *If You're an Egalitarian, How Come You're So Rich?*. Cambridge: Harvard University Pres.s

———. 2009. *Why Not Socialism?*. Princeton: Princeton University Press.

Colletti, Lucio. 1972. *From Rousseau to Lenin*. New York: Monthly Review.

Collier, Andrew. 1981. "Scientific Socialism and the Question of Socialist Values." In John Mepham and David-Hillel Ruben, eds., *Issues on Marxist Philosophy* Vol. IV, Brighton: Harvester.

Collier, Andrew. 1990. *Socialist Reasoning*. London: Pluto Press.

———. 1994. *Critical Realism*. London: Verso.

———. 2009. "Marx and Conservatisms." In Andrew Chitty and Martin McIvor eds., *Karl Marx and Contemporary Philosophy*. London: Palgrave.

Collins, Henry. 1961. "The Case for Left Reformism." *International Socialism* 1/6: 15–19.

———, and Chimon Abramsky. 1965. *Karl Marx and the British Labour Movement*. London, Macmillan.

Connolly, James. 1987. "The Reconquest of Ireland" In Michael O'Riordan ed. *James Connolly Collected Works*, Vol. I. Dublin: New Books: 185–280.

Critchley, Simon. 1999. *The Ethics of Deconstruction*. Edinburgh: Edinburgh University Press.

———. 2007. *Infinitely Demanding*. London: Verso.

Darlington, Ralph. 2008. *Syndicalism and the Transition to Communism*. Aldershot: Ashgate.

Delanty, Gerard. 2007. "T. W. Adorno as Critical Intellectual." In David Bates, ed., *Marxism, Intellectuals and Politics*. London: Palgrave: 119–134.

de Ste. Croix, Geoffrey. 1983. *Class Struggle in the Ancient Greek World*. London: Duckworth.

Deutscher, Isaac. 1959. *Trotsky: The Prophet Unarmed*. Oxford: Oxford University Press.

Dewey, John. 1973. "Means and Ends." Trotsky et al., *Their Morals and Ours*. New York: Pathfinder; 67–73.

Dobson, Andrew. 1993. *Jean-Paul Sartre and the Politics of Reason*. Cambridge: Cambridge University Press.

Doogan, Kevin. 2009. *New Capitalism?*. Cambridge: Polity.

Draper, Hal. 1977. *Karl Marx's Theory of Revolution Vol. I*. New York: Monthly Review Press.

———. 1978. *Karl Marx's Theory of Revolution*, Vol. II. New York: Monthly Review Press.

———. 1986. *Karl Marx's Theory of Revolution Vol. III*. New York: Monthly Review Press.

———. 1990. *Karl Marx's Theory of Revolution Vol. IV*. New York: Monthly Review Press.

———. 1992. "The Two Souls of Socialism." In Hal Draper, *Socialism from Below*. New Jersey: Humanities: 2–33.

Dunayevskaya, Raya. 1988. *Marxism and Freedom*. New York: Columbia University Press.

Dunn, Bill. 2004. *Global Restructuring and the Power of Labour*. London: Palgrav.e

———. 2009. *Global Political Economy*. London: Pluto.

Eagleton, Terry. 1990. *The Ideology of the Aesthetic*. Oxford: Blackwell.

———. 1993. "Deconstruction and Human Rights." In Barbara Johnson, ed., *Freedom and Interpretation*. New York: Basic Books: 121–145.

———. 1996. *The Illusions of Postmodernism*. Oxford: Blackwell.

———. 1997. *Marx and Freedom*. London: Pheonix.

———. 2003. *After Theory*. Harmondsworth: Penguin.

———. 2007a. "Lenin in the Postmodern Age." In Slavoj Žižek et al., eds., 2007, *Lenin Reloaded*. London: Duke University Press: 42–58.

———. 2007b. *The Meaning of Life*. Oxford: Oxford University Press.

———. 2009. *Trouble with Strangers*. Oxford: Blackwell.

Edgley, Roy 1990. "Marxism, Morality and Mr Lukes." In David McLellan and Sean Sayers, eds., 1990, *Socialism and Morality*. London: MacMillan, 21–41.

Eley, Geoff. 2002. *Forging Democracy.* Oxford: Oxford University Press.

Elliott, Gregory. 2006. *Althusser: The Detour of Theory.* Leiden: Brill.

Elster, John. 1985. *Making Sense of Marx.* Cambridge: Cambridge University Press.

Engels, Frederick 1947. *Anti-Dühring.* Moscow: Progress Publishers.

——. 1972. *The Origin of the Family, Private Property, and the State.* London: Lawrence and Wishart.

——. 1989a. "Letter to August Bebel" 18th–28th March 1875. In Karl Marx and Frederick Engels, *Collected Works.* London: Lawrence and Wishart. Vol. 24: 67–73.

——. 1989b. "A Fair Day's Wages for a Fair Day's Work." In Karl Marx and Frederick Engels, *Collected Works.* London: Lawrence and Wishart. Vol. 24: 376–378.

——. 1990. "A Critique of the Draft Social-Democratic Programme of 1891." In Karl Marx and Frederick Engels, *Collected Works.* London: Lawrence and Wishart. Vol. 27: 217–230.

——. 1991. "Letter to August Bebel" 12th October 1875. In Karl Marx and Frederick Engels, *Collected Works.* London: Lawrence and Wishart. Vol. 45: 97–98.

Erfurt Programme, The. 1891. At http://www.marxists.org/history/international/social-democracy/1891/erfurt-program.htm

Feenberg, Andrew. 1981. *Lukács, Marx and the Sources of Critical Theory.* Oxford: Rowman and Littlefield.

Ferguson, Iain. 2007. "Neoliberalism, Happiness and Wellbeing." *International Socialism* 2/117: 123–142.

Fisk, Milton. 1989. *The State as Justice.* Cambridge: Cambridge University Press.

Foote, Geoff. 1997. *The Labour Party's Political Thought.* London: MacMillan.

Foster, John Bellamy. 2000. *Marx's Ecology.* New York: Monthly Review.

Francis, Hywel, and David Smith. 1980. *The Fed.* London: Lawrence & Wishart.

Frank, Robert. 1999. *Luxury Fever.* New York: Free Press.

Fraser, Ian. 1998. *Hegel and Marx: The Concept of Need.* Edinburgh: Edinburgh University Press.

Fromm, Erich. 1966. *Marx's Concept of Man.* New York: Unger Press.

Fryer, Peter. 1997. *Hungarian Tragedy.* London: Index Books.

Gay, Peter. 1962. *The Dilemma of Democratic Socialism.* New York: Collier Books.

Geary, Dick. 1987. *Karl Kautsky.* Manchester: Manchester University Press.

Geoghegan, Vincent. 1996. *Ernst Bloch.* London: Routledge.

Geras, Norman. 1983. *Marx and Human Nature.* London: Verso.

——. 1989. "The Controversy about Marx and Justice." In Alex Callinicos, ed., *Marxist Theory.* Oxford: Oxford University Press: 211–267.

——. 1992. "Bringing Marx to Justice: An Addendum and Rejoinder." *New Left Review* 195: 37–68.

Geuss, Raymond. 2008. *Philosophy and Real Politics.* Princeton: Princeton University Press.

Gilbert, Alan. 1981. *Marx's Politics.* Oxford: Martin Robertson.

———. 1984. "Marx's Moral Realism: Eudaimonism and Moral Progress." In Terence Ball and James Farr, eds., *After Marx.* Cambridge: Cambridge University Press: 154–183.

Ginsberg, Paul. 2008. *Democracy.* London: Profile.

Gluckstein, Donny. 1985. *The Western Soviets.* London: Bookmarks.

Goldmann, Lucien. 1964. *The Hidden God.* London: Routledge.

———. 1971. *Immanuel Kant.* London: New Left Books.

———. 1968. "Is there a Marxist Sociology?." *International Socialism* 1/34: 13–21.

Gonzalez, Mike. 2005. "Bolivia: The Rising of the People." *International Socialism* 2: 108: 73–101.

———. 2009. "Chavez Ten Years On." *International Socialism* 2/121: 49–64.

Gotha Programme, The. 1875. At http://www.voiceoftheturtle.org/dictionary/dict_g1.php#gotha

Gould, Carol. 1978. *Marx's Social Ontology.* Cambridge: MIT Press.

Griffin, James. 1986. *Well-Being.* Oxford: Oxford University Press.

Gramsci, Antonio. 1971. *Selections from the Prison Notebooks.* London: Lawrence and Wishart.

———. 1977. *Selections from Political Writings 1910–1920.* London: Lawrence and Wishart.

———. 1978. *Selections from Political Writings 1921–1926.* London: Lawrence and Wishart.

———. 1995. *Further Selections from the Prison Notebooks.* Minneapolis: University of Minnesota Press.

———. 2007. *Prison Notebooks,* Vol. III. New York: Columbia University Press.

Grossman, Henryk. 1992. *The Law of Accumulation and the Breakdown of the Capitalist System.* London: Pluto.

Habermas, Jürgen. 1987. *The Philosophical Discourse of Modernity.* Cambridge: Polity.

Hall, Stuart. 1958. "A Sense of Classlessness." *Universities and Left Review* 5: 26–32.

———. 1959. "The Big Swipe." *Universities and Left Review* 7: 50–52.

Hallas, Duncan. 1969. "Building the Leadership." *International Socialism* 1/40: 25–32.

———. 1979. *Trotsky's Marxism.* London: Pluto.

———. 1985. *The Comintern.* London: Bookmarks.

Halliday, Fred. 1970. "Introduction," In Karl Korsch 1970, *Marxism and Philosophy.* London: New Left Books: 7–26.

Hallward, Peter. 2003. *Badiou: A Subject to Truth.* Minneapolis: University of Minnesota Press.

Hammer, Espen. 2006. *Adorno and the Political.* London: Routledge.

Hanson, Harry. 1957. "An Open Letter." *The New Reasoner* 2, Autumn 1957: 79–91.

Hardt, Michael, and Antonio Negri. 2000. *Empire*. Cambridge: Harvard University Press.

———. 2004. *Multitude*. New York: Penguin.

———. Negri 2009. *Commonwealth*. Cambridge: Harvard University Press.

Harman, Chris. 1983. "Philosophy and Revolution.," *International Socialism* 2/21: 58–87.

———. 1988. *Class Struggles in Eastern Europe 1945–1983*. London: Bookmarks.

———. 1996. "Party and Class." In Alex Callinicos, et al., *Party and Class*. London: Bookmarks: 15–37.

———. 1998. *The Fire Last Time: 1968 and After*. London: Bookmarks.

———. 2002. "The Workers of the World.," *International Socialism* 2/96: 1–45.

———. 2009. *Zombie Capitalism*. London: Bookmarks.

Harris, Nigel 1968. *Beliefs in Society*. London: Penguin.

———. 1978. *The Mandate of Heaven*. London: Quartet.

Harvey, David. 1996. *Justice, Nature and the Geography of Difference*. Oxford: Blackwell.

———. 2005. *A Brief History of Neoliberalism*. Oxford: Oxford University Press.

Haynes, Michael. 1985. *Nikolai Bukharin and the Transition from Capitalism to Socialism*. London: Croom Helm.

Hegel, Georg. 1952. *Philosophy of Right*. Oxford: Oxford University Press.

———. 1956. *The Philosophy of History*. New York: Dover.

———. 1969. *The Science of Logic*. London: Allen and Unwin.

Hilferding, Rudolph. 1981. *Finance Capital*. London: Routledge.

———. 1981. "The Materialist Conception of History." In Tom Bottomore, ed., *Modern Interpretations of Marx*. Oxford: Blackwell: 125–137.

Hobbes, Thomas. 1998. *Leviathan*. Oxford: Oxford University Press.

Hobsbawm, Eric. 1964. "Introduction" to Marx, Karl, *Pre-Capitalist Economic Formations*. London: Lawrence and Wishart.

———. 1986 "Revolution." In Roy Porter and Mikuláš Teich, eds., *Revolution in History*. Cambridge: Cambridge University Press: 5–46.

Holloway, John. 2002. *Change the World Without Taking Power*. London: Pluto.

———. 2010. *Crack Capitalism*. London: Pluto.

Hook, Sidney. 1962. *From Hegel to Marx*. Ann Arbor: University of Michigan Press.

Horkheimer, Max. 1972. *Critical Theory: Selected Essays*. New York: Herder and Herder.

Howard, M. C., and J. E. King. 1989. *A History of Marxist Economics: Vol. I*. Princeton: Princeton University Press.

Hudson, Wayne. 1982. *The Marxist Philosophy of Ernst Bloch*. London: Macmillan.

Hume, David. 1965. *A Treatise of Human Nature*. In Alasdair MacIntyre, ed., *Hume's Ethical Writings*. London: Macmillan: 177–252.

Hylton, Forrest, and Sinclair Thomson. 2005. "Chequered Rainbow.," *New Left Review* 2/35: 40–64.

Hyman, Richard. 1984. *Strikes.* London: Fontana.

James, Cyril Lionel Robert. 1992a. "Letter 10th February 1957." In Anna Grimshaw, Anna, 1992, ed., *The CLR James Reader.* Oxford: Blackwell: 264–268.

———. 1992b. "Lenin and the Vanguard Party." In Anna Grimshaw, ed., *The CLR James Reader.* Oxford: Blackwell: 327–330.

Jay, Martin. 1984. *Marxism and Totality.* Berkeley: University of California Press.

Jopling, David. 1992. "Sartre's Moral Psychology." In Christina Howells, ed., *The Cambridge Companion to Sartre.* Cambridge: Cambridge University Press: 103–139.

Kain, Philip. 1988. *Marx and Ethics.* Oxford: Oxford University Press.

Kamenka, Eugene. 1969. *Marxism and Ethics.* London: Macmillan.

Kant, Immanuel. 1933. *Critique of Pure Reason.* London: Macmillan.

———. 1948. *Groundwork of the Metaphysics of Morals.* London: Routledge.

Kautsky, Karl. 1892. *The Class Struggle.* At http://www.marxists.org/archive/kautsky/1892/erfurt/index.htm

———. 1918. *Ethics and the Materialist Conception of History.* Chicago: Charles H. Kerr.

———. 1953. *Foundations of Christianity.* S. A. Russell: New York.

———. 1983a. "The Revisionist Controversy." In Patrick Goode, ed., 1983, *Karl Kautsky: Selected Political Writings*: 15–31.

———. 1983b. "Life, Science and Ethics." In Patrick Goode, ed., *Karl Kautsky: Selected Political Writings*: 46–52.

Kellner, Douglas. 1984. *Herbert Marcuse and the Crisis of Marxism.* London: Macmillan.

Kelly, John. 1988. *Trade Unions and Socialist Politics.* London: Verso.

———. 1988. "Reply to Jack Robertson." *International Socialism* 2/42; 137–41.

Kenny, Mike. 1995. *The First New Left.* London: Lawrence and Wishart.

Kidron, Michael. 1961. "Reform and Revolution." *International Socialism* 1/7: 15–21.

———. 1968. *Western Capitalism Since the War.* London: Weidenfeld & Nicolson.

———. 1974. *Capitalism and Theory.* London: Pluto.

Knight, Kelvin. 2000. "The Ethical Post-Marxism of Alasdair MacIntyre." In Mark Cowling and Paul Reynolds, Paul, eds., *Marxism, the Millennium and Beyond.* London: Palgrave: 74–96.

———. 2007. *Aristotelian Philosophy.* Cambridge: Polity.

Kohan, Néstor. 2005. "Postmodernism, Commodity Fetishism and Hegemony." *International Socialism* 2/105: 139–158.

Kolakowski, Leszek. 1971. *Marxism and Beyond.* London: Paladin.

———. 1978. *Main Currents in Marxism* Vol. II. Oxford: Oxford University Press.

Korsch, Karl. 1970. *Marxism and Philosophy.* London: New Left Books.

Kouvelakis, Stathis. 2007. "Lenin as Reader of Hegel." In Sebastian Budgen, et al., eds., *Lenin Reloaded: Towards a Politics of Truth*. London: Duke University Press: 164–204.

Kuhn, Rick. 2007. *Henryk Grossman and the Recovery of Marxism*. Chicago: University of Illinois Press.

Kymlicka, Will. 2002. *Contemporary Political Philosophy*. Oxford: Oxford University Press.

Le Blanc, Paul. 1990. *Lenin and the Revolutionary Party*. New Jersey: Humanities Press.

Lebowitz, Michael. 2009. *Following Marx*. Leiden; Brill.

Lecourt, Dominique. 2001. *The Mediocracy*. London: Verso.

Lenin, Vladimir. 1960. "The Economic Content of Narodism." *Collected Works* Vol. 1: 333–507.

———. 1961a. "What is to be Done?" In Vladimir Lenin, 1961, *Collected Works*, Vol. 5: 517–520.

———. 1961b. "Philosophical Notebooks." *Collected Works* Vol. 38.

———. 1962. "The Reorganisation of the Party." In Vladimir Lenin, *Collected Works* Vol. 10: 29–39.

———. 1964. "Can the Bolsheviks Retain State Power?." *Collected Works* Vol. 26: 87–136.

———. 1968. "The State and Revolution." In Vladimir Lenin, *Selected Works*. Moscow: Progress Publishers: 263–348.

Levine, Andrew. 2003. *A Future for Marxism?*. London: Pluto.

Levitas, Ruth. 1990. *The Concept of Utopia*. Hemel Hempstead: Philip Allan.

Levitas, Ruth. 1997. "Educated Hope: Ernst Bloch on abstract and Concrete Utopia." In Jamie Daniel and Tom Moylan, 1997, *Not Yet*. London: Verso: 65–79.

Levy, Neil. 2002. *Sartre*. Oxford: Oneworld.

Lewontin, Richard, and Richard Levin. 2007. *Biology Under the Influence*. New York: Monthly Review.

Lih, Lars. 2006. *Lenin Rediscovered*. Leiden: Brill.

———. 2007. " 'Our Position in the Highest Degree Tragic': Bolshevik 'Euphoria' in 1920." In Mike Haynes and Jim Wolfreys, eds., *History and Revolution*. London: Verso: 118–137.

Lichtheim, George. 1964. *Marxism*. London: Routledge.

———. 1970. *A Short History of Socialism*. London: Weidenfeld and Nicolson.

Lomax, Bill. 1976. "The Workers Councils of Greater Budapest." *The Socialist Register* 1976: 89–110.

Löwy, Michael. 1979. *Georg Lukács—From Romanticism to Bolshevism*. London: New Left Books.

———. 1989. "The Poetry of the Past: Marx and the French Revolution." *New Left Review* 177: 111–124, p. 119.

———. 2003. *The Theory of Revolution in the Young Marx*. Leiden: Brill.

Lukács, Georg. 1970. *Lenin: A Study in the Unity of his Thought*. London: New Left Books.

———. 1971. *History and Class Consciousness*. London: Merlin Press.

———. 1972. *Political Writings 1919–1929*. London: New Left Books.

———. 1975. *The Young Hegel*. London: Merlin.

———. 1978. *The Ontology of Social Being: 2. Marx*. London: Merlin.

———. 1980a. *The Ontology of Social Being: 3. Labour*. London: Merlin.

———. 1980b. *The Destruction of Reason*. London: Merlin.

———. 2000. *Tailism and the Dialectic: A Defence of History and Class Consciousness*. London: Verso.

Lukes, Steven. 1973. *Individualism*. Oxford: Blackwell.

———. 1985. *Marxism and Morality*. Oxford: Oxford University Press.

Luxemburg, Rosa. 1986. *The Mass Strike*. London: Bookmarks.

———. 1989. *Reform or Revolution*. London: Bookmarks.

MacIntyre, Alasdair. 1964. "Against Utilitarianism.," In T. H. B. Hollins, ed., *Aims in Education*. Manchester: Manchester University Press: 1–23.

———. 1966. *A Short History of Ethics*. London: Routledg.e

———. 1970. *Marcuse*. London: Fontana.

———. 1971. "Hume on 'is' and 'ought.'" In Alasdair MacIntyre, *Against the Self Images of the Age*. London: Duckworth: 109–124.

———. 1972. "Justice: A New Theory and Some Old Questions." *Boston University Law Review* 52: 330–334.

———. 1973. "Ideology, Social Science and Revolution." *Comparative Politics* 5(2): 321–42.

———. 1979. "Review of John Dunn, *Western Political Theory in the Face of the Future*." *London Review of Books*, 20th December.

———. 1985. *After Virtue*. London: Duckworth.

———. 1988. *Whose Justice? Which Rationality?* London: Duckworth.

———. 1995. *Marxism and Christianity*. London: Duckworth.

———. 1998. "The Theses on Feuerbach: A Road Not Taken." In Kevin Knight, ed., 1998, *The MacIntyre Reader*. Cambridge: Polity: 223–234.

———. 1999. *Dependent Rational Animals*. London: Duckworth.

———. 2006a. *Ethics and Politics*. Cambridge: Cambridge University Press.

———. 2006b. "Outside Ethics." At http://ndpr.nd.edu/review.cfm?id = 5922.

———. 2008a. "Notes from the Moral Wilderness." In Paul Blackledgeand Neil Davidson, eds., *Alasdair MacIntyre's Engagement with Marxism: Essays and Articles 1953–1974*, Leiden: Brill: 45–68,

———. 2008b. "The 'New Left.'" In Paul Blackledge and Neil Davidson, eds., *Alasdair MacIntyre's Engagement with Marxism: Essays and Articles 1953–1974*. Leiden: Brill: 87–93.

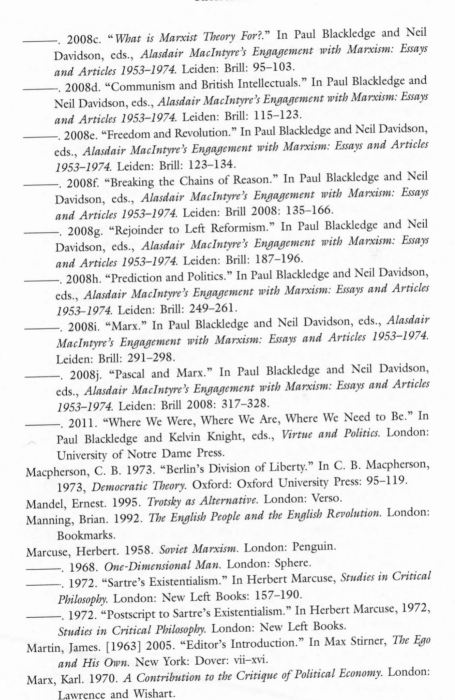

———. 2008c. "*What is Marxist Theory For?.*" In Paul Blackledge and Neil Davidson, eds., *Alasdair MacIntyre's Engagement with Marxism: Essays and Articles 1953–1974.* Leiden: Brill: 95–103.

———. 2008d. "Communism and British Intellectuals." In Paul Blackledge and Neil Davidson, eds., *Alasdair MacIntyre's Engagement with Marxism: Essays and Articles 1953–1974.* Leiden: Brill: 115–123.

———. 2008e. "Freedom and Revolution." In Paul Blackledge and Neil Davidson, eds., *Alasdair MacIntyre's Engagement with Marxism: Essays and Articles 1953–1974.* Leiden: Brill: 123–134.

———. 2008f. "Breaking the Chains of Reason." In Paul Blackledge and Neil Davidson, eds., *Alasdair MacIntyre's Engagement with Marxism: Essays and Articles 1953–1974.* Leiden: Brill 2008: 135–166.

———. 2008g. "Rejoinder to Left Reformism." In Paul Blackledge and Neil Davidson, eds., *Alasdair MacIntyre's Engagement with Marxism: Essays and Articles 1953–1974.* Leiden: Brill: 187–196.

———. 2008h. "Prediction and Politics." In Paul Blackledge and Neil Davidson, eds., *Alasdair MacIntyre's Engagement with Marxism: Essays and Articles 1953–1974.* Leiden: Brill: 249–261.

———. 2008i. "Marx." In Paul Blackledge and Neil Davidson, eds., *Alasdair MacIntyre's Engagement with Marxism: Essays and Articles 1953–1974.* Leiden: Brill: 291–298.

———. 2008j. "Pascal and Marx." In Paul Blackledge and Neil Davidson, eds., *Alasdair MacIntyre's Engagement with Marxism: Essays and Articles 1953–1974.* Leiden: Brill 2008: 317–328.

———. 2011. "Where We Were, Where We Are, Where We Need to Be." In Paul Blackledge and Kelvin Knight, eds., *Virtue and Politics.* London: University of Notre Dame Press.

Macpherson, C. B. 1973. "Berlin's Division of Liberty." In C. B. Macpherson, 1973, *Democratic Theory.* Oxford: Oxford University Press: 95–119.

Mandel, Ernest. 1995. *Trotsky as Alternative.* London: Verso.

Manning, Brian. 1992. *The English People and the English Revolution.* London: Bookmarks.

Marcuse, Herbert. 1958. *Soviet Marxism.* London: Penguin.

———. 1968. *One-Dimensional Man.* London: Sphere.

———. 1972. "Sartre's Existentialism." In Herbert Marcuse, *Studies in Critical Philosophy.* London: New Left Books: 157–190.

———. 1972. "Postscript to Sartre's Existentialism." In Herbert Marcuse, 1972, *Studies in Critical Philosophy.* London: New Left Books.

Martin, James. [1963] 2005. "Editor's Introduction." In Max Stirner, *The Ego and His Own.* New York: Dover: vii–xvi.

Marx, Karl. 1970. *A Contribution to the Critique of Political Economy.* London: Lawrence and Wishart.

———. 1972. *Theories of Surplus Value* Part III. London: Lawrence and Wishart.

———. 1973a. *Grundrisse*. London: Penguin.

———. 1973b. "Address of the Central Committee to the Communist League (March 1850)." In Karl Marx, 1973, *The Revolutions of 1848*. London: Penguin: 319–330.

———. 1973c. "The Eighteenth Brumaire of Louis Bonaparte." In Karl Marx, 1973, *Surveys from Exile*. London: Penguin: 143–249.

———. 1974a. "*Inaugural Address of the International Working Men's Association*." In Karl Marx, 1974, *The First International and After*. London: Penguin: 73–81.

———. 1974b. "Provisional Rules of the International." In Karl Marx,1974, *The First International and After*. London: Penguin: 82–84.

———. 1974c. "The Civil War in France." In Karl Marx, *The First International and After*. London: Penguin: 187–236. London: Penguin.

———. 1974d. "Critique of the Gotha Programme." In Karl Marx, *The First International and After*. London: Penguin: 339–359.

———. 1975a. "Critique of Hegel's Doctrine of the State." In Karl Marx, *Early Writings*. London: Penguin: 57–198.

———. 1975b. "On the Jewish Question." In Karl Marx, *Early Writings*. London: Penguin: 212–241.

———. 1975c. "Critique of Hegel's Philosophy of Right. Introduction." In Karl Marx, Karl, *Early Writings*. London: Penguin: 243–257.

———. 1975d. "Economic and Philosophical Manuscripts." In Karl Marx, *Early Writings*. London: Penguin: 279–400.

———. 1975e. "Critical Notes on the Article 'The King of Prussia and Social Reform by a Prussian.'" In Karl Marx 1975, *Early Writings*. London: Penguin: 401–420.

———. 1975f. "Theses on Feuerbach." In Karl Marx, *Early Writings*,.London: Penguin: 421–423.

———. 1975g. "Debates on Freedom of the Press." In Karl Marx and Frederick Engels, *Collected Works*. London: Lawrence and Wishart, Vol. 1: 132–181.

———. 1975h. "Letters from the Deutsch-Franzosische Jarbucher." In Karl Marx and Frederick Engels, *Collected Works*. London: Lawrence and Wishart, Vol. 3: 133–145.

———. 1976. *Capital*, Vol. I. London: Penguin.

———. 1978. *Capital*, Vol. II. London: Penguin.

———. 1979. "Russian Policy Against Turkey—Chartism." In Karl Marx and Frederick Engels, *Collected Works*. London: Lawrence and Wishart, Vol. 12: 163–173.

———. 1981. *Capital*, Vol. 3. London: Penguin.

———. 1984a. "The Poverty of Philosophy." In Karl Marx and Frederick Engels, *Collected Works*. London: Lawrence and Wishart, Vol. 6: 105–212.

———. 1984b. "Wages." In Karl Marx and Frederick Engels, *Collected Works*. London: Lawrence and Wishart, Vol. 6: 415–437.

———. 1985. "On Proudhon." In Karl Marx and Frederick Engels, *Collected Works*. London: Lawrence and Wishart, Vol. 20: 26–33.

———. 1987. "Letter to Engels, August 24th 1867." In Karl Marx and Frederick Engels, *Collected Works*. London: Lawrence and Wishart, Vol. 42: 407–8.

———. 1988a. "Economic Manuscripts of 1861–1863." In Karl Marx and Frederick Engels, *Collected Works*. London: Lawrence and Wishart, Vol. 30.

———. 1988b. "Letter to Schweitzer." In Karl Marx and Frederick Engels, *Collected Works*. London: Lawrence and Wishart, Vol. 43: 132–135.

———. 1994. "Economic Manuscripts of 1861–1864." In Karl Marx and Frederick Engels, *Collected Works*. London: Lawrence and Wishart, Vol. 34.

Marx, Karl, and Frederick Engels. 1973. "The Manifesto of the Communist Party." In Karl Marx, 1973, *The Revolutions of 1848*. London: Penguin: 62–98.

———. 1975. "The Holy Family." In Karl Marx and Frederick Engels, *Collected Works*., London: Lawrence and Wishart, Vol. 4: 3–211.

———. 1976. *The German Ideology*. In Karl Marxand Frederick Engels, Frederick, *Collected Works*. London: Lawrence and Wishart, Vol. 5: 20–539.

———. 1984. "Letter From the Brussels Communist Correspondence Committee to G. A. Kottgen," In Karl Marx and Frederick Engels, *Collected Works*. London: Lawrence and Wishart, Vol. 6: 54–56.

Mayer, Tom. 1994. *Analytical Marxism*. London: Sage.

McBride, William. 1991. *Sartre's Political Theory*. Bloomington: Indiana University.

McCarney, Joseph. 1990. *Social Theory and the Crisis of Marxism*. London: Verso.

———. 2000. *Hegel on History*. London: Routledge.

McLellan, David 1969. *The Young Hegelians and Karl Marx*. London: Macmillan.

———. 1979. *Marxism After Marx*. London: Macmillan.

McMylor, Peter. 1994.*Alasdair MacIntyre*. London: Routledge.

McNally, David. 1993. *Against the Market*. London: Verso.

———. 1997. "Language, History and Class Struggle." In Ellen Meiksins Wood and John Bellamy Foster, eds., 1997, *In Defence of History*. New York: Monthly Review Press.

Meikle, Scott. 1985. *Essentialism in the Thought of Karl Marx*. La Salle: Open Court.

Merquior, Jose. 1986. *Western Marxism*. London: Paladin.

Mészáros, István. 1975. *Marx's Theory of Alienation*. London: Merlin.

———. 1979. *The Work of Sartre*. London: Harvester.

———. 1986. "Marxism and Human Rights." In István Mészáros, 1986, *Philosophy, Ideology and Social Science*. Brighton: Wheatsheaf: 196–211.

———. 1995. *Beyond Capital*. London: Merlin.

———. 2005. *The Power of Ideology*. London: Zed.

Miéville, China. 2005. *Between Equal Rights*. London: Pluto.

Miliband, Ralph. 1985. "The New Revisionism in Britain." *New Left Review* 150, 5–26.

Mill, John Stuart. 1991. "Utilitarianism." In John Stuart Mill, 1991, *On Liberty and Other Essays*. Oxford: Oxford University Press.

Miller, Richard.1984. *Analyzing Marx*. Princeton: Princeton University Press.

———. 1989. "Marx and Aristotle." In Alex Callinicos, ed., *Marxist Theory*. 175–210.

Molyneux, John. 1986. *Marxism and the Party*. London: Bookmarks.

Moore, G. E. "Criticism of Mill's 'Proof.' " In Glover, *Utilitarianism and its Critics*. 21–23.

Murray, Patrick. 1988. *Marx's Theory of Scientific Knowledge*. New Jersey: Humanities Press.

Neale, Jonathan. 2008. *Stop Global Warming: Change the World*. London: Bookmarks.

Nederman, Cary. 2008. "Men at Work." *Analyse and Kritik*, Vol. 30, No. 1, 2008: 17–31.

Negri, Antonio. 2008. *Reflections on Empire*. Cambridge: Polity.

Nettl, Peter. 1969. *Rosa Luxemburg*. Oxford: Oxford University Press.

Nietzsche, Friedrich. 1967. *The Will to Power*, New York: Vintage Books.

Norman, Richard. 1983. *The Moral Philosophers*. Oxford: Oxford University Press.

Ollman, Bertell. 1976. *Alienation*. Cambridge: Cambridge University Press.

O'Neill, John. 1996. "Engels without Dogmatism." In Chris Arthur, Chris, ed., 1996, *Engels Today.*, London: Macmillan: 47–66.

Pannekoek, Anton. 1977. "The Theory of Capitalist Collapse." *Capital and Class* 1: 59–81.

———. 2003. *Workers' Councils*. Edinburgh: AK Press.

Parkinson, G. H. R. 1977. *Georg Lukács*. London: Routledge.

Pashukanis, Evgeny. 1978. *Law and Marxism*. London: Ink Links.

Paton, H. J. 1948. "Analysis of the Argument." In Kant, Immanuel, 1948, *Groundwork of the Metaphysics of Morals*. *London: Routledge*: 2–33,.

Peffer, Rodney. 1990. *Marxism, Morality and Social Justice*. Princeton: Princeton University Press.

Perkins, Stephen. 1993. *Marxism and the Proletariat*. London: Pluto.

Plekhanov, Georgi. 1976. *Selected Philosophical Works* Vol. II. Moscow: Progress Publishers.

Poster, Mark. 1975. *Existential Marxism in Postwar France*. Princeton, NJ: Princeton University Press.

Poster, Mark. 1979. *Sartre's Marxism*. London: Pluto.

Ramsay, Maureen. 1997. *What's Wrong with Liberalism?*. London: Leicester University Press.

Ratansi, Ali. 1982. *Marx and the Division of Labour*. London: Macmillan.

Rawls, John. 1971. *A Theory of Justice*. Oxford: Oxford University Press.

Rees, John. 1998. *The Algebra of Revolution*. London: Routledge.

———. 2000. " 'Introduction." In Georg Lukács, 2000, *Tailism and the Dialectic: A Defence of History and Class Consciousness*. London: Verso.

Reiman, Jeffrey. 1991. "Moral Philosophy.," In Terrell Carver, ed., 1991, *The Cambridge Companion to Marx*. Cambridge: Cambridge University Press: 143–167.

Reiman, Michal. 1987. *The Birth of Stalinism*. London: I. B. Tauris; Haynes.

Reiss, H. S. 1991. "Introduction." In H. S. Reiss, ed., 1991, *Kant's Political Writings*. Cambridge: Cambridge University Press.

Ricardo, David. 1973. *The Principles of Political Economy and Taxation*. London: Everyman.

Roberts, Marcus. 1996. *Analytical Marxism*. London: Verso.

Robertson, Jack. 1988. "Socialists and the Unions." *International Socialism* 2/41; 97–112.

Roemer, John. 1986a. "Introduction." In John Roemer, ed., 1986, *Analytical Marxism*. Cambridge: Cambridge University Press: 1–7.

———. 1986b. "Should Marxists be interested in exploitation?." In John Roemer, ed., *Analytical Marxism*. Cambridge: Cambridge University Press: 260–282

Rosdolsky, Roman. 1977. *The Making of Marx's Capital*. London: Pluto.

Rose, Hilary, and Steven Rose. eds. 2000. *Alas Poor Darwin*. London: Jonathan Cape.

Rose, Steven et al. 1984. *Not in Our Genes*. London: Penguin.

Rose, Steven. 1997. *Lifelines*. London: Penguin.

Ross, David. 1949. *Aristotle*. London: Methuen.

Rubin, Isaac. 1979. *A History of Economic Thought*. London: Ink Links.

Rudé, George. 1988. *The French Revolution*. London: Phoenix.

Salvadori, Massimo. 1979. *Karl Kautsky and the Socialist Revolution*. London: Verso.

Samuel, Raphael. 1959. "Class and Classlessness." *Universities and Left Review* 1/6.

Sartre, Jean-Paul. 1955. "Materialism and Revolution." In Jean-Paul Sartre, *Literary and Philosophical Essays*. London: Rider.

———. 1958. *Being and Nothingness*. New York: Philosophical Library.

———. 1963. *Search for a Method*. New York: Vintage Books.

———. 1968. *The Communists and Peace*. New York: George Braziller.

———. 1969. *The Spectre of Stalin*. London: Hamish Hamilton.

———. 1970. "Masses, Spontaneity, Party." *Socialist Register* 1970: 233–249.

———. 1974. "Determinism and Freedom." In Michel Contat and Michel Rybalka, eds., *The Writings of Jean-Paul Sartre, Vol. 2: Selected Prose*. Evaston: Northwestern University Press: 241–252.

———. 1976. *Critique of Dialectical Reason* Vol. I. London: Verso.

———. 1992. *Notebooks for an Ethics*. Chicago: University of Chicago Press.

———. 1995. *Anti-Semite and Jew*. Schocken Books.

Satterwhite, James. 1992. *Varieties of Marxist Humanism: Philosophical Revisionism in Postwar Eastern Europe*. Pittsburgh: University of Pittsburgh Press.

Sayer, Andrew. 2000. *Realism and Social Science*. London: Sage.

———. 2009. "Understanding Lay Normativity," In Sandra Moog and Rob Stones, eds., *Nature, Social Relations and Human Needs*. London: Palgrave.

Sayers, Sean 1998. *Marxism and Human Nature*. London: Routledge.

———. 2009. "Labour in Modern Industrial Society." In Andrew Chitty and Martin McIvor, eds., *Karl Marx and Contemporary Philosophy*. London: Palgrave.

Sayers, Sean 1998. *Marxism and Human Nature*. London: Routledge.

Schweppenhäuser, Gerhard. 2004. "Adorno's Negative Moral Philosophy." In Tom Huhn, ed., 2004, *The Cambridge Companion to Adorno*. Cambridge: Cambridge University Press: 328–353.

Schorske, Carl. 1983. *German Social Democracy, 1905–1917*. Cambridge: Harvard University Press.

Sedgwick, Peter. 1976. "The Two New Lefts." In David Widgery, ed., 1976, *The Left in Britain: 1956–1968*. London: Penguin.

Sen, Amartya. 1982. *Choice, Welfare and Measurement*. Harvard: Harvard University Press.

Sheehan, Helena. 1985. *Marxism and the Philosophy of Science*. New Jersey: Humanities.

Slote, Michael. 1997. "Virtue Ethics." In Marcia Baron et al., 1997, *Three Methods in Ethics*. Oxford: Blackwell: 175–238.

Smith, Adam. 1994. *The Wealth of Nations*. New York: The Modern Library.

Solomon, Robert. 1983. *In the Spirit of Hegel*. Oxford: Oxford University Press.

Soper, Kate. 1986. *Humanism and Anti-Humanism*. London: Hutchinson.

———. 1990. *Troubled Pleasures*. London: Verso.

Sparks, Colin. 1996. "Stuart Hall, Cultural Studies and Marxism." In D. Morley and K. Chen, eds., *Stuart Hall: Critical Dialogues in Cultural Studies*. London: Routledge.

Spinks, Lee. 2003. *Friedrich Nietzsche*. London: Routledge.

Stalin, Joseph. 1938. *Dialectical and Historical Materialism*. At http://www.marxists.org/reference/archive/stalin/works/1938/09.htm

Stedman Jones, Gareth. 1977. "The Marxism of the Early Lukács." *New Left Review* ed. *Western Marxism: A Critical Reader*. 11–60.

Steger, Manfred. 1996. "Introduction.: In Manfred Steger, ed., *Selected Writings of Eduard Bernstein*. New Jersey: Humanities Press.

Stirner, Max. 2005. *The Ego and His Own*. Trans. Steven Byington. New York: Dover.

Stone, Robert, and Bowman, Elizabeth. 1986. "Dialectical Ethics: A First Look at Sartre's Unpublished 1964 Rome Lecture Notes." *Social Text* 13/14: 195–215.

——. 1991. "Sartre's Morality and History: A First Look at the Notes for the Unpublished 1965 Cornell Lectures." In Ronald Aronson and Adrian van den Hoven, eds., *Sartre Alive*. Wayne State University Press: Detroit: 53–82.

Sturmthal, Adolf. 1964. *Workers Councils*. Cambridge: Harvard University Press.

Swarmi, Viren. 2007. "Evolutionary Psychology: 'New Science of the Mind' or 'Darwinian Fundamentalism?.'" *Historical Materialism* Vol. 15, No. 4.

Taylor, Charles. 1957a. "Marxism and Humanism." *The New Reasoner* 2, Autumn 1957: 92–98.

——. 1957b. "Socialism and Intellectuals." *Universities and Left Review* 2: 18–19.

——. 1975. *Hegel,*.Cambridge: Cambridge University Press.

Therborn, Goran. 1977. "The Frankfurt School." *New Left Review*, ed. 1977, *Western Marxism: A Critical Reader*. London: New Left Books: 83–139.

Thomas, Paul. 1980. *Karl Marx and the Anarchists*. London: Routledge & Kegan.

Thompson, Edward. 1957. "Socialist Humanism." *The New Reasoner* 1: 105–143.

——. 1958. "Agency and Choice." *The New Reasoner* 5: 89–106.

——. 1959. "Commitment in Politics." *Universities and Left Review* 6.

——. 1960. "At the Point of Decay." In Edward Thompson, ed., *Out of Apathy*. London, Stevens and Sons.

——. 1961. "The Long Revolution." *New Left Review* 1: 9.

——. 1978a. "The Peculiarities of the English." In Edward Thompson, *The Poverty of Theory and Other Essays*. London: Merlin.

——. 1978b. "An Open Letter to Leszek Kolakowski." In Edward Thompson, *The Poverty of Theory and Other Essays*.London: Merlin: 303–402.

Thompson, Paul. 1989. *The Nature of Work*. London: Macmillan.

Townsend, Jules. 1989. "Reassessing Kautsky's Marxism." *Political Studies* Vol. XXXVII, No. 4: 659-664.

Trotsky, Leon. 1972. *The Revolution Betrayed*. New York: Pathfinder

Tudor, Henry, and Leon Trotsky. 1973. "Their Morals and Ours." In Leon Trotsky et al., 1973, *Their Morals and Ours*. New York: Pathfinder: 13–52.

Tudor, Henry, and J. M. Tudor, eds. 1988. *Marxism and Social Democracy: The Revisionist Debate 1896–1898*. Cambridge: Cambridge University Press.

Tudor, Henry. 1993. "Introduction." In Bernstein, Eduard 1993, *The Preconditions of Socialism*. Cambridge: Cambridge University Press: xv–xxxvi.

Van der Linden, Harry. 1988. *Kantian Ethics and Socialism*. Indianapolis: Hackett.

Van der Linden, Marcel. 1997. "Socialisme ou Barbarie: A French Revolutionary Group (1949–65).," *Left History* 5.1.

Vincent, Jean-Marie, 2008. "Adorno and Marx." In Jacques Bidet and Eustache Kouvelakis, eds. 2008. *Critical Companion to Contemporary Marxism*. Leiden: Brill: 489–501.

Walicki, Andrzej. 1995. *Marxism and the Leap to the Kingdom of Freedom*. Stanford: Stanford University Press.

Weeks, John. 1981. *Capital and Exploitation*. Princeton: Princeton University Press.

Wiggershaus, Rolf. 1994. *The Frankfurt School,*. Cambridge: Polity.

Wilde, Lawrence. 1998. *Ethical Marxism and its Radical Critics*. London: Macmillan.

———. 2001. " 'Introduction." In Lawrence Wilde, ed., 2001, *Marxism's Ethical Thinkers*. London: Palgrave: 1–14.

Wilkinson, Richard. 2005. *The Impact of Inequality*. London: Routledge.

Williams, Bernard. 2006. *Ethics and the Limits of Philosophy*. London: Routledge.

Williams, Chris. 1998. *Capitalism, Community and Conflict: The South Wales Coalfields 1898–1947*. Cardiff: University of Wales Press.

Williams, Gwyn. 1975. *Proletarian Order*. London: Pluto.

Williams, Raymond. 1976. *Keywords*. London: Fontana.

———. 1979. *Politics and Letters*. London, Verso.

Wood, Allen. 1981. *Karl Marx*. London: Routledge.

———. 1990. *Hegel's Ethical Thought*. Cambridge: Cambridge University Press.

———. 2005. *Kant*. Oxford: Blackwell.

Wood, Ellen Meiksins. 1986. *The Retreat from Class*. London: Verso.

———. 1995. "A Chronology of the New Left and Its Successors, Or: Who's Old-Fashioned Now?." *Socialist Register* 1995.

Wright, Erik Olin. 1995. "What is Analytical Marxism." In Terrell Carver and Paul Thomas, eds., 1995, *Rational Choice Marxism*, London: Macmillan: 11–30.

———. 2010. *Envisioning Real Utopias*. London: Verso.

Wrigley, Chris, ed. 1993. *Challenges of Labour*. London: Routledge.

Žižek, Slavoj. 2000. "Georg Lukács as the Philosopher of Leninism." In Georg Lukács, *Tailism and the Dialectic: A Defence of History and Class Consciousness*. London: Verso.

———. 2001. *On Belief*. London: Routledge.

———. 2002. *Revolution at the Gates*. London: Verso.

———. 2004. "From Politics to Biopolitics . . . and Back." *The South Atlantic Quarterly* 103: 2/3.

———. 2006. *The Parallax View*. Cambridge: Massachusetts Institute of Technology.

———. 2007. "Introduction." In Robespierre, *Virtue and Terror*. London: Verso.

———. 2007. "Foreword" In Leon Trotsky, 2007, *Terrorism and Communism*. London: Verso.

———. 2007, "Resistance is Surrender," *London Review of Book.s* 15th November 2007.

———. 2008. *In Defence of Lost Causes*. London: Verso.

———. 2009a. *First as Tragedy, Then as Farce*. London: Verso.

———. 2009b. "Beginning Again." *New Left Review* 2/57: 43–55.

Index

Printed in Great Britain
by Amazon.co.uk, Ltd.,
Marston Gate.